Patriarchal Moments

Textual Moments in the History of

Political Thought

SERIES EDITORS
**J. C. Davis, Emeritus Professor of History,
University of East Anglia, UK
John Morrow, Professor of Political Studies,
University of Auckland, New Zealand**

Textual Moments provides accessible, short readings of key texts
in selected fields of political thought, encouraging close reading informed by
cutting-edge scholarship. The unique short essay format of the series ensures
that volumes cover a range of texts in roughly chronological order. The essays
in each volume aim to open up a reading of the text and its significance in
the political discourse in question and in the history of political thought more
widely. Key moments in the textual history of a particular genre of political
discourse are made accessible, appealing and instructive to students, scholars
and general readers.

Published

Utopian Moments: Reading Utopian Texts
Miguel Avilés & J. C. Davis

*Censorship Moments: Reading Texts in the History of Censorship
and Freedom of Expression*
Geoff Kemp

Revolutionary Moments: Reading Revolutionary Texts
Rachel Hammersley

Forthcoming
Feminist Moments: Reading Feminist Texts
Katherine Smits and Susan Bruce

Liberal Moments: Reading Liberal Texts
Ewa Atanassow and Alan S. Kahan

Patriarchal Moments

Reading Patriarchal Texts

Edited by
Cesare Cuttica and Gaby Mahlberg

Bloomsbury Academic
An imprint of Bloomsbury Publishing Plc

B L O O M S B U R Y

LONDON • OXFORD • NEW YORK • NEW DELHI • SYDNEY

Bloomsbury Academic

An imprint of Bloomsbury Publishing Plc

50 Bedford Square	1385 Broadway
London	New York
WC1B 3DP	NY 10018
UK	USA

www.bloomsbury.com

BLOOMSBURY and the Diana logo are trademarks of Bloomsbury Publishing Plc

First published 2016

British Library Cataloguing-in-Publication Data
A catalogue record for this book is available from the British Library.

ISBN: HB: 978-1-4725-8914-9
PB: 978-1-4725-8915-6
ePDF: 978-1-4742-3798-7
ePub: 978-1-4725-8917-0

Library of Congress Cataloging-in-Publication Data
Patriarchal moments : reading patriarchal texts / edited by
Cesare Cuttica and Gaby Mahlberg.
pages cm
Includes bibliographical references and index.
ISBN 978-1-4725-8914-9 (hb) – ISBN 978-1-4725-8915-6 (pb) –
ISBN 978-1-4725-8917-0 (epub) – ISBN 978-1-4742-3798-7 (epdf) 1. Patriarchy.
2. Patriarchy–Religious aspects. 3. Patriarchy in literature.
I. Cuttica, Cesare. II. Mahlberg, Gaby.
GN479.6.P37 2015
305.3–dc23
2015015243

Typeset by Integra Software Services Pvt. Ltd.

Contents

Contributors

Charlotte Alston Senior Lecturer in History at Northumbria University, UK; author of books and articles on Russia's revolutions and civil war, the post–First World War peace settlements, and the international influence of Tolstoy's thought. Her latest book is *Tolstoy and His Disciples: The History of a Radical International Movement*.

Paul Baines Professor of English at the University of Liverpool, UK; author of several books on eighteenth-century literature, including *The Collected Writings of Edward Rushton* and *The Complete Critical Guide to Alexander Pope*.

Asma Barlas Professor of Politics at Ithaca College, USA; author of '*Believing Women' in Islam: Unreading Patriarchal Interpretations of the Qur'an*; *Re-understanding Islam: A Double Critique*; and *Democracy, Nationalism and Communalism: The Colonial Legacy in South Asia*.

Federico Bonaddio Senior Lecturer in Modern Spanish Studies at King's College London, UK; editor of *A Companion to Federico García Lorca*; author of *Federico García Lorca: The Poetics of Self-Consciousness*.

Ruth Charnock Lecturer in English at the University of Lincoln, UK; author of ' "I want what everyone wants": cruel optimism in HBO's *Girls*' for *Gender and Austerity in Popular Culture* (forthcoming), and articles on Anaïs Nin and Joni Mitchell.

Catherine Conybeare Professor of Classics at Bryn Mawr College, USA; her most recent books are *The Laughter of Sarah: Biblical Exegesis, Feminist Theory, and the Concept of Delight* and *The Irrational Augustine*.

Cesare Cuttica Lecturer in British History at the Université Paris 8-Vincennes, France; author of *Sir Robert Filmer (1588–1653) and the Patriotic Monarch: Patriarchalism in Seventeenth-Century Political Thought*; editor of *Absolutism and Monarchism in Early Modern Europe* with Glenn Burgess.

Michelle Faubert Associate Professor of Romantic Literature, University of Manitoba, Canada, and Visiting Fellow, Northumbria University, UK; author of *Rhyming Reason: The Poetry of Romantic-Era Psychologists*; editor of Mary Wollstonecraft's novellas, *Mary* and *The Wrongs of Woman*; editor (with Thomas Schmid) of *Romanticism and Pleasure*; editor (with Allan Ingram) of *Medical Writings, Depression and Melancholy, 1660–1800* (vol. 2).

Edith Hall Professor of Classics at King's College London, UK. She is the recipient of the Erasmus Medal of the European Academy 2015. Her most recent book is *Introducing the Ancient Greeks*.

Karen Harvey Reader in Cultural History at the University of Sheffield, UK; author of *Reading Sex in the Eighteenth Century: Bodies and Gender in English Erotic Culture*, and *The Little Republic: Masculinity and Domestic Authority in Eighteenth-Century Britain*; editor of volumes of essays on the kiss and material culture.

Oliver Jahraus Professor of Modern German Literature and Media at Ludwig-Maximilians-University, Munich, Germany; author of *Franz Kafka* and *Die 101 wichtigsten Fragen: Deutsche Literatur*; co-editor of *Der erste Weltkrieg als Katastrophe*.

Daniel Laqua Senior Lecturer in European History at Northumbria University, UK; author of *The Age of Internationalism and Belgium, 1880–1930: Peace, Progress and Prestige*; editor of various publications on political activism and transnational history.

Sarra Lev Associate Professor of Rabbinics at the Reconstructionist Rabbinical College, Wyncote, USA; author of *They Treat Him as a Man and See Him as a Woman: The Tannaitic Understanding of the Congenital Eunuch* and *How the 'Aylonit Got Her Sex*.

Gaby Mahlberg Senior Lecturer in Early Modern British History at Northumbria University, UK; author of *Henry Neville and English Republican Culture: Dreaming of Another Game*, and with Dirk Wiemann co-editor of *European Contexts for English Republicanism* and *Perspectives on English Revolutionary Republicanism*.

Anne McLaren Senior Lecturer in Early Modern History at the University of Liverpool, UK; author of *Political Culture in the Reign of Elizabeth I: Queen and Commonwealth 1558–1585*, and articles on early modern political thought.

J. K. Numao Assistant Professor of Foreign Languages and Liberal Arts at Keio University, Tokyo, Japan; author of articles on Locke and his contemporaries.

Sandrine Parageau Assistant Professor of British History at the University of Paris Ouest Nanterre, France; author of *Les Ruses de l'ignorance. La contribution des femmes à l'avènement de la science moderne en Angleterre*, and of articles on early modern natural philosophy and intellectual history.

Jordan Pascoe Assistant Professor of Philosophy at Manhattan College, USA; author of several articles on Kant, women and race.

Deborah W. Rooke Research Fellow at the Oxford Centre for Christianity and Culture, Regent's Park College, Oxford, UK; editor of *A Question of Sex? Gender and Difference in the Hebrew Bible and Beyond* and *Embroidered Garments: Priests and Gender in Biblical Israel*; prospective editor of the *Oxford Handbook of the Hebrew Bible, Gender and Sexuality*.

Jonathan Scott Professor of History at the University of Auckland, New Zealand; author, most recently, of *When the Waves Ruled Britannia: Geography and Political Identities, 1500–1800*. His book in progress is *Anglo-Dutch Early Modernity: The Geography of Invention, 1500–1800*.

Arnold Weinstein Salomon Distinguished Professor of Comparative Literature at Brown University, USA; author of *Recovering Your Story: Proust, Joyce, Woolf, Faulkner, Morrison*; *Northern Arts: The Breakthrough of Scandinavian Literature and Art from Ibsen to Bergman*; and *Morning, Noon and Night: Finding the Meaning of Life's Stages Through Books*.

Brett D. Wilson Associate Professor of English at the College of William & Mary, USA; author of *A Race of Female Patriots: Women and Public Spirit on the British Stage, 1688–1745* and of articles on Nicholas Rowe, Richard Steele and Hannah More.

Series Editors' Foreword

At the heart of the serious study of the history of political thought, as expressed through both canonical and non-canonical works of all kinds, has been the question (to which we all too readily assume an answer), 'How shall I read this text?' Answers have varied greatly over time. Once the political works of the past – especially those of Classical Greece and Rome – were read with an eye to their immediate application to the present. And, until comparatively recently, the canonical works of political philosophy were selected and read as expressions of perennial, abiding truths about politics, social morality and justice. The problem was that this made little or no concession to historically changing contexts, that the 'truths' we identified were all too often our truths. A marxisant sociology of knowledge struggled to break free from the 'eternal verities' of political thought by exploring the ways in which past societies shaped their own forms of political expression in distinctive yet commonly grounded conceptions of their own image. The problem remained that the perception of what shaped past societies was all too often driven by the demands of a current political agenda. In both cases, present concerns shaped the narrative history of political thought off which the reading of texts fed. The last half century has seen another powerful and influential attempt to break free from a present-centred history of political thought by locating texts as speech acts or moves within a contemporary context of linguistic usage. Here the frequently perceived problem has been (a by-no-means inevitable) narrowing of focus to canonical texts, while the study of other forms of political expression in images, speech, performance and gesture – in all forms of political culture – has burgeoned independently.

We have, then, a variety of ways of approaching past texts and the interplay of text and context. The series 'Textual Moments in the History of Political Thought' (in which this present volume is the fourth to be published) is designed to encourage fresh readings of thematically selected texts. Each chapter identifies a key textual moment or passage and exposes it to a reading by an acknowledged expert. The aim is fresh insight, accessibility and the encouragement to read, in a more informed way for oneself.

Patriarchalism, far too often relegated to the margins of the history of political thought, has arguably been one of the most powerful ideological shapers of the distribution of power and authority in the history of political and social life.

Its cultural and chronological sweep and endurance, which is reflected in the present volume of essays, is not to be underestimated. The idea that a superior claim to authority resides exclusively in male heads of households, and even that one of them may legitimately exercise sovereign authority over the rest, may look deceptively simple and even, from some perspectives, more than a little absurd if not distasteful. But whatever our immediate reaction to that notion, it is important to recognize patriarchalism's dominance in many cultures for much of recorded history along with its capacity to shape (some would say 'distort') innumerable lives of both those who claimed patriarchal authority and those who have been subjected to it. Ideas about nature and convention, as well as questions of complicity, subversion and resistance are bound up with the astonishing durability of patriarchal ideology. Reactions against patriarchalism, whether from those of a more consensual (contractarian?), liberal or feminist disposition have frequently been shaped by their struggles with its dominance and have often found it a difficult, if not daunting adversary. Above all, patriarchalist theory and its tenacious hold on civic, social and familial consciousness suggest that the remit of the history of political thought cannot be confined to a limited number of canonical texts but must embrace the social, political and cultural expression of ideas which enable some to exercise power over others and circumscribe ideas about legitimate authority and its limits or their absence. If then, we are to come to grips with past thinking about political life and the legitimate exercise of power in social entities ranging from the family to communal organizations and beyond to the state and even the multinational empire, we will, at some point, have to engage with patriarchal theory and its history.

In this collection, Cesare Cuttica and Gaby Mahlberg have brought together a team of international experts to explore afresh key texts in the history of patriarchal thought and the debates surrounding it. In the process we gain insight into the exposition, defence, clarification, modification and criticism of patriarchalist ideas from the Bible, the Talmud and the Qur'an to more recent questioning of patriarchalism's theoretical underpinnings and the price paid for adherence to patriarchalist ideology. Many of patriarchalists' claims have rested on readings and interpretations of 'authoritative' texts. Time and again in these essays we see how the reading of texts becomes crucial to the establishment of meaning and access to the power which the ideology of patriarchalism can endorse. It is perhaps therefore doubly appropriate that, in a series which invites us to consider again how best to read political texts, a volume should be devoted to patriarchalism.

J. C. Davis
John Morrow

Acknowledgements

It is always a pleasure to acknowledge the debts acquired in putting together a volume like this. First of all, we would like to thank the series editors, J.C. Davis and John Morrow, for getting us involved in this exciting project. They have been critical friends and creative partners throughout this undertaking. A big thank you also goes to Jyoti Basuita, Balaji Kasirajan and the whole team at Bloomsbury for all their help and efficiency in seeing this volume through the press. Last but not least, we would like to express our gratitude to all twenty-one contributors for their outstanding work and for the enthusiasm with which they embarked on this project from day one.

Brighton and Newcastle, March 2015
The Editors

Introduction

Cesare Cuttica and Gaby Mahlberg

Patriarchalism is omnipresent in the West and it pervades the texts that have shaped its culture. From the creation story in the Bible and the religious prescriptions to be found in the Qur'an and Talmud to the ancient authors, from the Church fathers to the treatises of Enlightenment philosophers, right up to modern fiction, male authority over women, children and other dependants has informed the nature of human relationships and the discourses about these relationships. This concept of power, implying a fatherly male domination of society, has never gone uncontested. Yet, the debate is far from resolved.

Patriarchalism might be dead, but patriarchy is alive and well:[1] the economic recession affecting most western democracies has shown that women are bearing the brunt of it in terms of unemployment rates, economic hardship and social discrimination or marginalization.[2] Moreover, women are not less, but more objectified in our contemporary culture, especially through advertising, TV, the Internet and through a 'commodity is everything' attitude thriving in the media.[3] Men's sexual exploitation of, and predatory attitudes towards, women are amply documented in news outlets.[4] Certainly part and parcel of the everyday experience of many women, the situations described above do not explain the complexity of patriarchalism as an array of values and of patriarchy as an ideological scaffolding whose foundations are rooted historically in various domains of public and private life. Eschewing a linear account of these two phenomena, our volume nevertheless takes a chronological approach in an attempt to understand how certain ideas of gender and gender-based politics/ policies, which are still afloat in our societies, originated, developed and changed over a long time span and how they did so in different contexts, and in a variety of media and genres.

This collection of short essays therefore offers fresh and novel readings of key texts in the history of patriarchalism as a concept of power[5] as our contributors draw attention to moments of contestation or re-negotiation of patriarchal parameters and their reflection in the printed word. They also provide a collage of patriarchal moments which defy traditional and widely accepted interpretative categories of what patriarchy and patriarchalism meant for the writers and texts here considered. Indeed, *Patriarchal Moments* often reveals unexpected sides to a thinker's standpoint on matters of family, politics and gender.

Nowadays, we might call ourselves 'feminist' or declare our support for the original agenda of feminism.[6] It would be more controversial, however, for someone in a western society to define themselves as 'patriarchalist' or to state their steadfast adherence to patriarchy and its values. Nevertheless, what is today an improbable scenario was the norm not so long ago.[7]

While 'patriarchy' refers to a social, economic, political, cultural and ideological structure in which women are held to be inferior to men (fathers, husbands, older brothers) and are subjugated to them as holders of authority, prestige and access to wealth,[8] patriarchalism – like absolutism, liberalism, etc. – entails a series of doctrines concerning power, liberty, the origins of political society, the method of government and so on. Therefore, it belongs to the field of political thought. 'Paternalism', meanwhile, represents 'an authoritarian and, at the same time, benevolent type of politics, a sort of charitable activity pursued from above and set out to help the people with purely administrative methods'.[9] This care of those in power (the fathers) for those in their care (the people) has often been perceived as patronizing or condescending.

Denoting an important doctrine in the history of western society and thought, the term 'patriarchalism' is used in different ways and fields. It is traditionally employed in the theological sphere where references are made to the Judaeo-Christian notion of God the Father and to the biblical patriarchs. In this context the word 'patriarch' as attached to biblical personages comes from the Septuagint version, where it is adopted in a broad sense to describe both religious and civic officials (e.g. in *Chronicles*). In a more restricted sense it is applied to the antediluvian fathers of the human race, and more particularly to the three great progenitors of Israel: Abraham, Isaac and Jacob. In the New Testament the term is also extended to the sons of Jacob and to King David.

In social theory, 'patriarchalist' commonly refers to a pre-modern societal organization grounded on the absolute authority of the male landowner over a large familial unit, including his wife and children as well as live-in servants. In economic parlance, 'patriarchalism' describes a specific structure of production and distribution of goods and labour characterizing the household as an entity. Political theorists generally associate it with a form of oppressive, archaic and anti-modern fatherly power. This kind of personal and personalized authority has generally been considered antithetical to a liberal, conventional and artificial conception of politics. Most importantly, feminist scholars depict patriarchalism as the quintessence of women's subjugation to men and their consequent oppression under a rigorous system centred on female obedience.

Patriarchalist theory has maintained the supremacy of monarchs, arguing that they derived their authority from Adam, to whom God had assigned indisputable power over all creatures. From the progenitor of humankind, power had passed to kings through the ancient patriarchs. On the whole, patriarchalism had a significant impact on the organization of politics, society and family in western history for it claimed that order and submission to higher authorities ought to be preserved in all human institutions. It followed that kings in the political realm, fathers in the family and masters in the household wielded the same authority over their subjects, wives, children and servants.

Historians such as Susan Amussen have shown that patriarchal doctrines and values were often conveyed through prescriptive 'household manuals',[10] while Gordon Schochet has traced patriarchalism in the political language adopted by Plato, Aristotle, Bodin, Locke and other thinkers to identify the household as 'the organizational precursor of the political order'.[11] By and large, the historiographical mainstream has focused univocally on patriarchalism's historical and anthropological connotations, failing to see it in relation to cultural meanings, metaphorical references and gendered paradigms permeating the wider intellectual contexts in which various patriarchal moments developed.[12]

Instead of viewing patriarchalism exclusively as a societal or legal phenomenon, *Patriarchal Moments* explores how patriarchal political thought participated in the multifarious configurations of cultural, aesthetic, moral, philosophical, theological and literary meanings throughout history. In other words, we think that patriarchalism was more than the codification of archaic beliefs failing to succeed in the theatre of ideas when confronted by modern philosophy, empirical science and social change. Patriarchal ideas indicated the primacy of the emotionally, culturally and socially decisive sphere of the family, and shaped the ways in which not only conjugal, filial and sexual relationships were thought and acted out, but also the manner in which political, theoretical and fictional approaches to reality were conceived and enacted. The use of patriarchal vocabulary and imagery moulded the concepts of, among others, fatherhood and motherhood, marriage and obedience, and masculinity and virility.

Feminist theories have played a fundamental role in interpreting the notion and practice of 'patriarchy' with its specific focus on women's oppression and gendered violence in both the public and private domains. Feminists have underscored the socially constructed nature of the hierarchy existing between men and women in which the former aim to preserve power over the latter through control in conjunction with employment, sexuality, culture, family structure and the State. This apparatus of oppression is seen as intertwined with the hegemonic role the heterosexual family plays as a major institution whose mechanisms of functioning perpetuate inequality.[13]

Furthermore, as Mary Beard has recently elucidated, from classical Greece onwards women have been denied a public voice: they have not been heard because the Homeric ideal of '*muthos*' meant that authoritative public speech was the prerogative of aristocratic and superior male actors in the political arena.[14] This principle of the Greek assembly also held true for the early Christian communities, as outlined by St Paul.[15] A long and persistent list of practices and prejudices across the centuries has thus prevented women from debating political, social and intellectual issues or from simply expressing an opinion.[16] Even when women have succeeded in speaking, their voices have been (and so often still *are*) described as 'loud cacophonous shrills', deprived of the authority-infused, deep and, therefore, respectable low-pitched voice of their male 'superiors'. Accused of emitting whinging and whining sounds and considered to be up to mere trivial chatting and ghastly gossiping, women have been excluded not only from (positions of) authority, but also from the discourse of authority belonging to the male world. In light of these historical processes, our volume contributes – among other things – to expose what Beard has recently called 'the unresolved gender wars that lay just below the surface of ancient [and modern] public life and speaking'.[17]

Complementing *Feminist Moments* in the present series,[18] which focuses primarily on gender relations, our volume integrates gender politics into a broader patriarchalist framework. It thus offers an aid to experts as much as students approaching patriarchalism-patriarchy for the first time to understand a significant portion of western civilization and its political culture. Drawing on a wide range of academic expertise, we have gathered contributions from international scholars of different methodological and intellectual traditions as well as institutional profiles, including historians, literary scholars, political scientists and theologians. In this respect, the following essays aim to illuminate a complex horizon of thought that is not only the subject of constant media scrutiny and political focus but that is also at the centre of attention within a growing public discourse. This collection cannot cover all cultures, periods and genres in equal measure, nor does it claim to reflect the entire history of patriarchalism. Instead, it attempts to add new insights to the debate about patriarchalism that is as old as humankind. Through its chronologically and contextually rich outlook, and its broad selection of key texts, *Patriarchal Moments* adopts historical depth to grasp continuity as well as change in, and explain their effects on, the development(s) of a patriarchal discourse across sundry strands of political, philosophical, literary and theological reflection in the West. Ultimately, this way of proceeding should enable us to show the impact notions of patriarchy and patriarchalism have on society at large, not just there and then but also *here* and *now*. More specifically, *Patriarchal Moments* stimulates important reflections on the tangled relations between patriarchalism and feminism. In fact, it endeavours to unfold the implications of patriarchy not just for subordinate women but for men too (e.g. sons, younger brothers). In so doing, the volume as a whole underscores how as a system of authority patriarchalism needs to be interpreted with an eye to a more wide-ranging set of manifestations than those usually – and too simplistically – linking it to its gender implications.

Our patriarchal journey begins with the three great monotheistic world religions: Judaism, Christianity and Islam. The contributions on these key religious texts all pay detailed attention to the context(s) in which they were composed as well as to the (allegedly) indisputable patriarchalist values. The latter co-existed with counter-narratives opposing them, which reveals the vulnerability of patriarchy. As Sarra Lev, Deborah Rooke and Asma Barlas show, such a tension is well alive in rabbinic literature, in the biblical Genesis story of Adam and Eve in the Garden of Eden, and in the much discussed and often misinterpreted text the Qur'an certainly is.

Taking into careful consideration both the context and the linguistic subtleties of key texts in the western philosophical tradition such as Aristotle's *Politics* (384–322 B.C.E.) and Augustine's *The City of God* (fifth-century A.D.), Edith Hall and Catherine Conybeare reach opposite conclusions on the two philosophers' views of women: while Aristotle has to be seen as 'the founding father of patriarchy in the field of political theory' (42), 'Augustine's vision of humans' is 'more dynamic and egalitarian' than assumed through 'a patriarchalist reading' of his work (48). In tune with Conybeare's insistence on the affective bond characterizing interaction between men and women, Karen Harvey focuses on William Gouge's *Of Domesticall Duties* (1622) as a typical household manual revealing how patriarchy in the early modern period involved not just the family as a private unit, but also society and the commonwealth at large.

In her analysis of John Knox's *The First Blast of the Trumpet Against the Monstrous Regiment of Women* (1558), Anne McLaren addresses the important issue of misogyny in conjunction with political, moral and gender opinions thriving in the sixteenth century. If in the midst of Knox's tract we find queens, Protestantism, dynastic troubles and political theory, the notorious patriarchalist thinker Sir Robert Filmer, author of the much-criticized *Patriarcha* (published in 1680), serves Cesare Cuttica to depict patriarchalism as a specific *political* language deployed at a time of key theoretical and practical debates in early modern England. Driven by a contextualist approach to the study of past ideas, Cuttica's chapter sheds light on the unexpected interplay of patriarchal and patriotic moments in early modern political parlance.

From Filmer to his arch-critics, Algernon Sidney and John Locke, patriarchalism assumes very different connotations. Jonathan Scott positions Sidney's posthumously published *Discourses Concerning Government* (1698) in three different contexts where the political and the personal are intertwined in crucial ways. Regarding Locke, J. K. Numao concentrates on the philosopher's less-studied *Some Thoughts Concerning Education* (1693) rather than on the generally praised anti-Filmerian *Two Treatises of Government* (1689). In unpacking Locke's attitude towards patriarchalism, Numao expounds the vital links between fatherhood, adulthood and friendship in relation to issues of political obedience and human development. With Brett Wilson's essay, we encounter the first woman in our volume, Mary Astell (1666–1731), who was a proto-feminist as well as a 'significant political thinker' (90), applying ideas about passive obedience to both the political and the personal spheres, while also paving the way for later women thinkers with more radical approaches.

Moving on to the eighteenth century, Alexander Pope's ethical poem *An Essay on Man* (1734) is read by Paul Baines as a text rich in political meaning(s), steering a middle course between Filmer and Locke. Pope can be seen as a rather ambiguous character and one whose work engenders new reflections on irony, filial adoration of fathers and natural law. From Pope to Jean-Jacques Rousseau's *Emile* (1762) another complex patriarchal moment develops. As Sandrine Parageau explains, politics, education, gender and metaphysical considerations all coalesce in Rousseau's analysis of what is both a 'love story' and a 'political treatise' illustrating his idea of the family (108). Most importantly, the *philosophe* wrote at a historical juncture when political patriarchalism became increasingly the object of vehement criticism and systematic confutation in eighteenth-century France. In particular, paternal images of monarchs were being 'progressively replaced with ideas of "fraternity"' as the model of the good society (113).

Michelle Faubert's essay on Mary Wollstonecraft's *Mary, A Fiction* (1788) meanwhile explores 'the relationship between women and the patriarchal laws and customs surrounding property and ownership in Romantic-era England' (123). Bringing together at the centre of our journey different patriarchal moments of fiction, property, class, identity and the "legal prostitution" of marriage (124), Faubert portrays Mary herself as a 'property to be traded' (124). Jordan Pascoe, on her part, engages with Immanuel Kant's perceived 'intellectual immaturity' of women (116): while highlighting the possibility of reading Kant's essay *What is Enlightenment?* (1784) as a feminist moment, Pascoe nevertheless concludes that Kant was 'sexist' (121) as he in essence still supported a patriarchal political order. The question as to what extent the followers of Henri de Saint-Simon might have been contributing to either the liberation or suppression of women is also an issue in Daniel Laqua's essay on Prosper Enfantin. In his address to the family of Saint-Simonians of 1831, Enfantin called for the liberation of women. Yet, his idea of liberation does not involve women's equality within the Saint-Simonian family. Thus, as Laqua demonstrates, Saint-Simonism was – confirming a major theme of *Patriarchal Moments* – at the same time 'patriarchal and anti-patriarchal', conservative and progressive (132).

Yet, as Charlotte Alston's essay on *The Kreutzer Sonata* (1889) points out, not all progressive ideas were equally well received by the public. Tolstoy's work is discussed as 'a frank critique of the state of late nineteenth-century marriage and the relationship between the sexes', which 'fed into and fuelled' debate in Russia, Europe as well as America (140). Despite criticizing men's sexual exploitation of women, Tolstoy denied an equal sexual freedom for women. Instead, he (controversially) advocated chastity as the highest ideal of purity. With Arnold Weinstein's reading of Henrik Ibsen's *Hedda Gabler* (1890), we enter a world of bourgeois submission of women to their stifling male-run environment where love and passion are frustrated, and tragic consequences are common: Hedda Gabler chooses suicide as her way to say no to patriarchal norms. Ibsen's famous play thus constitutes a significant patriarchal moment with its variegated spectrum of motifs including 'subjectivity', motherhood, political gestures, intellectual authorship and 'revenge' (151).

Our long journey concludes with three important works of the twentieth century. Oliver Jahraus considers Franz Kafka's *Letter to his Father* (1919) as the key literary document of a son's struggle against paternal power and his attempt to create and assert his own individuality against this higher authority, while Federico Bonaddio studies Federico Garcia Lorca's *Blood Wedding* (written in 1932) as an exposition of patriarchy's 'own tragic flaws' (165). Combining marriage, inheritance, virility, economic interests and matriarchal values, Lorca's play points to the 'tragic potential' inherent in patriarchy, as a result of which tragedy (death) strikes (165). Finally, Ruth Charnock shows how Angela Carter's *The Passion of New Eve* (1977) questions patriarchal power by way of castration, sterility and emasculation. However, patriarchy is not the only target of Carter's provocative novel: French feminists of the 1970s are in for a piercing attack, too. In substance, both patriarchy and its strenuous opponents fall prey to Carter's searing criticism.

Such a move can well be read as an invitation to be always openly critical and to be so in all directions. Critique of patriarchy goes hand in hand with critiquing its critics. These are two indispensable *moments* that guide our study of this historically contentious and socially relevant subject. Perhaps, we can say that this double-edged approach to patriarchalism (recognition of its strong sociopolitical foundations and persistence alongside multiple examples of resistance) entails the subversive dimension of interpreting such a complex *-ism*.[19] More generally, from the Bible and the Qur'an to Angela Carter, *Patriarchal Moments* invites readers to consider the important question of whether and when authoritative texts are open to more than one interpretation, a theme which runs through the volume and through the *Textual Moments* series as a whole. We always need to understand the circumstances in which the reading of texts may be said to shape ideology as well as the conditions under which ideology affects the reading of texts. The essays here presented therefore underline the essential role of context in the reading of texts as well as suggesting how reading and critiquing can be pursued in original and unexpected ways.

Of Women, Snakes and Trees: The Bible

Deborah W. Rooke

The LORD God said to the serpent, 'Because you have done this, cursed are you above all cattle, and above all wild animals; upon your belly you shall go, and dust you shall eat all the days of your life. I will put enmity between you and the woman, and between your seed and her seed; he shall bruise your head, and you shall bruise his heel'. To the woman he said, 'I will greatly multiply your pain in childbearing; in pain you shall bring forth children, yet your desire shall be for your husband, and he shall rule over you'. And to Adam he said, 'Because you have listened to the voice of your wife, and have eaten of the tree of which I commanded you, "You shall not eat of it," cursed is the ground because of you; in toil you shall eat of it all the days of your life; thorns and thistles it shall bring forth to you; and you shall eat the plants of the field. In the sweat of your face you shall eat bread till you return to the ground, for out of it you were taken; you are dust, and to dust you shall return'.[1]

From a woman sin had its beginning, and because of her we all die.[2]

Let a woman learn in silence with all submissiveness. I permit no woman to teach or to have authority over men; she is to keep silent. For Adam was formed first, then Eve; and Adam was not deceived, but the woman was deceived and became a transgressor. Yet woman will be saved through bearing children, if she continues in faith and love and holiness, with modesty.[3]

The Bible is the foundational document for two major world religions, and in its appropriation for western cultural life it has been a major influence for centuries, indeed, for millennia. But it is not a monolithic text; rather, it is a composite, a collection of writings referred to as 'books', which originated over an extended period of at least a thousand years. The books vary in their stances and outlooks,

so to choose a passage from one single book as in some sense exemplifying the
Bible's patriarchalism would be misleading. However, the three biblical passages
quoted above demonstrate the explanation that the early chapters of the Bible
offer for the patriarchal social structures to which its earliest audiences would
have been accustomed, together with reflections on that explanation from two
much later authors who have taken it up and drawn patriarchal implications
from it for their own audiences. In this way, all three main sections of the
vastly extended patriarchal moment known as the Bible are represented – Old
Testament, Apocrypha and New Testament – and with them the documents that
flowed out of Judaism and into Christianity. I shall offer some reflection on each
of the passages.

To begin with the Genesis passage, then, this is taken from the longer story
in Genesis 2–3 of how human beings were created by the deity and placed in
the Garden of Eden, first the man, to till and keep the garden, and subsequently
the woman, who is created from the man to be his helper. The outline of the
story is well known: the deity forbids the humans to eat the fruit of the tree of
the knowledge of good and evil that is growing in the garden, saying that on
the day they do so they will die (Gen. 2.16–17); but the snake tells the woman
that, far from being fatal, eating the fruit will make the humans wise like God.
So both she and the man eat the fruit, as a result of which they realize that they
are naked, and when later on God comes to find them in the garden they hide
from him because of their nakedness. God realizes that they have disobeyed
him and eaten the fruit, and there follows an exchange between humans and
deity about what happened: the man blames the woman for giving him the
fruit, and the woman blames the snake for tricking her into eating. This is the
point at which the extract above comes in: the snake, the woman and the man
in turn are all informed of the consequences of their actions in the imposition
of a punitive hierarchy whereby the man and woman are condemned to
toilsome gendered labours, the woman to subjection to the man, and the snake
to continual enmity with both. This is surely the fundamental patriarchal
moment for western culture and the Judaeo-Christian tradition, on which an
enormous edifice has been erected over the millennia.

Setting this patriarchal moment in its original context, though, is rather more
difficult. As already remarked, the Bible is a composite of texts – indeed, a composite
of composite texts – from a range of sources, locations and circumstances in
the ancient Near East and eastern Mediterranean. Most scholars agree that the
texts cover more than a millennium, from around the tenth century BCE for
the earliest Hebrew texts in the Old Testament to the early second century CE for the

latest Greek texts in the New Testament. For many of these texts, authorship and origin are unknown, and it is left to scholars to infer and reconstruct the detailed circumstances of composition from the form and content of the texts themselves, together with such information from broader cultural and archaeological evidence as may be available. The ahistorical nature of a text such as Genesis 2–3 makes it particularly difficult to contextualize, precisely because its lack of fixed historical referents gives it a timeless quality that allows it to function equally well in a variety of contexts. Nevertheless, although the exact compositional date and social setting of Genesis 2–3 are unknown, many scholars associate it with an early phase in the history of the ancient Israelites. The narrative envisages an agrarian lifestyle: the man, and subsequently the woman with him, is placed in a garden to till it and keep it (Gen. 2.8, 15), and sustains himself by eating from the trees in the garden (Gen. 2.16). Later on, when this idyllic scenario is shattered by the humans' illegitimate consumption of fruit from the tree of knowledge, the man is condemned to grow his own food from an uncooperative earth outside the garden (Gen. 3.18–19, 23). Despite the creation of animals in the narrative (Gen. 2.19–20), there is no hint in these two chapters of animal husbandry, or of the nomadic existence that might accompany sheep or goat herding; the situation in view here is of the (possibly recently) settled small farmer. This makes a date of origin in the late second or early first millennium BCE attractive, since this is the period when archaeology suggests that the people who came to be known as the Israelites were establishing themselves in the Levant in just such small agrarian settlements.

The assumption, then, is that we are dealing with a roughly 3,000-year-old narrative, and that it seeks to explain and justify what its originators experienced as the pattern of life: men cultivated crops, which was difficult and demanding; women bore children, which was painful and labourious, and were subject to their husbands; and all human beings had a relationship of mutual hostility with snakes. This pattern is certainly what is presented in the extract above as being divinely ordained. Such an understanding, however, raises the question of how the societal structure pictured in the extract relates to the depiction of human relationships in the earlier part of the narrative when the humans are first created, prior to their disobedience (Gen. 2). Is the final state of affairs a reaffirmation and enforcement of a patriarchy that was intended by the deity from the start; or is it a falling (or a deliberate moving) away from an initially egalitarian arrangement towards a more hierarchical relationship between the sexes? The narrative intention in Genesis 2 is usually understood as being to present males as prior to females in the order of creation, thereby asserting the male's superiority and making a patriarchal stance fundamental to the narrative.

However, some scholars have argued that the original solitary human should be understood as sexless, as an 'earth creature', because the term by which it is designated (*'adām*, human) is a pun on the name of the material out of which it is created (*'adāmâ*, earth). On this reading, man *qua* male is not created until the woman is made, since 'man' (male) and 'woman' (female) are relational concepts that do not exist in any meaningful way without each other: there is no such thing as 'man' without 'woman'. The problem with this reading, however, is that once the woman has been created, the now clearly male original human being is not referred to as *'îsh* ('man', as opposed to 'woman', *'isshâ*), but continues to be referred to as *hā-'ādām* throughout the narrative, even when paired with the woman. This implies that *hā-'ādām* is conceptualized as male from the start, which means that in Genesis 2 the male is indeed created first and the female is a variation on the male. Additionally, the episode describing the creation of woman (Gen. 2.18–23) is presented from the male rather than from the female point of view, and it is clearly indicated that the female, who fulfils the role of 'helper', is created for the benefit of the male (Gen. 2.18), not *vice versa*.

Thus, the account in Genesis 2 of the creation of the garden, of humans, and of animals gives a definite, if implicit, hierarchy. The human, conceptualized as male, is created first, and then the animals are created as his companions and helpers, although they prove unsuitable for the task. Finally the woman is created from the human as the ideal helper, bone of his bone and flesh of his flesh, of the same substance as the man but fulfilling the auxiliary role for which the animals were originally intended. This gives the implied order of precedence as man-woman-animals, or more accurately, God-man-woman-animals.

However, a resistant reading that refuses to follow the patriarchal grain of the text reveals just how arbitrary the hierarchy is. Nowhere does the male demonstrate any innate superiority to justify the presumed order of precedence. He is the first created life-form, and he assists God in naming the animals that are created for his benefit as well as defining the woman as woman (Gen. 2.19–23); but it is the woman who appears to have greater aspirations than the man in that she is the one who is persuaded by the snake to seek godlike wisdom by eating the forbidden fruit (see Gen. 3.4–6). She is attracted not simply by aesthetic and gustatory pleasures but by the hope of knowledge; and the man puts up no resistance to her whatsoever. Given that the man is later punished for listening to (that is, obeying) the voice of his wife instead of the voice of God (Gen. 3.17), his failure to countermand her suggestion indicates a failure in his supposed duty as authority figure in their relationship. It may also suggest that he is constitutionally unfit to be the authority figure; it certainly suggests that his maleness gives him no intrinsic ability, and therefore no natural right, to dominate the woman. The only thing that gives him the right to dominate her is that God has made her to be his helper, rather than the other way around. Here we see the ultimately arbitrary nature of patriarchy unmasked. In protesting so vehemently against the reversal of hierarchy that puts the snake over the woman and her over the man to the exclusion of God, and in making no attempt to endow the man with any significant attributes or characteristics beyond his maleness, the text unwittingly demonstrates that what it assumes to be the natural order of precedence is by no means natural but constructed. The penalties for the transgression are a strong explicit enforcing of the original implicit hierarchy, including God's position at its head, its constructed nature being amply demonstrated by the need for such reinforcement.

It seems, then, that throughout the narrative the ideal human society envisaged is one where male primacy, set in place by God, is aided and supported by women. However, such an arrangement is not a foregone conclusion. Genesis 3, with its tale of the snake, acknowledges the existence of differing sources of authoritative wisdom which result in a different hierarchy (here, snake-woman-man-God), and so it attempts to delegitimize some of them in favour of its preferred *status quo*. This can be seen from the fact that the snake is actually correct when it tells the woman that, despite God's words, the humans will not die if they eat the forbidden fruit (Gen. 3.4–5). Although most interpreters preserve the deity's integrity by reading God's threat of immediate death on eating the fruit (Gen. 2.17) as metaphorical or symbolic – after all, the Judaeo-Christian God cannot lie – the narrative makes equal if rather different sense when read as patriarchy claiming control of power by controlling access to knowledge. In support of this reading, it is noticeable that when God questions the humans over what they have done and then allocates the penalties detailed in the extract quoted above, the snake (unlike the humans) is given no chance to defend itself. Once the woman says that it persuaded her to eat, it is roundly cursed and set at permanent odds with the humans to prevent any further inter-species cooperation. Although Christian tradition in particular claims that the snake represents evil and is 'the devil in disguise', in the first-millennium BCE ancient Near East snakes had many positive connotations, including associations with wisdom, healing and rejuvenation. Breaking the link between humans and snakes thus means that neither the knowledge nor the immortality that God has denied the humans can become available to them from this alternative source. Equally noticeable, though often overlooked by the patriarchally orientated reader who accepts the hierarchical stance of the text, is the fact that the woman is not actually cursed. Both the snake and the man have penalties that begin 'Because you have done ... cursed ...'. The woman, on the other hand, is simply told without any preamble that God will increase her pain in childbirth and put her under her husband's domination. Although clearly punitive, this consequence is presented neither as the direct result of her actions nor as a curse. This can be seen as God's grudging acknowledgement that the woman has uncovered the truth, along with his desire to prevent her from interfering any further with the hierarchy that he has established. In sum, the message of Genesis 2–3 is that other configurations of authority are possible, but that – whatever benefits they bring – they ultimately lead to negative consequences. In order, therefore, to avoid such consequences the original authority configuration must be preserved. The difficult circumstances that are now experienced by men and women in relation to their life-tasks should be a reminder to them of what happens when authority structures are disrupted. In other words, the events in the garden and their results are a moment of contestation of patriarchy that shows it to be vulnerable. The end result is to reaffirm it, though at the price of revealing its essentially arbitrary nature.

But what of the notion of death that appears in the man's penalty (Gen. 3.19)? Is that not the punishment that was threatened for eating the forbidden fruit? And is that not indeed the woman's fault, as evidenced by God's accusatory words to the man? Certainly later readers saw it thus, as evidenced by the second and third passages quoted above, and by centuries of subsequent Christian tradition. However, to accuse the woman of *causing* by her actions a death that would not otherwise have afflicted humans at all is unwarranted, given that when such preconceived interpretations are abandoned it can be seen that the text itself does not set out to level such an accusation. First, in contrast to the punishments visited on the snake and the woman, both of whom are punished in their actual person (Gen. 3.14–16), God does not curse the man himself, but the ground on which the man is to work (Gen. 3.17). It thus makes better sense to read the comment about the man returning to dust (Gen. 3.19) not as part of his punishment – he dies because he is cursed – but as a reminder of his fundamentally human, as opposed to divine, nature: he may have godlike wisdom, but he is not a god, merely sculpted dust. This understanding is supported by the verses following the extract quoted above, where God declares that having eaten the forbidden fruit the human is now like him in knowing good and evil; so he must be prevented from eating the fruit of the tree of life, which also grows in the Garden of Eden, and thereby living forever (Gen. 3.22). This is the only thing that now separates humans from God (or gods): humans die, but gods do not; and to preserve that boundary God expels the human from the garden, away from the possibility of becoming immortal (Gen. 3.23–24). The text implies that the human has not yet eaten from the tree of life, because had he done so he would already be immortal; and this in turn implies that he was created mortal, not immortal. Immortality may have been theoretically within the humans' grasp, and their actions may have destroyed the opportunity for them to have it. But that is different from saying that their actions – or the woman's actions in particular – caused a change in their ontological status from immortal to mortal.

Nevertheless, the reading that death was brought on the human race by a woman has a long history, as is clear from the second patriarchal moment quoted above. Dating from the second century BCE, this is taken from a work that according to its own prologue was written in Hebrew by a Hellenistic Jew named Jesus Ben Sirah and translated into Greek by his grandson. The Greek version has been transmitted to us as part of the Septuagint, an ancient Greek translation of Judaism's Hebrew scriptures. The Septuagint dates from the third or second centuries BCE, and as well as translations of every book in the Hebrew canon it contains several works (including the Wisdom of Ben Sirah, from which the extract is taken) that are not present in the Hebrew collection. The Septuagint with its expanded table of contents was scripture for Greek-speaking Jews, and in the Hellenized culture of the eastern Mediterranean it was the scripture used by the earliest Christians, who were Jewish. Later it was combined with the documents that eventually formed the New Testament to produce a distinctively Christian Bible. Although the fifteenth-century Christian reformer Martin Luther and his Protestant followers rejected the Septuagint – and thereby its additional books – in favour of the Hebrew scriptures as the true basis for the Christian Bible, Catholic and Orthodox Christianity have continued to revere the Septuagint's additional books, known as the Apocrypha or Deutero-canonical works, as part of the canon of scripture. So despite being largely overlooked by Protestant Christianity, the Wisdom of Ben Sirah is a part of the Judaeo-Christian scriptural tradition, hence its inclusion here.

The verse cited is the earliest known reference to the traditions in Genesis 2–3. It comes as part of a series of didactic comments on good and bad wives and how they bring prosperity or pain to their husbands (Sir. 25.13–26.16). The series as a whole is at best patriarchal and at worst positively misogynistic, from an author who was writing for the education of young Jewish men, and in doing so reflected the general sentiments of his own patriarchal era. The verse quoted above is, however, highly unusual in presenting such a negative assessment of the woman's role in Eden, since other similar allusions to the Genesis traditions in subsequent Judaeo-Christian texts hold Adam or humans in general rather than Eve alone responsible for the entry of sin into the world. That said, Ben Sirah's negative attitude was reflected some 200 years later by the New Testament writer of the first letter to Timothy, as quoted in the third moment above. This writer's proclamations were made in the context of the emergence of the Jewish sect that would later become Christianity, and although there is no external evidence of the letter's context it may well have been a local response to the influence of heterodox Gnostic groups who, believing that material, bodily existence (and thus physical reproduction) was evil, sought instead spiritual enlightenment via esoteric knowledge and also allowed women to be teachers. The relevance of Eve, constructed as a woman who sought and transmitted what turned out to be illegitimate knowledge, is evident in such a situation. The writer of 1 Timothy claims to be the apostle Paul, the mid-first-century CE Jewish convert whose surviving letters with their exposition of the significance of Jesus' life and death are the earliest foundational documents of Christianity. But the sentiments expressed in 1 Timothy differ in significant ways from those in other letters written by Paul. Among those differences is this idea that the woman, not the man, was deceived and became a transgressor, so she needs to remain silent, learn in humility and bear children. Elsewhere, Paul requires women to cover their heads when speaking in church (1 Corinthians 11.3–15), but clearly envisages them having the right to pray and prophesy in mixed gatherings in public.[4] Paul himself also attributes the original transgression to the man Adam (Romans 5.12–19; 1 Corinthians 15.22) rather than to the woman, which is another significant difference from the sentiments expressed in 1 Timothy. Unfortunately, it is the more negative version of events that has had the greater impact on social mores both inside and subsequently outside the church, one suspects because in the early days of Christianity it was more compatible with the pre-existing social structures, and allowed churches to exist more easily within those structures without attracting unwanted hostility.

In summary, then, our three biblical moments demonstrate the increasingly patriarchal trajectory of an already patriarchal tradition. It is not the only trajectory of the Adam and Eve story in the Bible, but it is the one that has had the most enduring effect. And yet the two best-known instances of it (Genesis and 1 Timothy) both appear to have arisen from moments of contestation. They thus affirm a patriarchal world order while unwittingly betraying to the discerning reader its vulnerability.

The Talmud: A Tale of Two Bodies

Sarra Lev

I.   R. Yohanan opened [his exposition]: ' "You have beset me behind and before (ahor vakedem tzartani)" (Ps. 139:5)…'

II. R. Yirmiyah b. Leazar said: 'When God created (Heb. bara) adam, God created it an androgynus[1] as it says, "Male and female God created them and… called their name Adam." (Gen. 5:2)'

III. R. Shmuel b. Nahman said: 'When God created adam, God created it double-faced, then split her/him and made him/her two backs, here and there.'

IV. They objected: 'But it is written, "God took one of his ribs (tzela)…!" (Gen. 2:21)'

V.   He answered: 'from [adam's] sides, as it says, "And for the second side (tzela) of the tabernacle…" (Ex. 26:20)'

VI. R. Tanhuma in R. Banayah's name and R. Berekhiah in R. Leazar's name said: 'God created [adam] an unformed mass [golem], and it was stretched from one end of the world to the other, as it says, "Your eyes saw my unformed substance (g-l-m)." (Ps. 139:16)'

VII. R. Yehoshua b. R. Nehemiah and R. Yehudah b. R. Shimon in R. Leazar's name said: 'God created [adam] encompassing the entire world…'

VIII. R. Leazer said: '[Adam] was the last in the work of the last day, and the first in the work of the last day. R. Shimon b. Lakish said: The last in the work of the last day and the earliest in the work of the first day. That is the view of R. Shimon b. Lakish, who says: "And the spirit of God hovered" (Gen. 1:2) refers to the soul of the first adam…'

IX. Rav Nahman said: 'Last of all of the deeds [of creation] and first in punishment.'

X.   Rav Shmuel b. R. Tanhum said: 'So too, [human] praise is [uttered] last, as it is written, "Halleluyah. Praise God from the heavens"… and after that,

"*Praise God from the* earth"...*and only after that*, "*Kings of the earth and all peoples.*" *(Ps. 148:1–11)*'

XI. *R. Simlai said:* '*Just as [human] praise comes only after that of cattle, beasts, and fowl, so too [human] creation comes after that of cattle, beasts, and fowl. First it says* "*And Elohim said: Let the waters crawl with live crawling creatures, and fowl shall fly over the land...*" *(Gen. 1:20) and after [the creation of] all of the others,* "*LET US MAKE ADAM...*" *(Gen. 1:26–27)*'[2]

Do not be dismayed. What you read above is *midrash* (pl. *midrashim*), one of the most complex genres in Hebrew literature to negotiate, and one of the richest to mine. This chapter will do both, step by step. But first, a few words about *midrash* itself.

Midrash is a text *about* a text. Its purpose is to expound upon the biblical text and to bring to light what it 'really' says. Many *midrashim* seem to have little loyalty to the 'plain meaning' of the biblical text they are explaining. One could even claim that the closer a *midrash* is to the plain meaning of the text, the less 'midrashic' it really is. The underlying premise of *midrash* is that Scripture, having been written by God, is perfect. Thus, when Scripture *looks* imperfect, it is actually trying to tell us something. The *midrash* is used to reveal that hidden message. This has the potential to (and often does) open up what we might today think of as 'unexpected' readings.

'Looking imperfect' for the rabbis consisted of any number of possible factors. Something that could have been written more concisely, for example, is considered imperfect – if it could have been said in fewer words, the unnecessary words must convey information. The existence of these extra words (or even letters) must be explained, or expounded by *midrash*. So too, if a verse is unclear, seemingly out of place, or theologically untenable, it constitutes an opportunity for *midrash*. The biblical stories of creation are filled with these midrashic opportunities.

The first chapters of Genesis are usually read as a continuous narrative, but there are, in fact, *two* stories of creation. In the first (Gen. 1:1–2:4a), male and female are created together, while in the second (Gen. 2:4b–25), female is created out of male. The rabbis consider the stories separately at times, and together at times. The biblical stories of creation lay the foundation for patriarchy. The first prescribes human domination of the planet – God creates an '*adam*', a word that functions both as a proper name (Adam) and as the word for 'human' or for 'first human' (*the adam*) in biblical and rabbinic literature.[3]

God gives the *adam* dominion over the earth and its inhabitants. The second Genesis narrative constructs men's domination of women – God creates a *man*, sees that *he* is lonely and, in response, creates *him* a woman, from *his* rib. Woman is subsequent to, derivative of and made for man.

The early rabbis used their interpretations of biblical text to establish and maintain their hold as experts on the Bible, and thus, their authority. One might (rightly) assume, therefore, that it would be in their interest to uphold these patriarchal underpinnings of human mastery and male primacy. And yet, counter-narratives and openings for counter-narratives do appear in rabbinic literature. This chapter will explore a single text that exemplifies the ongoing tension between rabbinic narratives that construct or uphold patriarchy, and those that contest it.

The text that we will study is called a *petihta* (homiletical *midrash*). It appears in *Bereshit* (Genesis) *Rabbah*, a fifth-century C.E. compilation of *midrash* from the Land of Israel. Each chapter of Bereshit Rabbah (BR) begins with several *petihta'ot* (pl.), each of which opens with a verse from the *Ketuvim* and weaves a homily that closes with a verse (or verses) from the *Torah*.[4] That verse from the *Torah* is the key to every *petihta*. In our case, the closing verse establishes *adam's* (humans') dominion over all the earth and continues to describe the creation of the *adam*:[5]

> (26) And Elohim said, "Let us make *an adam* in our image, as our likeness and let *them* have dominion over the fish of the sea, and over the birds of the skies, and over the cattle, and over all the earth, and over every creeping thing that creeps upon the earth. (27) So God created *the adam* in *His* image, in the image of Elohim *He* created *him*; male and female *He* created *them.*" (XI).

Several midrashic 'problems' appear here. Most notably, the *adam* is described using both singular and plural pronouns, and as both 'man' and 'male and female'. This ambiguity is revisited in the individual *midrashim* that make up the *petihta*.

The verse from *Ketuvim* that opens the *petihta* is Ps. 139:5: 'Behind and before you have closed me in (*ahor vakedem tzartani*)' (see I). This *petihta* is composed of a series of short *midrashim*[6] about the creation of the first human, in which the rabbis play on the Hebrew word for 'closed me in', (*tzartani*) because of its similarity to the word for 'formed me', (*yetzartani*). Thus, they read the verse as if to say, 'You have *formed* me behind and before', (also translated '*early* and *late*' or '*west* and *east*') linking the verse from Psalms with the formation of the first human. The play on *tzartani* carries through the individual *midrashim*, each one providing a different understanding of what it means to be formed 'behind and before', 'early and late', or 'west and east'. These *midrashim* alternate between a more traditional patriarchal trope (describing humanity (and/or man) as superior), and the notion that humanity is distinctly common, or even inferior. These narratives with their patriarchal outlook and their counter-narratives form the warp and woof of this colourful tapestry, in which no sooner has the reader followed one thread, than she encounters another of an entirely different colour.

The interlaced counter-narratives were not necessarily intentional disruptions of the rabbis' patriarchal values, nor do they demonstrate a different value system. However, through the rabbis' commitment to the enterprise of *midrash*, counter-narratives were created, whether intentional or not.[7] Let us then examine the *midrash* above, in order to understand the narrative and counter-narrative that appear in this rabbinic homily. In his opening to the *petihta* (I), R. Yohanan explains this contradiction through the Hagiographic verse (Psalms 139:5): if one merits, one is superior – one receives a reward in this world ('behind') and in the world to come ('forward'). If one does not merit, one is inferior (will be held accountable).

However, one need not accept the framing of R. Yohanan as that which guides these individual *midrashim*, even if that is how the redactor of the *petihta* combined them. Rather, each *midrash* can also be read individually as a statement about the creation of (hu)mans as told in Genesis, and thus, as a statement about patriarchy. In what follows, we will walk through the *midrashim* that appear in the *petihta*, concentrating on the first parts (II–V), which directly speak to the patriarchal framework of male dominion over female.

The *midrash* of R. Yirmiyah ben Leazar (II) is arguably the most radical, explaining that the first human, the *adam*, is created as a single body composed of male and female. R. Shmuel b. Nahman's statement (III) is ostensibly a follow-up to that declaration, describing the creation in more detail: *How* was this two-sexed *adam* created? With two faces, back to back ('behind and before'), so that God could split the 'double body' down the middle and come out with two human bodies.

This story of creation closely resembles that which Aristophanes proposes in Plato's *Symposium*, in which humans were created back to back in a single body with two faces, two sets of limbs and two sets of genitals. In his version, some were male and female (these were called *androgynus*), some male and male, and some female and female. In order to reduce the strength of humans, Zeus halved these bodies, creating what are now (single-sexed) humans. According to Aristophanes, each individual human has for evermore been drawn to the particular sex from which he or she was initially separated.[8]

But why does R. Yirmiyah posit this story? His interpretation is based on a textual problem, similar to that which we noted in Genesis 1:26. Genesis 5:1–2 reads: 'In the day when Elohim created *adam*, in the likeness of Elohim God created *him*; male and female God created *them*, and blessed *them*, and called *their* name *adam*, in the day when *they* were created.' Is *adam* a 'he' or a 'they?' What does it mean to say that God created *them* male and female and then 'called *their* name *adam*?' R. Yirmiyah resolves these questions by ignoring the patriarchal tropes of the secondary and derivative creation of woman, and offering a different story of creation, one that brilliantly explains the enigmatic verses.

R. Yirmiyah's solution is not benign. In his version of the story, the first creation consists of a single male-and-female body. Woman's creation does not emerge from man, or even follow that of man. The creation of man and woman is simultaneous, throwing a wrench into the entire story of human creation.

But that is not all that R. Yirmiyah achieves through his interpretation. He also manages inadvertently to disrupt another baseline understanding that patriarchy has always taken for granted – the hierarchical binary. If patriarchy is based on the premise that there are males and females, and female is secondary, then any suggestion of a third sex/gender option is itself a disruption of the norm. And yet, R. Yirmiyah's story of human creation integrates the intersexed *androgynus* into the very origin of creation, making his/her creation primary, preceding the secondary 'two sex' arrangement.

As we said, this *petihta* is composed of warp and woof, and thus R. Yirmiyah's narrative does not hang in the air for long before his radical reformulation of woman's creation is challenged. An anonymous 'they' objects (IV): Your egalitarian story doesn't hold! The biblical text clearly says that the woman was taken from one of *adam's* ribs!

There are two objections here – one textual and the other ideological. The textual problem is simply that R. Yirmiyah's story (supported by R. Shmuel) is a far stretch from the text of the second chapter of Genesis, in which woman is built from man's rib following *his* creation. However, the genre of *midrash* frequently veers from the main story, so that textual problems alone should hardly provoke this reaction. This is where the ideological objection enters the picture, balking at the idea that women and men may be formed from precisely the same cloth at precisely the same moment.[9] R. Yirmiyah and R. Shmuel have strayed not only from the biblical text, but also from the *status quo*.

R. Shmuel's response to the anonymous objection (V) elegantly draws on the description of the building of the tabernacle in Exodus 26. Verses 18–19 describe the plans for the south wall of the tabernacle – twenty boards with two silver sockets each. Verses 20–21 then state: 'And for the second side (*tzela*) of the tabernacle on the *north* edge, there shall be twenty boards, and their forty sockets of silver …' The word *tzela* thus has *two* meanings, one anatomical ('rib') and the other architectural ('side'). The 'objectors' read *tzela* in its anatomical sense, but R. Shmuel reads the word in its architectural sense. R. Shmuel's answer plays several functions. To begin with, the body of the first human is analogized to the tabernacle. But more importantly, that body (like the tabernacle) is symmetric – one side male, one side female – and *both* sides, analogized to God's holy dwelling place.

With all of this, it is important to remember that although R. Yirmiyah's counter-narrative significantly undermines certain elements of patriarchy, it assumes and supports other elements of that system, in particular, heteronormativity. In contrast to Aristophanes' story where bodies were initially sometimes 'double male' or 'double female', in R. Yirmiyah's *midrash* there is no suggestion of more than one (male/female) original body. Although his *midrash* does not include Aristophanes' claim that the split bodies are eternally drawn to one another, the rabbinic narrative is based directly on the biblical one in which 'a man shall leave his father and his mother and cleave to his wife, and they shall be one flesh' (Gen. 2:24). This *midrash* cannot be separated from that larger narrative in which those two (male and female) bodies (again) become 'one flesh'.

Following R. Yirmiyah and R. Shmuel's *midrash*, comes another that potentially contests the patriarchal narrative, though it too has multiple interpretations. R. Tanhuma and R. Berekhiah suggest that the *adam* was not a human body at all, but a *golem*, stretched from one end of the earth (or universe) to the other (VI). The root (*g-l-m*) of the word *golem* means raw material. In this *midrash*, the *adam* is presented as a giant mass of raw material, covering the planet. While this *midrash* does not directly call into question the traditional gender paradigm, it does challenge some basic tenets of the biblical creation story, including its presentation of a sovereign (male) human. In this description, *adam* is not 'human' at all, but simply raw material. Rather than master and ruler, *adam* must be formed and worked by one more powerful. The image of *adam* as *golem* also raises the possibility that neither sex nor gender is original to creation. That is to say, the initial creation that was to become human was an undifferentiated blob – unsexed, and certainly un-gendered.

The suggestion that this *golem* stretches from one end of the world to the other is again an interpretation of 'behind and before'. In this *midrash*, however, the words *ahor vakedem* are more aptly translated 'west and east', evoking a vast horizontal expanse. Thus, despite its characteristics as counter-narrative, this *midrash* does lend itself to a patriarchal viewpoint as well – painting the *adam* as larger than life (*all* life, quite literally). While this *midrash* demotes the *adam* from its status as ruler, it allows this *golem* to occupy *all possible* space.

What comes next in the sequence of *midrashim* (VII) is ambiguous. R. Yehoshua b. R. Nehemiah and R. Yehudah b. R. Shimon state: '[God] created [the *adam*] encompassing (*maleh*) the entire world.' What does the word 'encompassing' mean here? Do we hold onto the image of the *adam* stretching over the entire world, filling all space, or might the original *golem* body *include* that world within it? That is, does that first *adam*, in fact, *contain* the raw material for the *entirety* of creation, plant, animal, water and sand? The Hebrew word 'maleh' indicates that *adam* is *filled with* the entire world, not separate from it, or lord over it, but composed *of* it.

Once again, however, it is also possible to read R. Yehoshua and R. Yehudah (VII) not as asserting *adam*'s embodiment of all things, but rather *his* immensity in comparison with all things. If there is nothing outside of that *adam*, then *golem* or not, *he* is the locus of all power, or in essence, *he* is *everything*.[10] What follows adopts this very interpretation, reading *maleh* not as 'being filled by the world', but as 'filling the world'. A series of biblical verses is proffered, 'proving' that the *adam* filled every space on earth, including the space between the earth and the heavens. This is followed by a *midrash* (not quoted) in which R. Leazar suggests that *adam*'s creation took place both at the earliest and at the latest moment of the last day.[11] R. Shimon ben Lakish (VIII) pushes this idea to its limits: *adam*'s creation was 'the earliest act of the *first* day'. The combination of these three *midrashim* positions the *adam* as spanning all existing space, and all existing time – elevating human primacy to mythical proportions.

It is directly following this grandiose description of *adam*'s vastness that Rav Nahman steps in (IX) to reclaim the words 'behind and before' as counter-narrative. The *adam*, he asserts, is 'last ("behind") of all of the deeds [of creation] and first ("before") in punishment'. Rav Nahman's terse statement instantly (and quite literally) shrinks the massive *adam* down to size. The *adam* is not first in creation, but last! The only thing for which *adam* can claim primacy, according to Rav Nahman, is punishment – not a legacy of which to be proud, and certainly not one that either explicitly or implicitly vests humans or men with power or authority.

The *petihta* ends on a similar note, not by praising the grandeur of men or humans, but by setting them in their 'rightful place' in creation – last. Rav

Shmuel b. Rav Tanhum (X) points to humans as having been the last of all the creations to praise God. God's *quid-pro-quo* response, says R. Simlai (XI), is to create humans *last*, not as the grand finale of all creation, but as a castigation.[12]

The *petihta* does not close with an image of the superiority or power of *man* over all others (women, other-sexed/gendered and all creatures who roam the earth). However, although *man* loses his privileged place in creation in these last three *midrashim*, woman fares no better. For Rav Nahman (IX), Rav Shmuel (X) and R. Simlai (XI), she does not even appear any longer as the final stage of creation. If these last three *midrashim* diminish 'man' by positioning him last in the order of creation, then woman's inferior status (and certainly that of a 'third sex/gender') is highlighted both by her assumed place in that order and by her outright absence in the *midrash*.

As we noted, the key to a *petihta* is its closing verse (XI), in our case two verses – Genesis 1:26–27: 'And Elohim said, "Let us make *an adam* in our image ... and let *them* have dominion ... So God created *the adam* in *His* image, in the image of Elohim *He* created *him*; male and female *He* created *them*."' The confusion that this verse in Genesis evokes is twofold. We noted already that it calls into question the sovereignty of men over women: Did God create *adam* a 'him' or a 'them?' But by the end of this *petihta*, we are left wondering not only about *adam*'s place in relation to gender, but also about *adam*'s place in relation to all creation. Are humans truly meant to be sovereign over the earth and all her creatures? While the *petihta*'s closing Biblical verse (Gen. 1:26) describes the dominion of *man*, these last few *midrashim* leave us in doubt. *Man* is last in creation, last to praise God and first to be punished – not really the material for a supreme ruler.

BR 8:1 leaves us sitting in a moment of tension between the archetypal (patriarchal) creation narrative and alternatives to that narrative. Although we rarely find evidence that the rabbis of late antiquity advocated for (or even contemplated) fundamental changes to societal patriarchy, the genre of *midrash* did present some unique opportunities to express alternative world views. Through *midrash* the rabbis wrestled with biblical texts that did not 'make sense', and sometimes produced alternative narratives as a by-product of that enterprise. *Midrash* thus had the potential to open up worlds that the rabbis' legal and social systems did not. While it is true that none of these alternative worlds is wholly free from the patriarchal paradigm, each of them cuts away at the overgrowth and offers us a glimpse of the road not taken.

Patriarchalism and the Qur'an[1]

Asma Barlas

Say: He is God,
The One and Only;
God, the Eternal, Absolute;
He begetteth not,
Nor is He begotten;
And there is none
Like unto Him (112).[2]
* * *

Men are [qawwamuna 'ala] women [on the basis] of what Allah has [faddala]
some of them over others, and [on the basis] of what they spend of their
property (for the support of women). So good women are [qanitat], guarding
in secret that which Allah has guarded. As for those from whom you fear
[nushuz] admonish them, banish them to beds apart, and … separate [daraba]
them. Then, if they obey you, seek not a way against them (4:34).[3]
* * *

For Muslim men and women,–
For believing men and women,
For devout men and women,
For men and women who are
Patient and constant, for men
And women who humble themselves,
For men and women who give
In charity, for men and women
Who fast (and deny themselves).
For men and women who

Guard their chastity, and
For men and women who
Engage much in God's praise
For them has God prepared
Forgiveness and great reward (33:35).[4]
* * *

In this chapter, I examine oppositional readings of Islam's scripture, the Qur'an, as a patriarchal and also as an anti-patriarchal text, and since it does not have a single 300-word-long passage that fits into either category, I will be quoting partial lines, single words and shorter verses, including the three cited above. Historically, however, Muslims have interpreted it as privileging men, which is why the history of Qur'anic exegesis is more than a moment, or series of moments, of 'patriarchalism'. It is, rather, a millennium-long history of Muslim patriarchy itself. And this in spite of the fact that there are fewer than a dozen lines and words in a text of about 80,000 words and 6,000 verses that are said to favour men. In recent years, therefore, some Muslim women have also offered anti-patriarchal readings of the Qur'an, which have, in turn, inspired some secular Muslims, especially third-generation feminists, to rebrand it as being incurably patriarchal, although they never say what they mean by patriarchy itself.

Clearly, these irreducible differences tell us about the range of Muslim attitudes to their religion but they also reflect how the Qur'an is interpreted, in what contexts and by whom. The *how* is crucial because while there are certainly some words and lines in it – moments, really – that speak to male authority, there are also teachings that are opposed to patriarchy. By this term I mean two distinct types of male authority over women. One is rule by the father/husband, which, in some of its religious iterations, draws on images of God as Father/male. The other is the politics of sexual differentiation that privileges men in their biological capacity as males. The Qur'an itself does not use words like 'sexual differentiation', 'male privilege', or 'father-rule', but I will be discussing its teachings in light of this comprehensive definition of patriarchy. I begin by reviewing its 'patriarchal moments', and then analyse what I consider to be some anti-patriarchal teachings; I end with a note on method.

The one verse that is quoted most often in defence of male privilege is 4:34 (cited above) which most Muslims interpret as saying that God prefers (*faddala*) men to women, that men are women's guardians (*qawwamun*), that good wives are obedient (*qanitat*) and that husbands can beat (*daraba*) those who are not (*nushuz*). However, all five Arabic keywords have several other meanings as well, and so these are not the only possible, or plausible, choices.

For instance, al-Tabari, a medieval exegete, took *qawwamun* to mean financial maintainers, which is also how some contemporary feminists, notably, Riffat Hassan and Azizah al-Hibri, read it. They also point out that the first line of the verse is descriptive, not normative, 'since obviously there are at least some men who do not provide for women'.[5] Moreover, since men can only be *qawwamun* 'in matters where God gave *some* of the men more than *some* of the women *and* in what the men spend of their money, then clearly men as a class are not "*qawwamun*" over women as a *class*'.[6] (In their interpretation, *faddala* alludes to resources and not to God's partiality to men.) Incidentally, this is the sole use of *qawwamun* in the Qur'an, as Zainah Anwar and Ziba Mir-Hosseini note. 'In relation to marriage,' they say, 'it uses two other terms over twenty times: *ma'ruf* (good way, decent) and *rahmah wa muwadah* (compassion and love)'.[7] Yet, Muslim family law revolves around the concept of male guardianship over women. As to *qanitat*, Amina Wadud believes it means obedience to God since the Qur'an does not compel a wife to obey her husband; she therefore also reads *nushuz* as denoting marital discord and not a wife's disobedience to her husband.[8] This seems right since the Qur'an also refers to a husband's *nushuz* (4:128), which Muslims never interpret as a man's disobedience to his wife.

Lastly, there is *daraba*, which the Qur'an uses over a dozen times for everything from strike/beat to leave/go away. Laleh Bakhtiar uses 'go away' and, although her choice is against the grain of the Muslim exegetical tradition, it is not outside all tradition.[9] There are also *hadith* (narratives) that the Prophet never struck his own wives and forbade men to strike theirs. More to the point, the Qur'an does not permit violence against a wife in any other instance. About marriage it says: '[God] created for you helpmeets from yourselves that ye might find *sukun* in them, and He ordained between you love and mercy' (30:21).[10] *Sukun* implies not only a sense of peace but also of sexual fulfilment.[11] Even where love is in short supply and husbands dislike their wives, the Qur'an still tells them to 'consort with them [wives] in kindness, for if ye hate them it may happen that ye hate a thing wherein Allah hath placed much good' (4:19).[12] Indeed, even in those cases where spouses are each other's 'enemies', the Qur'an urges them to be mutually forgiving and forbearing (64:14).[13] In light of the rest of its teachings, then, 4:34 becomes anomalous when we pick the most punitive meaning of *daraba* and, in truth, there is no compulsion to do so when the Qur'an itself recommends looking for the text's 'best' meanings (29:18).[14]

A line that is also read as affirming male superiority is: 'men are a degree above women' (2:228). However, the only context in which the Qur'an says this is when it speaks about a couple who has separated, pending their divorce. During this period, it says, they can reunite 'if they desire a reconciliation. And they [women] have rights similar to those [of men] over them *in kindness*, and men are *[darajah]* above them'.[15] The 'degree' husbands enjoy, therefore, is only in cases of divorce and reconciliation.

A word that also evokes patriarchal interpretations is *harth*: 'Your women are a *harth* for you (to cultivate) so go to your tilth as ye will, and send (good deeds) before you for your souls' (2:223).[16] *Harth* is usually taken to mean sowing and therefore as indicating vaginal intercourse, though some men think it means a wife is her husband's property to treat as he likes. However, this is a patriarchal fantasy because not only does the Qur'an counsel mutuality in a marriage but it also warns husbands against lewd behaviour (5:6). Furthermore, it does not describe any human being as property even when it speaks about slaves to its first audience, a seventh-century tribal Arab slave-owning patriarchy. Lastly, the Qur'an also speaks of paradise as *harth* (42:20), which cannot possibly be taken to mean land, property or sowing. I therefore read it as a metaphor for sexual pleasure given Islam's positive view of sexual desire.[17]

Finally, Muslims claim that one man equals two women because the Qur'an gives him double a woman's share in inheritance, treats his evidence as more important than hers and caters to his sexual needs through polygyny. All these are glib generalizations, however. Only a son gets double what a daughter does from their parents' property; parents get equal shares from their child's. Also, while two women can take the place of one man as witnesses to a financial deal, a wife's evidence outweighs her husband's if he accuses her of adultery. (A man must either produce four male witnesses, or swear four times to this effect himself, but, if his wife swears her innocence four times, there the matter ends.) As to polygyny, the Qur'an permits only *some* wards of female orphans to marry more than one orphan if doing so will secure justice for *her*. However, even in such situations, it says monogamy is better for the wife (4:3). This is the extent of 'patriarchal moments' in the Qur'an, and I will now look at some teachings that run counter to patriarchal ideologies and practices.

The Qur'an's approach to fathers differs from that of religious and traditional patriarchies in two ways. First, it does not patriarchalize God. This is a critical point since men claim power when 'the source of ultimate value is ... described in anthropomorphic images as Father or King'.[18] As should be clear from verse 112 cited at the outset, however, the Qur'an explicitly says that God is not father or son or, for that matter, like any other being. Since God is incomparable, it even forbids using similitude for God (16:74), or trying to define God (37:180). These prohibitions mean the Qur'an's own gendered language about God is just that: language; it is not a claim that God is a male.

Second, the Qur'an does not endorse father-rule. In fact, it criticizes those who follow the 'ways' of their fathers and warns of '(The coming of) a Day/ When no father can avail/Aught for his son, nor/A son avail aught/For his father' (31:33). To this end, it tells children *not* to obey their parents (not just their fathers), 'If they strive/To make thee join/In worship with [God]/Things of which thou hast/No knowledge' (31:14–15).[19]

This conflict between monotheism and patriarchy – that is, between what believers owe to God and to their fathers – is also the motif of Abraham's story. As a youth searching for the one true God, Abraham breaks with his father, and also the idols his father worships, as the condition for submitting to God. And when his father has him thrown into a fire, it is God who saves him. Since God is not father in Islam, I interpret this rescue not as affirming God as patriarch but as displacing father-rule altogether. Abraham's attempted sacrifice of his own son years later also shows that, far from exalting fathers, the Qur'an limits their authority and subordinates it to God's. Thus, Abraham not only does not have the right to kill an unwary son (he can only proceed with the sacrifice after his son freely consents to it), but, in the end, he cannot kill even a willing son since God saves him from *Abraham*. He does not therefore have the absolute power fathers did in traditional and religious patriarchies or even his namesake does in the Biblical narrative.[20]

I believe what makes the Qur'an's episteme anti-patriarchal is not only its descriptions of God and its attitude to fathers but also the fact that it does not ascribe 'psycho-social distinctions' between women and men to their biological differences, as do patriarchal religions.[21] Even its 'patriarchal moments' do not claim that sex/gender differences make men and women unequal. In fact, the Qur'an does not map cultural symbolism (gender) onto biology (sex), which means there is 'no *concept* of woman' or of 'gendered man' in it.[22] Nor is there a 'hierarchy of being',[23] which means it also does not discriminate between women and men on the basis of their sexual identities. To the contrary, it consistently affirms their ontological equality in describing human creation, moral personality and religious praxis.

The absence of a sexual hierarchy is apparent in the Qur'an's declaration that God 'created you/From a single Self/Created, of like nature, [its mate]' (4:1).[24] Many Muslims who believe that God made men in 'His' image refuse to accept this ontology of a single self and insist that Eve (who is not named in the Qur'an) was created from Adam's rib, an idea borrowed from the Bible by some exegetes. Others, meanwhile, claim that men and women are only equal in the religious sphere and not in the social or marital. The Qur'an, however, does not bifurcate these three domains. For instance, when it talks about *sukun* between a wife and husband, it explicitly references their origins in a single self. Similarly, when it speaks of God's vicegerents (*khalifa*) on earth, it refers to both women and men whom it also calls each other's guardians: 'The Believers, men/And women, are *awliya*,/One of another: they enjoin/What is just, and forbid/What is evil' (9:71–72).[25] *Awliya* means having *walayah*, or custody of/ guardianship over, another. In effect, guardianship is mutual despite Muslim insistence on interpreting *qawwamun* as meaning that men are women's guardians and 'in charge' of them.

Finally, the Qur'an 'pairs' women and men when outlining the nature of moral personality and the scope of religious obligations, as 33:35, quoted at the beginning of this essay, demonstrates. Muslims, however, discount such verses and focus on the Qur'an's 'patriarchal moments' instead. So, I will end with a critique of this predilection on the part of conservatives and secular Muslims and feminists alike.[26]

Contrasting the Qur'an's anti-patriarchal teachings with its 'patriarchal moments' may seem like waging an interminable and unproductive war of verses since people will select those that resonate most with their own sensibilities. Yet, it would be absurd to think that there are not better or worse ways to interpret texts. The Qur'an itself praises 'Those who listen to the Word and follow the best (meaning) in it' (39:18).[27] (Since notions of what is best are likely to depend on time and circumstance, interpretations of the Qur'an will also always be time and context-bound.) In addition, it urges Muslims to read the 'whole of it' (as a textual unity), and to privilege its foundational verses over allegorical ones (to read it intratextually). However, those who interpolate male privilege into the Qur'an usually ignore these basic hermeneutical principles.

First, they treat words as if they have one fixed meaning, precluding others even if these yield better readings and/or readings that are more congruent with the totality of the Qur'an's teachings. Examples would be *qawwamun*, *daraba* and *harth*. Second, they read the text selectively which generates a fragmentary and sometimes a patently false understanding of it, as, for instance, when 'degree' is taken to mean that men are ontologically superior to women, or when deceptive generalizations are made about marriage, inheritance and evidence. Third, they disregard the Qur'an's foundational verses – about creation, moral personality and mutual guardianship – which affirm the ontic equality of women and men while overstating the significance of allegorical allusions, such as the one to wives as *harth*. They also ignore the range of the Qur'an's rulings on evidence, inheritance and marriage that do not fit into the template of male privilege and underscore only those that do, often at the cost of ignoring the intent of specific verses (like the one on polygyny) and of holding the Qur'an hostage to a few words and verses. Finally, those who read male privilege into the Qur'an do not differentiate between teachings that apply to Muslims across time and space and those that were directed at its first (seventh-century) audience. This collapse of the universal and the particular results in part from an unwillingness 'to reckon with moving time'.[28] In other words, it is not just questionable textual practices but also the failure to contextualize its teachings that ties the Qur'an in perpetuity to a long defunct patriarchy. However, trying to make it 'immune from history' also makes the Qur'an's 'own history irrelevant', argues Kenneth Cragg. This idea, he says, 'emerges indisputably from the Quranic text itself', which stresses 'the necessarily periodic and contextual nature of its contents'.[29] I believe its 'patriarchal moments' are in the nature of these 'periodic and contextual' contents since they pertain to a historical situation in which men had a certain type of authority over women. That the Qur'an takes this authority as a given does not mean it upholds patriarchy. To the contrary, as I have argued, its core teachings incline against the ideology of male supremacy propagated by religious, traditional and secular patriarchies. It is, rather, the belief in the idea of fixity, of both time and text, that results in interpretations which tie the Qur'an to a seventh-century patriarchy, thus prolonging its life much beyond its historical origins, prime and logic.

However, as I see it, Muslim patriarchies are hanging by one of the flimsiest ideological threads in history. This is not only because they have hung an ontology of sexual oppression on a scandalously few lines in the Qur'an but also because they have done so by suppressing all that is egalitarian in Islam and by corrupting our very conception of God. For observant Muslims, the Qur'an is the word of a God who, the Qur'an says, does not transgress against the rights of another (God is just), forbids coercion in religion and is beyond sex/gender. I fear that as long as we continue to project sexual partisanship and injustice onto this God by interpreting the Qur'an as a patriarchal text, we will be no better than the 'illiterates who know not the Book/But [see therein their own] desires,/And they do nothing but conjecture' (2:78).[30]

Citizens But Second Class: Women in Aristotle's *Politics* (384–322 B.C.E.)

Edith Hall

Since then household governance falls into three parts – the first, the relation of master to slave (which has been discussed already), the second, the paternal relationship, and the third, the marital relationship – a man also rules his wife and children, both categories as free persons, but not with the same form of rule. He rules his wife as a citizen and his children as a monarch, because the male is by nature better suited to leadership than the female, unless the union is somehow contrary to nature, and the more senior and developed person is more suited to leadership than the younger and immature. Although in most constitutions with citizenship the roles of ruler and ruled shift from one person to another, and they are considered equal by nature and not to differ from one another at all, nevertheless, at the time when one is ruling over the other, they endeavour to create a distinction by means of regalia and titles and honours, just as Amasis described it in his speech about the basin used for washing feet: the male always holds this position in relation to the female. But the rule of a man over his children is that of a king, because the male parent is ruler on the grounds of both affection and seniority, and that is the monarchical type of government [...]

And of this we straightway find an indication in connection with the soul; for the soul by nature contains a part that rules and a part that is ruled, to which we assign different virtues, that is, the virtue of the rational and that of the irrational. It is clear then that the case is the same also with the other instances of ruler and ruled. Hence there are by nature various classes of rulers and ruled. For the free rules the slave, the male the female, and the man the child in a different way. And all possess the various parts of the soul, but possess them in different ways; for the slave has not got the deliberative part at all, and the female has it, but without full authority, while the child has it, but in an undeveloped form.[1]

Aristotle prescribes that men should rule women because the male is 'by nature better suited to leadership than the female', and because men hold seniority over women and are 'more developed'. Male rule over women is founded in nature and any subversions of this natural hierarchy deviate from nature. The requirement for men to rule women is reflected in the constituent parts of the soul and how they differ in men and women: men are naturally superior to women in their capacity for deliberation.

No passage in ancient Greek or Roman literature has exerted more influence on subsequent justifications of patriarchy. Its impact can be traced from the Church Fathers and Thomas Aquinas to Hegel, Schopenhauer and Nietzsche. Yet Aristotle's argument is more complex than my summary implies. In recommending that men's rule over women should be like a magistrate's rule over a city-state, rather than a king's rule over his subjects, or a master's over his slaves, he indicates that the male–female relationship is *less unequal* than the father–child relationship or the master–slave relationship. Women should be like citizens of city-states in some respects, but they are to be excluded permanently from ruling magistracies and from executive power. This lesser inequality rests on another distinction: women are distinguished from children and slaves in that they have *some* capacity for deliberation, even if it lacks authority.

The remainder of this essay consists of three sections. The first offers a brief account of Aristotle's life and times and how this may have informed his political theorization of the position of women. The second locates the excerpt in the context of the preceding argument of Aristotle's *Politics*. The third explicates the excerpt, including the reference to Amasis, and its fit with other Aristotelian discussions of male–female relationships.

The passage is extracted from the first of the eight books of the *Politics* of Aristotle (384–322 BCE). Aristotle studied under Plato at the Academy in Athens, where he will have discussed the place of women in society. He was appointed tutor to Alexander, later known as 'the Great'. Once Alexander had succeeded to the throne and embarked on his conquest of the Persian Empire, Aristotle moved back to Athens in 335 BCE. It was then that he probably completed most of his treatises, including the *Politics*, which is intended to guide statesmen, reflecting the elite circle in which he moved.

Aristotle's life experiences influenced his political thought. Since even free women in all ancient Greek city-states were excluded from most dimensions of political life, it is unremarkable that Aristotle regards women as incapable of most public activities in which he expects free men to engage. He criticizes, while borrowing extensively, Plato's *Republic*, *Statesman*, and *Laws*. Although, in his *Republic*, Plato had discussed many topics explored in Aristotle's *Politics*, the latter is the first extant treatise entirely devoted to political philosophy. Plato, for example, had envisaged the possibility that in a hypothetical ideal republic of the future there could be women among the enlightened oligarchy, or 'guardians', trained on account of their philosophical ability to participate as equal members of a full-time ruling class. But Aristotle's *Politics* systematically defines an achievable contemporary household, shared by men and women, and justifies the hierarchical relationship between them.

Politics Book I first explains political philosophy as the study of the sovereign city-state (*polis*), which Aristotle defines as a community, or partnership. Citizens pursue, in partnership, a common good, or end (*telos*), which is virtue and happiness on both an individual and a collective level. Aristotle then addresses (in order to refute) the popular view that political rule is identical to any other kind of rule – whether of kings over their subjects, men over women and children, or masters over slaves. To show how each type of rule differs, he describes the evolution of city-states from two fundamental partnerships 'between people who can't exist without one another' (27). He identifies these two partnerships as (1) those of men and women, indispensable for human reproduction, which is an imperative because people like to leave behind them someone else like themselves; and (2) those of 'natural ruler' and 'naturally ruled' (i.e. masters and slaves), indispensable for human survival. These two partnerships join to form a household, the purpose of which is to meet the practical needs of life (food, shelter, etc.). Families then join other families to create villages, and eventually villages fuse with other villages to form a city-state. The city-state reaches a greater level of self-sufficiency than is possible in a village. Although it originally evolves because it is easier to create conditions supportive of life in a partnership of several villages than in a single village, it achieves something new: the goal of merely living is replaced by the goal of 'living well'. This does not mean living comfortably or pleasurably, but in accordance with virtue in order to achieve the chief end of humans, which Aristotle sees as happiness and becoming the best possible human. Politics is inseparable from ethics because a well-run city-state is one which enables its citizens to lead good lives.

Aristotle has already stated that the political community, the city-state, has a certain priority over either the household or the individual. Since it ultimately derives from familial partnerships, which depend on natural instincts, it is a *natural* organism rather than a man-made cultural artefact. So man is '*by nature* a political animal' (28). He has offered the analogy of the physical body and its several parts. If a body is destroyed, then each of its parts, including its limbs, is destroyed. No limb can survive without being connected to a functioning body, just as no individual can survive if unattached to any city-state (29). In the establishment of male–female and master–slave partnerships among human beings, nature was aiming at the formation of city-states, the optimal contexts for all humans (who have certain qualities which set them apart from other animals) to achieve perfection. These qualities include speech, reason, and the ability to distinguish good from bad, and just from unjust. Humans pass laws to ensure that justice is upheld and to support the pursuit of virtue, which is more important than the pursuit of wealth or security.

Aristotle has proceeded to defend the naturalness and justice of slavery, which (at least in some circumstances) he regards as mutually beneficial to master and slave. Aristotle views those who are suited by nature to slavery as under-endowed in the capacity to reason, and therefore only able to flourish if humans with superior reason tell them what to do. Such people, he says, are suited to labour, or 'animate tools'.[2] Since slaves were household possessions, Aristotle then moves to a discussion of the management of the household, the *oikos*, where the production and processing of victuals and textiles took place (the words for 'household' and 'management' combined to produce the term *oikonomika* or *economics*). Economics is discussed in tandem with business activities, and Aristotle argues that the pursuit of 'the good life' is more important than making money.

Aristotle now addresses the governance of women and children. The three relationships which constitute the household are the master–slave relationship, the paternal relationship and the marital relationship. (Aristotle assumes that his reader is a free male householder and excludes from consideration the other three relationships which we know, from other ancient sources, were fundamental to households' happiness: those between women and children, women and slaves, and children and slaves.[3]) He declares a qualitative difference between a man's rule over his family members and his slaves, since wives and offspring are free. But there is also a difference between the way a man rules his wife and his children – as the opening excerpt shows.

Aristotle envisages a situation in which a female is better suited to leadership than a male, but only to dismiss this situation as 'contrary to nature'. He might have cited the matriarchal tribeswomen of myth, the 'unnatural' Amazons, who were believed eventually to have been raped or seduced into submission and to have settled down into 'natural' patriarchal relationships. But Aristotle knows that in all periods of Greek history there were successful female leaders, such as Queen Artemisia of Caria, an admiral in the Persian King Xerxes' fleet.[4] In the next book of the *Politics* he criticizes the Spartans for allowing their womenfolk excessive power and freedom (85–8). He here simply pre-empts any counter-argument, which might cite examples of effective female leaders.

In the sentences omitted from the excerpt, Aristotle argues that although slaves, women and children can participate to an extent in virtues such as courage, temperance and justice, since they have some limited capacity for reason, they do so in a different way from men. Where the excerpt restarts, Aristotle proposes the real distinction between the ruling householder and other household members: he alone possesses a *fully developed* rational faculty. It consists of the ability to deliberate and come to reasoned decisions about action. The word for deliberation, *bouleuesthai*, derives from the same root as the Greek word for the civic Council (*boule*), whose role was to deliberate about how the community should act. In all households only ruling males are competent deliberators, which legitimizes their exclusive rule at home and eligibility to participate in power in the public sphere. Deliberation is a central topic in Greek ethics long before Aristotle; women were held to be incapable of it.[5] Yet Aristotle does not deny the deliberative capacity to women and children altogether, as he does to slaves. In children it is undeveloped, but (exclusively in boys, we must assume) has the potential to mature with them. In women, the ability to deliberate is described not as 'undeveloped' but as 'lacking authority'.

Aristotle's choice of term here, *akuros*, makes this sentence one of the most debated in ancient Greek. *Akuros* denotes the opposite of *kurios*, which means 'having power', 'having authority', 'being entitled', 'decisive', 'trustworthy', 'ordained', 'ratified', 'lawful', 'valid', or even 'authentic'. Aristotle is saying that women's deliberative faculty means one or more of the following: 'powerless', 'lacking authority', 'unentitled', 'indecisive', 'untrustworthy', 'not ordained', 'unratified', 'not grounded in law', 'invalid' or 'inauthentic'. It is not clear whether Aristotle means that the capacity is present in women but not legally acknowledged, or whether it is not acknowledged *because* in women it is by nature untrustworthy and indecisive. Some scholars, who argue that Aristotle is, for a man of his time, surprisingly enlightened about women, favour the former interpretation. My own view is that he indeed believed women's deliberations to be untrustworthy and indecisive, which is why he thought that women were not entitled to equality with men, either in the miniature city-state, which constituted the household, or in the institutions where decisions were made on behalf of the whole *polis*. The word *kurios*, used as a noun, also denoted the legal position of a male 'guardian' of a female. Every citizen woman in classical Athens had a *kurios* – her father until she married (in Athens often as young as thirteen), her husband, or in the absence of either a husband or father, her brother or uncle. Her *kurios* not only provided for her but also had power over her. He represented her in financial dealings and in the courts of law.[6] Women's souls, like their persons, needed a *kurios* – an authoritative male agent to validate their decisions and deeds.

Yet women are not to be subordinated to the absolute sovereignty (albeit affectionate) which characterizes a man's control of his children. Aristotle *is* giving women a more consequential role in suggesting that a wife's relationship with her husband bears at least some comparison with the relationship between two equal citizens of a city-state. Within the community of the household, Aristotle is inventing a new civic status, which did not exist anywhere in reality: it is citizenship, but one in which women are permanently debarred from decision-making bodies and magistracies with executive power. As Aristotle says, 'in most constitutions with citizenship the roles of ruler and ruled shift from one person to another, and they are considered equal by nature and not to differ from one another at all'. In such constitutions, when a man became a magistrate, he was temporarily granted insignia of office, titles and privileges for the duration of his rule over other citizens. Aristotle suggests that husbands appoint themselves magistrates in perpetuity, as if assuming forever the regalia, titles and privileges of power. This relationship 'is unlike the civic partnership in that the freedom of man and wife cannot be expressed in functional interchangeability'.[7]

In illustration, Aristotle cites the Egyptian King Amasis, who had been made famous a century before by Herodotus.[8] Amasis was a commoner who had become king. At first, despised by his subjects for his humble origins, he 'won them over to himself by wisdom and not by wilfulness'. One of his kingly possessions was a golden foot-basin in which he and his dinner-guests washed their feet and urinated. He had it melted down and turned into the image of a god. The Egyptians worshipped it and paid it honour. Amasis then summoned his people, and revealed the truth about the divine image; he compared himself with the basin, since he had once been treated with indignity as a commoner, but now deserved honour as their king.

Aristotle's choice of anecdote is subtle. The figure from history he chooses to illustrate the husband's right to rule over women is a commoner who had won the right to rule and be paid respect through merit and superior wisdom rather than birth-right or autocratic conduct. Just so, a husband's role as ruler, and the respect paid to him, although natural, are neither a birth-right nor for ceremonial show, but predicated on his superior wisdom. Amasis' lack of concern with material possessions and public display (the gold basin, slightly comically, represents the 'regalia' of the official in the city-state which Aristotle has been discussing) and his conversion of financial wealth into a symbol of piety also implicitly colour Aristotle's portrait of the perfect household community and its idealized male ruler.

This passage in Aristotle has found defenders even among recent scholars who would never condone sexism in the modern world. Some point to Aristotle's theory of the complementarity of the sexes, elaborated in his works on biology, zoology and ethics. In the *Nicomachean Ethics*, for example, he states that the difference between justice in the household and political justice lies in the way that offices are assigned; within the household, roles and responsibilities are assigned in recognition of the complementarity of the sexes, but in the political sphere as a reward for an individual man's excellence.[9] Different skills, he says later in the *Politics*, are required from men and women under the same heading 'household management', since it is the task of men to acquire goods and of women to guard them with vigilance (110). Other apologists for Aristotle's view of women point to his statement that both women *and* children must be educated in a way which promotes the well-being of the city-state as a whole, since for a community to be excellent it needs to have excellent children and women (51). They also cite Aristotle's recommendations concerning the appropriate ages at which men and women should marry in order to maximize conjugal harmony. He prefers a husband and a wife reach the end of their fertility simultaneously, which requires that men marry considerably younger women. But he also recommends that women marry much later than was the usual practice – at eighteen – in order to aid procreation (it is implied that he believed, correctly, that it is less dangerous for an older teenager to carry a child than a younger one), and to enhance the woman's chance to improve and grow in excellence (292–3). Apologists for Aristotle's attitude to women also compare him with Plato; they argue that although Plato's Socrates envisages in the *Republic* the hypothetical possibility that a few women might have philosophical talents qualifying them as guardians, the general tenor of remarks on women elsewhere in Plato is infinitely more derogatory than in Aristotle.[10] The younger philosopher, it has been suggested, at least envisages a real, contemporary marriage in which the wife has some kind of agency in that she can attain excellence crucial to the happiness of the household as a whole.

Aristotle was prolific. His arguments concerning women's capacities and relations with men, whether considered biologically or socially, pervade all his treatises. But it is this passage in the *Politics* which ultimately justifies *both* women's exclusion from political life in the city-state *and* their second-rate status as citizens in the mini-city of the household. The justification lies in woman's allegedly inferior capacity for deliberation. Those who would argue that Aristotle's gender theory is more nuanced or enlightened than we might otherwise expect, from a man raised under ancient Greek patriarchy, should consider the ultimate consequence of applying his recommendations in any community:

> the existence of fifty percent of the species is legally and economically subordinated to the benefit of the remaining fifty percent. The social system depends on women to give up their public rights and autonomy to the benefit of the private security granted by the status of minority they must have for life.[11]

Men who try to live considered lives in accordance with virtue have no doubt always been kinder to their wives than those without such a commitment. But critics who would try to turn Aristotle into anything other than the founding father of patriarchy in the field of political theory need to remember his pithy, epigrammatic statement on gender relations in the *Politics* just a few chapters before the more extended discussion in the excerpt which has been discussed here: 'the male is by nature superior and the female inferior, the male ruler and the female subject' (33). That is Aristotle's bottom line.

Augustine's *The City of God* (fifth century A.D.): Patriarchy, Pluralism and the Creation of Man

Catherine Conybeare

[I]t is not hard to see how much better it is that God multiplied the human race from the one man whom He created first, than it would have been had He originated it from several. As to the other animals, he created some solitary and, as it were, lone-ranging: that is, more inclined towards solitude.... Others he made gregarious, and these congregate together and prefer to live in company.... But in neither case did God produce these from a single individual. Rather, he commanded that several should come into being at once. Man, however, whose nature was to be in a manner intermediate between angels and beasts, God created in such a way that, if he remained subject to his Creator as his true Lord, and if he kept His commandments with pious obedience, he should pass over into the company of the angels and obtain, without suffering death, a blessed immortality without end. But if he offended the Lord his God by using his free will proudly and disobediently, he should live, as the beasts do, subject to death: the slave of his own lust, destined to suffer eternal punishment after death. God therefore created only one single man: not, certainly, that he might be alone and bereft of human society, but that, by this means, the unity of society and the bond of concord might be commended to him more forcefully, mankind being bound together not only by similarity of nature, but by the affection of kinship. Indeed, God did not even create the woman who was to be united with the man in the same way as He created the man. Rather, it pleased Him to create her out of the man, so that the human race might derive entirely from the one man.[1]

This passage comes from the twelfth book of twenty-two in Augustine of Hippo's 'great, uphill work' (*magnum opus et arduum*), *The City of God*. Augustine began to compose the work in 413 CE, in direct response to the sack of Rome – still the symbolic, if not the political, centre of the empire in which he lived – by the Goths in 410. The first three books seem to be composed in the white heat of rage against 'those who favour their own gods' against the divine founder of the City of God (*CG*, preface); the subsequent seven are a more systematic re-examination of Roman history and demolition of her conventional beliefs. It is in the eleventh book that Augustine turns to a spacious exposition of God's creation and ordering of the universe, and of humanity's place in the divine plan: this preoccupies him for the rest of the work.

The excerpt quoted here seems, at first reading, paradigmatic of the patriarchalism with which the present volume is concerned. It describes the moment of God's creation of the first man: its purpose and process. It sets man in the context of the hierarchical divine order: God, angels, man, beasts. It promises to man the possibility of attaining 'the company of the angels'. And it insists on the priority of man's creation, and the fact that woman was created 'out of the man'. I shall not treat here of the role of God in this arrangement. His governing presence – whether or not you wish to call it patriarchal – is not in doubt for Augustine. Nor shall I treat of the angels, and the potential of a life (or afterlife) in their company. My focus is on the description of man's creation, and its implications for his place in the earthly political order.

Man is, it seems, created alone as a patriarchal presence. Augustine goes out of his way to observe that birds and beasts, whether their habit is solitary or gregarious, were not created alone, but in groups. Man's duty is to govern the beasts and to prove himself superior to them by the right exercise of his free will. The beasts are not singled out and differentiated as man is; his sovereign self is unassailable from that moment of singular creation onwards. The previous chapter ends, 'In order that there might be [a] beginning, therefore, a man was created before whom no man existed' (*CG* 12.21).

Moreover, Augustine has preferred the account of the creation of woman given at Genesis 2:22 to the apparently more egalitarian one in Genesis 1:27. Genesis 1:27 suggested that man and woman were made simultaneously, both according to God's image: it reads, 'And God created man in his own image, in the image of God He created him; male and female He created them.' Genesis 2:22, on the other hand, lays out a hierarchical order: 'And God built the rib which He had taken from Adam into a woman, and led her to Adam.' The suppression of the more egalitarian version in favour of the story about the patriarchal bestowal of a wife purpose-built for Adam would seem to clinch the charges of patriarchalism in Augustine. As an author who has himself been lambasted through the centuries as the origin of much that is wrong in Christian doctrine, Augustine here offers a hierarchical interpretation of a patriarchal order - or so it seems. But we should look again. And looking again, we shall see that Augustine is striving towards a vision far more inclusive and less hierarchical – in short, far less patriarchal – than he is generally given credit for. This we see both in the specifics of his language and in his broader vision of how people (not just men) come together in community.

First, throughout this passage, instead of using the marked word *vir* which denotes someone biologically male, Augustine is at pains to use the more generic word for man, *homo*. In the singular form, this can generally be translated 'person'; in the plural, *homines*, 'humankind'. In other words, *homines* may include women as well. That Augustine is well aware of this distinction is shown in the final book of the *City of God*. Commenting on a passage of Paul which talks about striving to become a 'perfect man' (Ephesians 4:13), he writes:

> Suppose … that the 'perfect man' passage is indeed meant as a reference to the form in which each of us is to rise: even in this case, what is to prevent us from understanding the word 'man' [*vir*], here used instead of 'person' [*homo*], as applying to the woman also? For in the saying, 'Blessed is the man [*vir*] who feareth the Lord', women who fear the Lord are surely also included (*CG* 22.18).[2]

Here, Augustine is striving for inclusiveness even against the grain of the apparently restrictive term *vir*, so we may readily infer that the *homo* of book 12 is to be read with an eye to inclusion. It is also notable that nowhere in this account does Augustine give Adam a name: in fact, Adam is not named until the middle of book 13 (in the context of Adam and Eve's shame at their nakedness, *CG* 13.15).

This alone would mean little, for it is still the creation of Adam, and its precedence over Eve, that is being paraphrased in our passage. The important section explains why God created only 'one single man' (*unum ac singulum*): 'that, by this means, the unity of society and the bond of concord might be commended to him more forcefully, mankind being bound together not only by similarity of nature, but by the affection of kinship'. Augustine takes the biblical passage that is normally cited to justify woman's subjection to man and instead uses it to prove that every human being is always already born into a web of relationality. Far from man being sovereign and alone, his interrelation with woman is predetermined by their shared flesh, and the affective bonds that link them become the basis of all human sociality.

The fact that individual humans, rather than being autonomous and self-sufficient, are from the beginning interdependent and stand in relation to others has enormous importance for Augustine's ideas of political organization. We learn about the necessary human qualities of sociality partly in their absence, when Augustine describes 'a creature depicted in poetry and fable: a creature so unsociable and wild that people have preferred to call him a semi-man rather than a man'. This is the monster Cacus, who is depicted in the eighth book of Virgil's *Aeneid*:

> he had no wife with whom to give and receive caresses[3]; no children to play with when little or instruct when a little bigger; and no friends with whom to enjoy converse … (*CG* 19.12).

This is the ideal, evoked in its absence: conversation, affection, playfulness, teaching: sociality constantly enacted through interlocution and interrelation. Augustine goes on to observe that 'pride is a perverted imitation of God. For pride hates a fellowship of equality under God, and wishes to impose its own dominion upon its equals, in place of God's rule' (*CG* 19.12). Here is the 'lust for mastery' (*CG* preface; compare *CG* 3.14) which disarranges God's order and perverts human relations. Yet Augustine continues:

> Therefore, [pride] hates the just peace of God, and it loves its own unjust peace; but it cannot help loving peace of some kind or other. For no vice is so entirely contrary to nature as to destroy even the last vestiges of nature (*CG* 19.12).

Peace is the result of 'bringing suitable things suitably together' (*CG* 19.12), and it is the foundation of God's entire ordering of the world:

> The peace of a household is an ordered concord, with respect to command and obedience, of those who dwell together; the peace of a city is an ordered concord, with respect to command and obedience, of the citizens; and the peace of the Heavenly City is a perfectly ordered and perfectly harmonious fellowship in the enjoyment of God, and of one another in God (*CG* 19.13).

This, clearly, is not an argument for equality as such, the desire for a 'fellowship of equality under God' notwithstanding: it is an argument for equity, for each human being to have their own place in a balanced and peaceful community. But it is, at the same time, a vision of humans as always in relation to each other, with their ensuing obligations and responsibilities.

Augustine, in book 19, is revising Cicero's definition of a people (*populus*) in his *Republic*, and he uses this revision to ground his notion of human relationships. The similarities are strong, but the differences between the two are instructive: in fact, they trouble the idea of patriarchal social structures. Cicero defines the people as 'the gathering of a multitude, brought into association by consent to the law and common utility'.[4] Augustine, on the other hand, defines the people as 'the gathering of a *rational* multitude, brought into association *through the harmonious sharing of the things it loves*' (CG 19.24).[5] In Cicero, no claim is made for the ratiocinative powers of the general throng (Cicero's overall vision of the organization of the state is highly paternalistic), and they are brought together by the claims of law and expediency. For Augustine, the role of the rational soul, whose domain is both cognition and action, is crucial; and not law or expedience, but the objects of love serve as the bonds that unite the people.[6]

All this is assisted by the notion invoked in the very title of Augustine's work: the city, *civitas* in Latin. The earthly and the heavenly cities are intertwined in this life, he tells us, to be untangled only in the next. He conceives of the cities not as things of bricks and mortar, but as gatherings or communities of citizens, *cives*. The word *civitas*, in fact, means not just 'community' or (in later Latin) 'city', but 'the state of being a citizen'. This emphasis on the people that compose the city, rather than the city as place or material object, lends itself to a dynamic and inclusive notion of community. Yes, the *cives* are ordered in right relation to each other; but they comprehend both men and women – and, indeed, angels: anyone with a rational soul – and they are founded on relationality.[7] This takes us back to our original excerpt, that God created woman from man so that 'the unity of society and the bond of concord might be commended to him more forcefully': for this is what grounds the *civitas*.

As mentioned earlier, immediately before this excerpt comes the statement, 'In order that there might be [a] beginning ... a man was created before whom no man existed' (CG 12.21). This seems at first sight a claim for a certain patriarchal supremacy. And yet, this is a favourite passage of Hannah Arendt, who quotes it in Latin: '[Initium] ergo ut esset, creatus est homo, ante quem nullus fuit'.[8] In *The City of God*, the context is the creation of man *ex nihilo*, and the beginning refers to the balanced cycle of creation of the souls of the redeemed and the damned. But Arendt observes, 'This beginning ... is not the beginning of something but of somebody, who is a beginner himself'; and she links it to the uniqueness of any human being within the human condition of plurality.[9] Furthermore, she links the beginning 'of somebody' to her whole concept of action: for action is the starting of something new and unexpected. It is the iteration of the principle of freedom that was created when man himself was created. Plurality, meanwhile, is linked to speech; for it is interlocution, for Arendt, that recognizes the simultaneous individuality and plurality of human beings.

It may seem anachronistic to read *The City of God* through Arendt; but Arendt was intellectually formed through her reading of Augustine, and her appropriation of his underlying structures is often revealing. Here, she points us to the significance of the creation of man – that is, *homo*, not *vir* – as a unique and single being: that both his own uniqueness and the ensuing plurality of human beings are recognized and held in constant dynamic tension with each other. For Arendt, the dynamic tension is sustained by speech; for Augustine, as we have seen in the Cacus passage, by speech and love. Finally, she can help us see the importance of Augustine's description of the province of the rational soul, which is cognition and action (*CG* 19.13). 'Action' is, in Arendt's theory, something quite particular, and it is not entirely applicable to Augustine; but the presence of action in the rational soul – which is the part of God's order that raises humans above beasts – points again to the dynamic individuality and freedom of human beings, while cognition points to the understanding and language that always bring humans into relation to each other (Arendt's plurality) and to God.

We cannot argue that Augustine's vision of humans in the world, and of their political organization, is not hierarchical. It is. But it is far more dynamic and egalitarian, through its recognition of others in their common humanity, than would be suggested by a patriarchalist reading. Indeed, as we have seen, it simply cannot support the blunt patriarchalism that careless readers have attributed to him. Augustine's vision of humans, from their creation forwards, eschews the notion of 'a self on one's own', to use the words of Charles Taylor,[10] in favour of an insistence on the shared bonds of affection and kinship. And it emphasizes, always, the power and potential of a relationality that subverts the power structures of patriarchal domination.

Men, Women and Monsters: John Knox's *First Blast of the Trumpet* (1558)

Anne McLaren

Nature I say, doth paint [women] forth to be weak, frail, impatient, feeble and foolish: and experience hath declared them to be inconstant, variable, cruel and lacking the spirit of counsel and regiment. And these notable faults have men in all ages espied…, for the which not only they have removed women from rule and authority, but also some have thought that men subject to the counsel or empire of their wives were unworthy of all public office. For thus writes Aristotle in the second of his Politics: what difference shall we put, says he, whether that women bear authority, or the husbands that obey the empire of their wives…? For what ensues [from] the one, must needs follow the other, to wit, injustice, confusion and disorder …

What would [Aristotle] (I pray you) have said to that realm or nation, where a woman sits crowned in parliament amongst the midst of men [?]…I am assuredly persuaded that if any of those men, which illuminated only by the light of nature, did see and pronounce causes sufficient, why women ought not to bear rule nor authority, should this day live and see a woman sitting in judgment, or riding from parliament in the midst of men, having the royal crown upon her head, the sword and scepter borne before her, in sign that the administration of justice was in her power: I am assuredly persuaded, I say, that such a sight should so astonish them, that they should judge… albeit the outward form of men remained, … their hearts were changed from the wisdom, understanding, and courage of men, to the foolish fondness and cowardice of women.[1]

John Knox (c1514–72) was one of the leading lights of the Protestant reformation in Scotland and England. He wrote voluminously and influentially, but *The First Blast of the Trumpet Against the Monstrous Regiment of Women*, written in 1558, remains the work for which he is best known, if not, indeed notorious. Controversial at the time, it seems to us now to signal something important and revealing about attitudes towards women in the early modern period. In his opening salvo Knox claims that the empire of a woman is 'repugnant to nature' because of her inherent deficiencies:

> For who can deny but it repugneth to nature, that the blind shall be appointed to lead and conduct such as do see? That the weak, the sick, and impotent persons shall nourish and keep the whole and strong, and finally, that the foolish, mad and frenetic shall govern the discrete, and give counsel to such as be sober of mind? And such be all women, compared unto man in bearing of authority (10.v–r).

Men who accept or collude in women's rule are not simply misguided. They have become lower than 'brute beasts' or – worse still – 'slaves of Satan' (30r, 30v). These are strong words – hateful even. But was Knox a misogynist – a man who hated women – or did his fiery denunciation of female rule in the *First Blast* draw on entrenched patriarchal views and values?

To answer this question, we need to understand what the world looked like to Knox and other radical Protestant reformers in 1558. They saw themselves as a godly minority – prophets, even, like the Biblical figures of old – fighting the 'evil empire' that was the Roman Catholic Church. By the time Knox wrote, that empire seemed to be on the verge of eradicating Protestantism altogether from its strongholds in Scotland and England. In large measure its success resulted from dynastic chance. Both countries were divided between adherents of the 'old' and 'new' religions: Catholicism and varieties of Protestantism. It happened that two women who were proponents of the 'old' religion, the Catholic queens Mary Queen of Scots and Mary Tudor, had recently inherited the Scottish and English crowns. They then married the Catholic kings of what were at that time the two most powerful countries in Europe, France and Spain. The Scottish queen lived in France at the court of her husband, Francis II. In her absence, her mother, the Catholic Frenchwoman Mary of Guise ('that crafty dame', according to Knox's characterization), acted as regent on her behalf (48v). In England Mary Tudor gained the throne in 1553 after a failed Protestant coup. By 1558 she had re-established Catholicism in England and had married the Spanish king Philip II. Mary Queen of Scots, Mary of Guise, Mary Tudor – these were the three 'mischievous Marys' whom Knox excoriated in the pages of the *First Blast*; and we must remember that 'mischief', then, was associated not with gentle mayhem but with witchcraft and demonic possession, just as 'craft' denoted the deceit, guile and cunning commonly displayed by practitioners of the black arts (42v).

So the prospects for the survival of what Knox and his fellows regarded as the 'True Church' looked bleak. It appeared overwhelmingly likely that the Catholicism embraced by all three Marys would triumph in both kingdoms. This outcome would be confirmed when the marriages of the Scottish and English queens produced male offspring, if not before. The resulting Catholic line of descent would establish both realms as securely Catholic nations as well as satellites to those major Catholic European powers, whose military power could, if necessary, be mobilized to protect the new *status quo*. True, in England there was one Protestant hope: the last of Henry VIII's surviving heirs, Mary's half-sister Elizabeth Tudor. Should Mary Tudor die without issue, Elizabeth *might* inherit the English throne. But looking at the situation in 1558 this must have appeared to be a remote possibility. Mary Queen of Scots was young and likely to bear children to carry the line. Moreover she herself had a strong dynastic claim to succeed in her own right, in preference to Elizabeth.

In this political context of impending night, what were godly Protestant men to do? How were they to fight to secure the true faith? One answer was to use the power of the printing press to motivate the male readers – whom I think we can assume Knox addressed – to adopt, and act on, revolutionary ideas. This is what John Knox set himself to do in the *First Blast*. These ideas challenged the right to rule of monarchs who were deemed to be ungodly, even when their dynastic claims to kingship were impeccable.

In the sixteenth century this was indeed revolutionary. 'Touch not mine anointed' was the word of God and a ubiquitous mantra. All men knew that the office of kingship was ordained by God, just as His divine aura protected individual kings. Their pedigree – their birth and breeding – confirmed a status that was almost divine. From that eminence they functioned as both the embodiment and guarantor of social order. It did not require much imagination to fear that an assault on the authority of kings could easily segue into attacks on other kinds of 'divine right' that, in the view of the age, conformed both to the law of nature and God's revealed will: the power of the nobility, for example; even the authority of husbands over wives, or, more generally of men over women.

Knox was not alone in writing works that hammered out how it might be possible for men to stand up to their kings; ideas that we collectively denominate 'resistance theories'. But we can see immediately how difficult the task would be. For Knox and his fellows, ungodly rulers were those who refused to embrace Protestantism. But this was a minority view. Knox wrote in a society where religious views, although hotly contested, were in flux, and where the generality of men remained wedded to the principle of hereditary succession, regardless of the ruler's faith. He could not, therefore, 'preach to the converted' – few in number on both counts – without running the risk of alienating many, perhaps most, of his readers. To be effective he had somehow to move beyond the narrow confines of anti-Catholic diatribe and make a more inclusive case. That case would have to persuade his readers that rebelling against certain rulers, even to the point of deposing or killing them, could be right and necessary, and, importantly, reassure them that acting against the Lord's anointed in this way would not inevitably unleash social anarchy.

This conundrum explains, I think, important features of the argument that Knox advances in the *First Blast*. First, it explains why he begins by launching a generalized assault on female rule as contrary to the word of God, before moving on to identify and demonize Mary Tudor and Mary Queen of Scots, the particular regnant queens he has in his sights. For everyone, Protestant and Catholic alike, could accept two propositions: first, that God's word should be law; and second, that women's inferiority was God-ordained, as was, in consequence, their subordination to men. As we shall see, it also helps us understand the next stage of his argument, as he moves to position the two Marys as so far beyond the pale of the generality even of women that they stand as exemplars of the ungodly rulers whom it would be laudable to kill.

It also explains why Knox does not restrict his argument to the word of God as revealed in the Bible. Biblical strictures predominate in his text, but he reinforces the universality of his case by drawing upon influential voices from classical antiquity. As we see in the extract quoted above, an important element of his argument is that women's inferiority has been recognized in all times and places. It is God-ordained, but it is also 'natural', and this is why the sages of classical antiquity (exemplified by Aristotle) could appreciate the enormity of women's rule despite living in a pagan age. And he again draws on Aristotle to hammer home the correspondence between the microcosm of the household and the macrocosm of the state – a truism of the age – in terms that privilege male authority absolutely. The ancients recognized the disastrous effects of female rule, but they were also alert to the dangers that lurked when women exercised control indirectly, by lording it over the men who should be their masters:

> And these notable faults have men in all ages espied … , for the which not only they have removed women from rule and authority, but also some have thought that men subject to the counsel or empire of their wives were unworthy of all

public office. For thus writes Aristotle in the second of his *Politics*: what difference shall we put, says he, whether that women bear authority, or the husbands that obey the empire of their wives...?

The result in both cases is 'injustice, confusion and disorder'. '[I]lluminated only by the light of nature', the Greeks disallowed all varieties of female authority, he concludes (11v-r). The subtext here is that Knox's contemporaries, men who are privileged to live in the light of Christ, have even more reason than did the ancients to band together to preserve male hegemony, political and cultural.

Knox begins his attack on female rule in a subsection entitled 'The First Blast to Awake Women degenerate'. By 'degenerate' Knox does not *primarily* mean that women are morally depraved, although undoubtedly he plays on the word's ambiguity. Instead, in the first instance he uses it to remind men about the consequences of the fall of humankind as recounted in the pages of Genesis. No orthodox Christian would deny that humankind had 'degenerated' – that is, fallen from their original glory – when Adam and Eve disobeyed God in the Garden of Eden. Similarly, no orthodox Christian of that time would deny that Eve, in seducing Adam to eat the forbidden apple, bore the primary responsibility for that primal act, or that the punishment that God then set Eve remained in force for all women, and would do until the second coming. Even before the fall, '[i]n her greatest perfection woman was created to be subject to man', Knox reminds us.

> But after her fall and rebellion committed against God ... she was made subject to man by the irrevocable sentence of God, pronounced in these words: ... With sorrow shalt thou bear thy children, and thy will shall be subject to thy man: *and he shall bear dominion over thee* (14v).[2]

What does this mean if not that God 'hath dejected all woman [*sic*] from empire and dominion above man'? he demands (14v).[3]

But Knox must address a problem that arises with this line of attack. For the Bible also provides instances where women not only exercise political authority, but do so with God's approval. Famous examples include Huldah and Deborah, Old Testament professed prophets who guided their people at God's behest. Might not these instances of divine intervention justify female rule? Might not either or both of the Queen Marys be one of those exceptional women, singled out by God for His special providence? In a Bible-centred society, where monarchs were regarded as nearly allied to God, this was a powerful counter-case – one that was to fuel the effusive identification of Elizabeth Tudor with Deborah when she succeeded Mary to the English throne (1558).

Thus Knox is forced to acknowledge that the Biblical strictures he cites are not categorical. 'I except', he says, 'such as God by singular privilege, and for certain causes known only to himself, hath exempted from the common rank of women' (10r-v). But he then uses the ambiguity of 'degenerate' to dismiss this objection by focusing on the character of the English and Scottish queens. It is at this point that his attack on female rule moves from the general to the particular, as he conflates and demonizes the two Marys. Mary Tudor is a 'wicked woman, yea ... a traitoress and bastard' (2r). She and her cousin Mary Queen of Scots are 'degenerate' in the sense of morally debased, made kin twice over through their commitment to wickedness. They have compounded their inheritance as daughters of Eve by wilfully following the example, not of Huldah and Deborah, but of the Old Testament tyrant queens Jezebel and Athaliah. Jezebel and her daughter Athaliah were regarded as witches, hence at war with God. By the time Knox wrote both had become bywords for monstrous tyranny and God's immediate protection: both were executed by godly men following God's decree.

Executed – but not, finally, eradicated. Rather, Knox finds that they have come to life again, housed in the bodies of Mary Tudor and Mary Queen of Scots, in whom 'we ... find the spirit of Jezebel, and Athaliah' (41.v). For Knox, this immediate identity confirms that the English and Scottish queens are, like them, tyrants rather than legitimate rulers, 'monsters' rather than women. Moreover, it powerfully reveals the necessity for men who would be godly to similarly act against 'these Jezebels'. They must emulate the example of the Old Testament prophets and rid the earth of the 'mischievous Marys'. For in the Bible is it not written 'thou shalt not suffer a witch to live'? (*Exodus* 22:18).

So was Knox a misogynist? I think the answer to that question must be no. There is no evidence that he hated women. Indeed, Patrick Collinson has shown how warm and cordial his relations with women in his church congregations were, even how at points he looked to them for spiritual enlightenment and consolation.[4] However, there is no denying that in the pages of the *First Blast* he drew on and powerfully amplified misogynist views. At the extreme such views depict women as 'monsters' or witches: less than human beings who are allied to the devil in an ongoing war against God and man. Looking for ammunition to persuade men of all religious opinions to disallow the rule of ungodly kings, Knox focused on these ideas rather than on the two queens' Catholicism to ground his argument. Arguably the consequences of this 'turn' are still discernible in English-speaking polities, both in how women in power are presented – and, more tellingly, the terms in which they are attacked.

Like the majority of humankind throughout history, Knox and his contemporaries inhabited a profoundly patriarchal world. That world turned on the rooted conviction that men were superior to women in every way, and that all good order, familial and political, depended on them holding the reins of power. These linked beliefs reach back at least to classical antiquity. They changed form with the introduction of Christianity, but they survived, and maintained their predominance during the early modern period, when Knox wrote. The line between patriarchalism and misogyny can be a fine one and very much depends on cultural circumstance. In the pages of Knox's work we can see an influential instance of one shading into the other, as Knox tries to rouse his fellow men to follow the trumpet of God.

Love and Order: William Gouge, *Of Domesticall Duties* (1622)

Karen Harvey

I remember that when these Domesticall Duties *were first uttered out of the pulpit, much exception was taken against the application of a wives subjection to the restraining of her from disposing the common goods of the family without, or against her husbands consent. But surely they that made those exceptions did not well thinke of the* Cautions *and* Limitations *which were then delivered, and are now againe expresly noted: which are, that the foresaid restraint be not extended to the* proper goods of a wife, *no nor overstrictly to such* goods as are set apart for the use of the family, *nor to* extraordinary cases, *nor alwaies to an* expresse consent, *nor to the* consent of such husbands as are impotent, or farre and long absent. *[…] I take the maine reason of the many exceptions which were taken, to be this, that wives duties (according to the Apostles method) being in the first place handled, there was taught (as must have beene taught, except the truth should have beene betrayed) what a wife, in the uttermost extent of that subjection under which God hath put her, is bound unto, in case her husband will stand upon the uttermost of his authority: which was so taken, as if I had taught that an husband might, and ought to exact the uttermost, and that a wife was bound in that uttermost extent to doe all that was delivered as dutie, whether her husband exact it or no. But when I came to deliver husbands duties, I shewed, that he ought not to exact whatsoever his wife was bound unto (in case it were exacted by him) but that he ought to make her a joynt Governour of the family with himself […].*[1]

William Gouge's *Of Domesticall Duties* is one of the most sophisticated post-Reformation conduct books written in English and the first substantial Puritan analysis of household duties. The book is a weighty tome both in topic and physical size. The first edition of 1622 ran to 693 pages and this was supplemented by 23 pages of family prayers by the third edition of 1634. This is a large book to digest, to be sure. Yet William Gouge (1575–1653), a famous Puritan preacher in London, intended his work not as a philosophical text on which high-minded readers would ruminate at their leisure. Rather, Gouge designed the book as a daily guide to family life. Books such as this on the family engaged with some of the most pressing public and political matters of the time. The late sixteenth and early seventeenth centuries were characterized by demographic and economic change which had further divided the rich and poor in England. This generated social disorder, or fear of that disorder, and long-held views that the family was central to social and political order meant that attention became focused acutely on the family and the maintenance of its government.[2] It was in this context that, '[c]ontemporary writers constructed a household that was a microcosm of the whole kingdom, hierarchically ordered by bonds of obedience'.[3]

The opening of Gouge's book belies this larger context, though, and roots the work firmly in the practical life of people's families in a London parish. Gouge's dedication to his parishioners at St. Ann Blackfriars church in London flatters its readers, as all dedications must. The first sentence of the dedication – and thus of the book – characterizes the relationship between Gouge and the men and women who thronged St. Ann Blackfriars in a striking way, as one of '*intire love*' (i). Gouge here foregrounds the affective nature of human relationships, as he goes on to do in his discussion of the family. Yet the remainder of the dedication and large sections of the main text suggest conflict with these parishioners as much as harmony. Indeed, the book was clearly rooted in a dynamic relationship between this charismatic preacher and his congregation. Gouge first presented these ideas orally, in sermons, and the community of his congregation then discussed them. *Of Domesticall Duties* was a series of sermons to Londoners before it was a patriarchal text. Gouge's description of the sermons and ensuing debate show that his initial emphasis on a husband's principal authority over the family was not met with universal acceptance:

> I remember that when these Domesticall Duties *were first uttered out of the* pulpit, *much exception was taken against the application of a wives subjection to the restraining of her from disposing the common goods of the family without, or against her husbands consent.* (iv)

It is surely a reflection of the strength of opposition he faced, his desire to satisfy his congregation, his wish to make his book relevant and useful, as well as his belief in a husband's ultimate authority as Christian truth, that Gouge subsequently amended his book. Indeed, for all the significance of this text as a patriarchal landmark, it is remarkable that it contains a retraction of some of his comments about women: '[t]his just Apologie I have been forced to make, that I might not ever be iudged (as some have censured me)* an hater of women' (v). His initial response to the complaints in the printed version was this: God has put wives under the subjection of their husbands' ultimate authority; yet I do not say that a husband should exercise that ultimate authority to exact entire subjection but rather that 'he ought to make her a ioynt Governour of the family with him selfe' (v). To pacify his detractors further he then combed his manuscript and added an asterisk in the margin at every point where the duties of wives were to be matched by the corresponding duties of husbands and compiled these corresponding duties in a table. This table conveyed in visual form the unequal yet harmonious balance that wives and husbands should carry in their joint governorship of the household (viii–ix).

Understanding this direct engagement with the readers of his book is key to the interpretation of the text. Gouge's experiences of his parishioners drove him to write a book that was practical. He was conscious that 'the worke may seeme at first sight to be too copious' (ii) and anxious that readers would find it 'tedious' (iii). And so he used a form to render the book more digestible and navigable, with eight clear chapters (or treatises) each with short numbered paragraphs and marginal pointers that were laid out in tabular form at the start of the main text. All of this would, he hoped, enable the reader, to 'more readily finde out such particular points as you desire most especially to read' (vi). Historians might be inclined to reach for Gouge as an example of 'prescriptive literature' which provided men and women with an idealized model of a godly life. Yet the provenance of the text, as well as Gouge's insistence that the book be useful, should caution us before we relegate *Of Domesticall Duties* to a realm of mere 'prescription'. Such books were not inflexible ideals but derived from and interacted with everyday practice in dynamic ways: they provoked reflection and opposition as well as aspiration.[4] Gouge's own concerns are clear evidence that not all women – or men – lived the family lives he wished for them. As a 47-year-old father of eleven, married to Elizabeth (née Caulton) for eighteen years, Gouge was surely familiar with the challenges of keeping both order and affection in a busy household.[5]

Identifying readers of early modern books with confidence is difficult. Two of the three digitized copies available on Early English Books Online belonged to male readers, though these copies surely had other readers and listeners.[6] William Gouge did not direct *Of Domesticall Duties* at either male or female readers; the book was neither a tool with which men were to govern or educate

their wives nor a simple conduct book. Instead, Gouge pictured his readership as
the whole community of his parishioners: husbands, wives, children, masters and
servants. This broad intended audience – in practice limited to the comfortably
off 'metropolitan bourgeoisie'[7] – reflected Gouge's underlying patriarchal vision,
one in which the distinct spheres of family, household, church, commonwealth
and society nevertheless shared the same principles of Christian love and order.
His parishioners of St. Ann Blackfriars were, of course, a microcosm of the larger
commonwealth.

Gouge gets to the heart of this vision by providing answers to a series of
rhetorical questions:

> *oh if the head and severall members of a family would be perswaded every of*
> *them to be conscionable in performing their owner particular duties, what a sweet*
> *society, and happy harmony would there be in houses? What excellent seminaries*
> *would families be to Church and Commonwealth? Necessary it is that good order*
> *be first set in families: for as they were before other polities, so they are somewhat*
> *the more necessary: and good members of a family are like to make good members*
> *of Church and common-wealth.* (ii)

Of Domesticall Duties is thus a classic patriarchal text that slips back and forth
between a literal and analogous relationship between the family and wider social
entities: 'a familie is a little Church, and a little common-wealth, at least a lively
representations thereof, whereby trial may be made of such as are fit for any
place of authoritie, or of subjection in Church or common-wealth' (18). In the
order of the family lay the order of the state or commonwealth. Yet it denies the
depth of Gouge's comprehension of human relationships and the human soul to
reduce his book to one about order. The family was distinct for Gouge because
it was constituted above all out of affective relationships, not just ones of order
and hierarchy.

Of Domesticall Duties is structured according to Ephesians 5:22–6:9,
passages in the New Testament which treat directly of wives, husbands,
children, parents, servants and masters. The first of the book's eight treatises
grounds the *Of Domesticall Duties* in scripture. At 178 pages in the first
edition, this is by far the longest chapter and the most significant to laying
out the supporting architecture of Gouge's vision for the household. It
establishes two important principles that run throughout the eight treatises:
first, that there are general Christian duties to be performed by all persons
(faith and obedience, for example); second, that distinct groups of people have
particular duties related to their place in the divine order. These particular
duties require that each individual be cognizant of her or his place in three

separate degrees or orders: husbands and wives, parents and children, masters and servants. As Gouge puts it, 'A bad husband, wife, parent, childe, master, servant, magistrate or minister, is no good Christian' (17). This first treatise establishes the particular duties of husband and wife, starkly summed up in the two words, 'love' and 'feare': '*Love* as sugar to sweeten the duties of authoritie, which appertaine to an husband. *Feare* as salt to season all the duties of subjection which appertaine to a wife' (128). The virtuous balance in the marital relationship rests on emotion and the duties of husbands and wives are characterized by feelings, feelings made palpable by Gouge's invocation of the sense of taste.

The second treatise lays out the good grounds for marriage and then the 'common mutuall duties' of man and wife (179). This second part is remarkable. It represents a significant addition to the brief injunctions in Ephesians, which say nothing of the duties husband and wife bear each other or the duties they exercise in unison. Indeed, this is the only treatise that does not begin with a quote from Ephesians, though it is supported by other biblical references throughout. In its insistence on both the mutual respect of husband and wife and their joint responsibility to others in the family, the section was perhaps written in response to the criticism generated by the original sermons. The vision of the marital relationship is one of mutual care. First are those common duties which are absolutely necessary for marriage to exist: '*Matrimonial Unity*' and '*Matrimonial Chastity*'. Second are those common duties which are needful for marriage to be comfortable: '*A loving affection of one to another*' and '*A provident care of one for another*' (213). The striking feature of this section, and one which echoes the dedication, is the balance of pairs. This repetition of pairings expressed Gouge's vision of the equal significance of husband and wife and their joint governance of the household.

The particular and distinct duties of wives and husbands are the subject of treatises 3 and 4, respectively. Women's subjection to their husbands should be complete (268–9). Their submission takes the form of women's attenuation of their external actions: she should be mild in her countenance, courteous in manners, modest in dress and reverent in speech (278–85). This extensive system of bodily fashioning assumes a husband's superiority in all things. It is for this reason that historians commonly use Gouge to illustrate the dominant view of women as subject to their husbands.[8] But Gouge knew that not all men warranted this complete subjection:

> it oft falleth out that a wise, vertuous, and gratious woman, is married to an
> husband destitute of understanding, to a very natural (as we say) or a frenzy

man, or to one made very blockish, and stupid, unfit to manage his affaires
through some distemper, wound, or sicknesse. (287–8)

Gouge equips his patriarchal system with adaptive devices that take account of
the real (flawed) men and women in his community and the tensions inherent
in prescribing a joint partnership of unequals. The book could be seen as
one of many with internal contradictions.[9] Maintaining the delicate balance
was typical of household manuals which sought to combine male superiority
with the realities of everyday life, different callings and the equality of souls:
'The husband had to be the head, but to recognize the practical and spiritual
importance of the wife; he could not have too much power.'[10] Gouge's language
struggled to accommodate the complexities of this relationship and those
of the family overall; rather than a sustained analogy he deploys a series of
distinct metaphors to convey the intricate ordering of a series of relationships.
In this third treatise on wives' duties, it is with the metaphor of the human
body that Gouge tries to express the ideal marital relationship as based on
the husband's superiority: 'This metaphor sheweth that to his wife he is at the
head of a natural body, both more *eminent* in place, and also more *excellent* in
dignity: by virtue of both which, he is ruler and governour of his wife.' (343)
Gouge draws explicitly on both nature and scripture as authority, as do all early
modern writers who envisage social order as a Great Chain of Being; in so
doing he ensures that the challenge of a wife to her husband's authority is both
ungodly and monstrous.

If wives are counselled to submit, men are counselled to love. The fourth
treatise prepares the husband to be the family head but the emphasis is on the
tenor of that role rather than the particular tasks that such a husband might
enact. One of Gouge's primary concerns is to dissuade men from 'the furious,
and spightfull actions of many unkinde husbands (*heads too heady*) whose
favours are buffets, blowes, strokes, & stripes' (389). Gouge is unequivocal:
men should not beat their wives (389–93). Instead, they should be tender
like birds that protectively spread their wings over their young (421). This
metaphor is revealing. It couches a husband's love towards his wife in terms of
a parent protecting a child. Furthermore, Gouge remarks, the metaphor itself –
the very words – comes directly from God (408). The metaphor encapsulates
patriarchalism though Gouge reserves the metaphor for the marital relationship
and does not use it in the subsequent chapters on children and parents. It was
particularly within marriage that relationships were bound by emotion as
well as power and duty. Indeed, Gouge saw these features as indivisible; they
constitute what Victoria Kahn has called 'affective duties'.[11]

And yet the chapters on the duties of children, parents, servants and masters are indispensable to the larger vision. Each individual possessed duties particular to their role in the household hierarchy. Children, for example, were to regard their parents with love, obedience, submission and care. While the differences between husbands and wives were apparent when Gouge laid out their duties to each other, from a child's perspective they were as one:

> children are not to looke to that difference that is betwixt their parents in that mutuall relation that is betwixt husband and wife, but to that authority which both parents have over their children: and so carry an equall respect to both (485).

Following Ephesians, it was the duty of parents to nourish children's bodily needs, to nurture with discipline and instruct them in the ways of God (497–8). Yet Gouge draws on other scriptural authorities for his claim that in fact all these duties stem from natural affection or love (498–9). No such affective duties were required of either servants or masters. Fear and faithfulness characterize service, while masters are counselled to wisely maintain their authority over servants and use them well (647).

Sitting out with the affective core of the family, these relationships might appear peripheral. And yet they were exemplary. Duty to masters was duty to Christ and 'in rebelling against their master they rebel against Christ' (641). By the same token, masters were to be forever mindful (to know) that 'God will doe the same things to all sorts of masters that they doe to their servants' (693). Wives and husbands were at the heart of the family but that could only function if each individual performed their role as laid down by nature and by God. Early modern patriarchy was not a ladder but a 'grid of power'.[12] For a Puritan preacher this grid stretched through society, the commonwealth and the family but was seeded in the individual's Christian heart. This was why William Gouge styled himself, 'The Watch-man of your soules' (vii). *Of Domesticall Duties* thus marks the moment when patriarchalism combined the social, political, religious and individual within the family.

Filmer's *Patriarcha* (1680): Absolute Power, Political Patriarchalism and Patriotic Language

Cesare Cuttica

An implicit faith is given to the meanest artificer in his own craft. How much more is it, then, due to a prince in the profound secrets of government. The causes and ends of the greatest politic actions and motions of state dazzle the eyes and exceed the capacities of all men, save only those that are hourly versed in managing public affairs. […] I am not to question or quarrel at the rights or liberties of this or any other nation. My task is chiefly to inquire from whom these *first* came, not to dispute what or how many they are, but whether they are derived from the law of natural liberty or from the grace and bounty of princes. My desire and hope is that the people of England may and do enjoy as ample privileges as any nation under heaven. The greatest liberty in the world (if it be duly considered) is for people to live under a monarch. It is the Magna Carta of this kingdom. All other shows or pretexts of liberty are but several degrees of slavery, and a liberty only to destroy liberty. […] Late writers have taken up too much upon trust from the subtle schoolmen, who to be sure to thrust down the king below the pope, thought it the safest course to advance the people above the king, that so the papal power may *more easily* take place of the regal. *Thus* many an ignorant subject hath been fooled into this faith, that a man may become a martyr for his country by being a traitor to his prince; whereas the new coined distinction of subjects into royalists and patriots is most unnatural, since the relation between king and people is so great that their well-being is reciprocal.[1]

Notorious as the arch-villain of the history of early modern political thought whose sole merit was to have been picked by the philosopher John Locke (1632–1704) as the main target in the *Two Treatises of Government* (1689), the author of these lines is the Kentish gentleman and scholar Sir Robert Filmer (1588–1653). Filmer has been depicted as a narrow-minded representative of a patriarchal society; as a conventional absolutist; or, simply, as the exponent of archaic beliefs which failed to succeed in the theatre of ideas when confronted by the *typhoon* of modern philosophy, empirical science and social change. His best-known work is *Patriarcha* (published in 1680, but ready for publication in the early 1630s), which was vehemently attacked at the time of the Exclusion Crisis (1679–81) not only by Locke, but also by the republican writer Algernon Sidney (1623–83) and the Whig thinker James Tyrrell (1642–1718). The list of Filmer's later detractors includes minds of the calibre of the natural-rights theorist Jean Barbeyrac (1674–1744), the highly influential *philosophe* Jean-Jacques Rousseau (1712–78), the jurist John Millar (1735–1801) as well as sundry modern commentators.[2]

The name 'Filmer' came to be associated with the patriarchalist theory since he insisted on the political role of Adam as first king on earth to whom God had assigned absolute power over all creatures and from whom power had then passed to kings through the ancient patriarchs. In consequence, *Patriarcha* was considered as the ideological bedrock of patriarchalism with its strenuous defence of the superiority of monarchy. In addition, the text was seen as a strong justification for the dominion of fathers/husbands over their children/wives and of masters over their servants. Filmerian patriarchalism was also portrayed as the epitome of a personal and personalized authority antithetical to an artificial and liberal conception of politics; as the quintessence of women's subjugation to men; and as a specific structure of production and labour characterizing the household.[3]

Given these considerations, it might seem odd that, at first sight, the passage here presented does not appear to have much to do with any explicit patriarchalist agenda. There is no mention of Adam's power nor reference to ancient patriarchs. And yet these lines take us to the core of *Patriarcha*'s message, goals and targets as set out by Filmer in early seventeenth-century England. The reason for choosing them is that their author's ideas have for a long time been interpreted out of context, as if they belonged to the empyrean world of eternal philosophical problems. In fact, this paragraph plunges us in the midst of the debates and controversies around which Filmer conceived his treatise. In turn, this contextual approach enables us to revise the key aspects of the language of one of the most important – but often misread – political theories adopted in early modern European culture.

Patriarchalism articulated a specific vision of politics through rational arguments, historical research and analogical reasoning. Filmer did not transpose social prejudices into his political theories. Rather, he employed a conservative vocabulary with a radical meaning. In substance, 'anthropological' and 'ideological' readings of patriarchalism need to be replaced with interpretations that highlight its *political* dimension. And it is from this angle that the following pages consider this intellectual category. By focusing on its specifically political features, patriarchalism emerges not simply as a strong reaction to the idea that a voluntary contract formed civil society or merely as a fierce rejection of the concept that human consent was the wellspring of government. This was the theoretical performance that patriarchalist theorists played when it came to analysing the origins of political society. In fact, what was fundamental for Filmer was the method of governing a polity, which entailed a different representation of power. Patriarchalism as a forceful theory of absolute and arbitrary government was a version of the theory of the divine right of kings, but it was not the same as frequently and wrongly claimed. In this respect, while the latter doctrine argued that kings had been entrusted with power either directly by God or indirectly through the irrevocable mediation of the people, the patriarchalist Filmer rejected all forms of popular participation in politics and made Adam the exclusive founder of political authority. Moreover, if contemporary royalist thinkers like John Hayward (1564?–1627), Adam Blackwood (1539–1613) and John Barclay (1582–1621) admitted that men had originally been free and had, therefore, set up different kinds of government, Filmer denied that a state of nature had ever existed (3). Likewise, he rejected Thomas Hobbes' (1588–1679) claims that in the beginning people had been free of government and that as such polities stemmed from a contract.

Contrary to received scholarly views, contractualists were not the sole target of patriarchalists. A major part of their criticism in early seventeenth-century England discredited claims that Parliament was the true representative of the people. This conflict centred on the identity of the nation. Its key element was the identification of the head of the nation either with Parliament as the cornerstone of liberties or, instead, with the absolute monarch as *pater patriae*. This last image is here taken as the theoretical fabric of what we call *political patriarchalism*. The extract above captures very well the nature of this paradigm. Indeed, it encapsulates its pivotal features. To its analysis we now turn.

Written at some stage in the 1620s,[4] namely at a time of conflict between King Charles I Stuart (who reigned between 1625 and 1649) and an increasingly defiant Parliament whose Petition of Right (1628) tried to limit the monarch's prerogative, these lines – which did not appear in print for another fifty years given that in 1632 *Patriarcha* was refused the licence to be published – express Filmer's preoccupation with (what he and many monarchists perceived as)

growing opposition to monarchy in the country. A number of MPs – encouraged
by monarchomach literature and Dutch ideas of resistance – became more vocal
about kingly abuses such as imprisonment without cause shown, billeting of
troops, heavy and unjustified taxation. In brief, many representatives of the so-
called 'common people' began to contest the *absolute* policies enacted by Charles
and his dismissal of the rule of law, especially his trampling upon the rights and
liberties of freeborn Englishmen. Often depicting themselves as true patriots,
whose objective was to protect England and its immemorial customs from
arbitrary power and royal conduct now seen as popish (Catholic), a significant
portion of the politically active nation advanced a more controlling role for the
parliamentary assembly. With *Patriarcha*, Filmer formulated one of the strongest
responses to this discourse and, notably, to the rhetoric of civic participation
voiced by the self-appointed patriotic stalwarts.[5] Our passage exemplifies this
Filmerian strategy.

In stark contrast to what he saw as the inflammatory propaganda of
rebellious hotheads, Filmer maintained that the absolute monarch made
everyone equal because he was the only superior in the body politic. For
this reason, the nation was and ought to be powerless to control and judge
his decisions. Politics was not for all. It was a complex domain that required
specific competence. Both the *separateness* of the monarch and the *separateness*
of power were indispensable and irrevocable conditions for the working of all
good politics. Dismissing the role of Parliament as the main defender of the
English people, Filmer aimed at demonstrating that in any nation it was kings
who conceded rights and liberties to the people. And this was so because the
will of the sovereign not only gave being to the law, but coincided with the law.
Absolute monarchies were superior because in them the king was '*lex loquens* –
a speaking law' (40). The patriarchal monarch was also *legibus solutus*, that
is unrestrained by external or internal authorities: in the former case, Filmer
had in mind the Pope, while in the latter he referred to intermediary bodies or
(worse) the people through their representatives.

To further clarify Filmer's position with regard to these issues, it is
important to remember that the principal goal of *Patriarcha* was to assert
'The *Naturall* Power of Kinges Defended against the Unnatural Liberty of
the People' (1). Completely at odds with natural rights theorists, for him
men were born dependent on those who had begotten them. The 'tenet' that
mankind was 'naturally endowed and born with freedom from all subjection,
and at liberty to choose what form of government it please [...] according
to the discretion of the multitude' was 'first hatched in the schools [of the

Jesuits] and hath been fostered by all succeeding papists for good divinity'. Yet Filmer was quick to add that also the 'divines [...] of the reformed churches have entertained it, and the common people everywhere tenderly embrace it as being most plausible to flesh and blood, for that it prodigally distributes a portion of liberty to the meanest of the multitude' (2). Filmer not only criticized Catholic and Protestant thinkers, but targeted the 'common people'. These were urbanized parliamentary countrymen who, on Filmer's account, represented a much threatening category of subjects since, following their immoderate love of liberty, they irresponsibly conceded political space to the rabble. In choosing these targets Filmer articulated his discourse on two different levels. First, he engaged in a well-established philosophical dispute on the origins of government and the natural role of men in assigning power to governors. Second, he addressed his critique to a 'vulgar opinion [that] hath of late obtained great reputation' and of which '[i]t is hard to say whether it be more dangerous in divinity or dangerous in policy' (3).

Thus, in the first case Filmer attacked those who spread the 'pestilent' theory of 'the supposed natural equality and freedom of mankind'. Among these were 'both Jesuits and some over zealous favourers of the Geneva discipline'. He singled out Robert Parsons (1546–1610), George Buchanan (1506–82), Robert Bellarmine (1542–1621) and John Calvin (1509–64) as supporters of the right of the people to depose and punish their rulers in case the latter bypassed the law. In substance, these two groups enslaved kings by giving them two awful masters: the Pontiff and the people. In the second case, Filmer did not need to look for sophisticated treatises to discover how widespread 'the whole fabric of this vast engine of popular sedition' had become (3). It was, in fact, sufficient to pay attention to one particular opinion held by many people in England (5). This was the conviction that to sacrifice oneself for one's country was the highest action, even when this meant to justify the killing of evil fathers on the basis of the formula *pro rege et patria*. Against such subversive contentions, Filmer carved out an image of the monarch, which, by relying on the socially and emotionally powerful motifs of family and fatherhood, made of him the protector of the fatherland. After all, '[a]s the father over one family, so the king, as father over many families, extends his care to preserve, feed, clothe, instruct and defend the whole commonwealth' (12). Its calling on this persuasive rhetoric demonstrates that *Patriarcha* was a vigorous attempt to regain for the monarchical cause those who had become dissatisfied with Charles I's policies. Moreover, the theoretical medium of the family as the entity where social life had at first originated constituted the antithesis of the bellicose condition of total anarchic freedom to be found in the state of nature. The Adamite narrative of the origins guaranteed a safe platform from which man's polity had stemmed and developed.

Turning more directly to the disputes afloat at his time in England, Filmer viewed the idea that somebody might become a martyr by posing as the guardian of the nation against its king as poisonous because it mirrored the attitudes of Roman republicans whose iconic martyr was Brutus, the murderer of Caesar. Grounded on Cicero's *De Officiis* (44 B.C.) and the ideal of virtuous citizenship, the patriot narrative – according to Filmer – encouraged citizens to fulfil their duty towards the *patria* by overthrowing the legitimate ruler when they thought it necessary. This political activism threatened to irreparably taint the unity of the kingdom, which for Filmer was enshrined in the monarch. By seizing upon republican and godly patriotism, these divisive spirits made the king the mere figurehead of the English nation, replaced him with the authority of Parliament and questioned the inviolability of his prerogative. Accordingly, Puritan and quasi-republican types considered the people above the king (just as papists argued that the Pope was superior to secular monarchs), so that the former could judge the latter and re-appropriate the power they claimed to have conceded to the sovereign. Filmer believed that this seditious opinion had become so popular that 'many out of an imaginary fear pretend the power of the people to be necessary for the repressing of the insolencies of tyrants, herein they propound a remedy far worse than the disease' (33). For him, a considerable number of theorists as well as sundry MPs demagogically lured ignorant subjects into the deceptive belief that liberty (other than that provided by the king) was everything. However, what they proposed – Filmer caustically remarked – was no more than a theatrical staging of a fake liberty: indeed, they engendered a form of modern slavery. Only under the protective wing of the fatherly ruler could Englishmen be at peace and thrive in freedom. Being guided by the 'natural law of a father', a patriarchalist monarchy was the best form of government to guarantee people's prosperity and preserve the wealth of the kingdom. As he put it, even usurpers and tyrants were 'bound to preserve the lands, goods, liberties and lives of all their subjects, not by any municipal law of the land, but by the natural law of a father' (42). At a historical juncture of mounting disaffection towards a Stuart monarchy making itself unpopular through taxes like the Forced Loan (1626–7) and through poor diplomacy abroad, Filmer stressed that harmony could only be found in an absolute monarchy where political matters were left to the control of the supreme, patriotic *and* fatherly king.

By defining the role of the caring father, Filmer retraced the original moment of the foundation of political dominion. Above all, he employed this image to depict the patriotic king. As he put it, 'many a child, by succeeding a king, hath the right of a father over many a grey-headed multitude, and hath the title of *pater patriae*' (10). At this point, Filmer had consolidated in the most stringent way the indissoluble link between fatherhood, household, patriarchy and kingly care for the polity and its subjects. By identifying king and nation, he rejected the opinion fostered by quasi-republican and godly patriots, public men and MPs that love of country meant primarily allegiance to Parliament. Filmer had no doubt that people had to obey the king if they truly wanted to promote the interests of their country. Therefore, being faithful to the country as conceived by the 'common people' meant to be unfaithful to the sovereign. This was so because the latter *was* the country and as such could not be dissociated from the representation of the national commonweal. In consequence, those who aspired to become martyrs for their native land by fighting the king (in Parliament, in the localities and in print) inevitably betrayed the true *pater patriae*. Patriarchalism offered thus a powerful answer to the humanist and republican tenet whereby *amor patriae* was intertwined with *caritas*, which implied the dangerous equation of the self-sacrifice of the citizen dying *pro patria* with Christ's death for the salvation of humankind.

The excerpts that open this essay cast light on Sir Robert Filmer's *Patriarcha* as a thorough and radical expression of *political patriarchalism*. Filmer deployed the latter as a weapon against patriots and Jesuits during a historical phase of increasingly heated ideological battle between absolutists and their adversaries. He targeted these two camps because their works put forward theories that were at loggerheads with his absolute and Adamite vision of power and authority. Thus, patriarchalism served Sir Robert to contest patriotic contentions making Parliament the cornerstone of the kingdom's political identity, and to dismantle popish arguments whereby the Pope controlled monarchs and was their superior. The fatherly account of politics delineated in *Patriarcha* was a response to these two discourses: above all, it was a statement or a re-assertion of who held ultimate power. In order to avoid the lethal political scenario in which patriots and Jesuits had the upper hand, Filmer re-considered the role of the fatherly sovereign and fostered his patriotic aura. For this reason, Filmerian patriarchalism needs to be read as a forceful attempt at rethinking the nature of power. As a result of its making Adam's fatherly might the essential model of kingship, *Patriarcha* provides a rich account of statecraft whose fundament was the principle of the patriarchalist sovereign as founder of the State and father of the fatherland. And this, in turn, has to be interpreted as a move to make the ruler coincide *tout court* with the polity and to represent the will of the king as the supreme authorizing political and legal voice in the body politic.

Together with presenting a contextual reading of a much referred to but little studied patriarchal moment, this essay hopes to have shown the – unexpected – interplay of patriarchalism and patriotism in early modern political thought. Ultimately, this perspective also helps us to understand why thinkers of the status of John Locke felt it imperative to counter Filmer's patriarchalist arguments.

Patriarchy, Primogeniture and Prescription: Algernon Sidney's *Discourses Concerning Government* (1698)

Jonathan Scott

CHAPTER ONE SECTION 8: There is no natural propensity in Man or Beast to Monarchy.

I see no reason to believe that God did approve the government of one over many, because he created but one; but to the contrary, in as much as he did endow him, and those that came from him, as well the youngest as the eldest line, with understanding to provide for themselves, and by the invention of arts and sciences, to be beneficial to each other; he shewed, that they ought to make use of that understanding in forming governments according to their own convenience, and such occasions as should arise, as well as in other matters; and it might as well be inferr'd, that it is unlawful for us to build, clothe, arm, defend, or nourish ourselves, otherwise than as our first parents did, before, or soon after the Flood, as to take from us the liberty of instituting governments that were not known to them. If they did not find out all that conduces to the use of man, but a faculty as well as a liberty was left to everyone, and will be to the end of the world, to make use of his wit, industry, and experience, according to present exigencies, to invent and practise such things as seem convenient to himself and others of the least importance; it were absurd to imagine, that the political science, which of all others is the most abstruse and variable according to accidents and circumstances, should have been perfectly known to them who had no use of it; and that their descendants are obliged to add nothing to what they practiced. (121)[1]

Algernon Sidney (1623–83) wrote his *Discourses* with ill-concealed anger. The opinions of his opponent, 'brutally ignorant, or maliciously contentious'

(102) 'deserve[d] scorn and hatred' (101), and rather to be answered 'with stones than words'. He meant it, and paid the price, having the manuscript ruled as a sufficient witness to treason, before being beheaded on Tower Hill in December 1683. But his words survived, and over the century following their publication no political tract had a more powerful impact across both Europe (including Britain) and America.

One reason for the *Discourses'* percussive force, the verbal equivalent of an extended physical assault, was that it drew upon three intertwining contexts, each a deep repository of feeling and experience. The first was polemical: the *Discourses* was one of several replies to Sir Robert Filmer's *Patriarcha*, first published in 1680 but probably written half a century earlier, and so associated by Sidney, as also by John Locke, with the religious and political policies of Charles I's personal rule.[2] Nobody, he asserted, had dared to 'publish doctrines so contrary to commonsense, virtue, and humanity, till these times. The production of Laud, Manwaring, Sybthorpe, Hobbes, Filmer, and Heylyn seems to have been reserved as an additional curse to compleat the misery of our age and country' (11). This emphasis on the Caroline episcopate underlined Sidney's understanding of these doctrines as at root religious, not simply political. And this was a particular and severe understanding of what contemporaries condemned as 'popery and arbitrary government': that of a radical 'experimental' Calvinist. In a groundbreaking article Michael Winship has for the first time identified and analysed Sidney's theology (unchanged between his two major works, the earlier being *Court Maxims*). In so doing he has laid to rest the whig account of Sidney as an Enlightenment-friendly post-godly 'arminian'. To the contrary he was a religious as well as political disciple of Sir Henry Vane the younger (1613–62). Thus when Filmer attacked Calvin, Sidney responded that he was a '"glorious servant of God"', and 'when insisting that the observation of the Sabbath is a perpetual divine law', that he was 'willing' to take the '"reproach"' of being called 'a Puritan and a Calvinist'.[3] More important, Winship has pointed out, Filmer's claim that humanity had a natural propensity to monarchy was dismissed partly on the grounds that

'Even if humanity did have that propensity... it would demonstrate nothing. Men have always been wicked liars, none do good, and evil thoughts proceed out of their hearts continually', Sidney claims, stringing together Genesis 6:5, Psalms 116:11 and 14:3, and Matthew 15:19 without acknowledgement. He then loosely channels Romans 6 to demonstrate that grace alone can deliver people from this corruption... The spiritual man's 'proceedings can only be referred to God, and that only so far as he is guided by the spirit'. The 'natural man', by contrast, 'is in perpetual enmity against God without any possibility of being reconciled to him, unless by destruction of the old man, and the regenerating or renewing him through the spirit of grace'.[4]

Thus Sidney's first business was to reveal 'whose throne he [Filmer] seeks to advance, and whose servant he is, whilst he pretends to serve the king' (7). Soon after Sidney would go to his death expressing confidence that

God ... will in his mercy speedily visit his afflicted people ... [in] that his cause, and his people is more concerned now then it was in former time. The lust of one man and his favyrites was then only to be set up in the exercise of arbitrary power over persons and [e]states; but now, the tyranny over consciences is principally affected, and the civil powers are stretched into this exorbitant height, for the establishment of popery.[5]

Under Charles I, this was to say, popery was to be a means to arbitrary power. Between 1681 and 1683, with Charles II inaugurating a second personal rule with the support of France, the reverse was true.

This brings us to the *Discourses'* second context, what Sidney called 'that OLD CAUSE in which I was from my youth engaged, and for which thou hast often and wonderfully declared thyself'.[6] The lord had declared himself amid the soldiers of Parliament, Colonel Sidney included, as they had vanquished a king who was an instrument of the Devil. Sidney had taken his seat at the helm of the Free State which replaced Stuart monarchy in 1649. Thereafter he had personally experienced the difference between what the quote above calls 'the government of one over many' and one which had used a God-given 'faculty as well as a liberty' of 'instituting governments that were not known' to their predecessors. Had there been any doubt about the superiority of a rational meritocracy over a patriarchal dynasty the spectacular contrast between the dismal military record of Charles I abroad and at home and the republic's conquest of Ireland (1649), Scotland (1651) and defeat of the Dutch at sea (1654) more than sufficiently cleared it up, for Sidney at least. Thus it was from his pen that there emerged some of the most stirring utterances of a newly created ideology. This was not that the republic's military successes reflected an array of new-found resources, but rather that it was a consequence, as Machiavelli had insisted it would be, of the replacement of monarchy by a republic.

When [the Dutch Admiral Maarten] Van Tromp set upon [the English Admiral Robert] Blake in Foleston-Bay, the parliament had not above thirteen ships against threescore ... to oppose the best captain in the world ... But such was the power of wisdom and integrity in those who sat at the helm, and their diligence in chusing men only for their merit was blessed with such success, that in two years our fleets grew to be as famous as our land armies; the reputation and power of our nation rose to a greater height, than when we possessed the better half of France ... All the states ... of Europe ... sought our friendship; and Rome was more afraid of Blake and his fleet, than they had been of the great king of Sweden, when he was ready to invade Italy with a hundred thousand men. (278–9)

Then, following the republic's collapse and the restoration of monarchy (1660), Sidney had endured a seventeen-year exile, being granted leave to return to see his dying father in 1677. The eruption the following year of a major crisis and the publication of *Patriarcha* two years later showed that the struggle was not over, nor was Sidney's moral and ultimately military obligation to engage.[7]

The third life-defining context for Sidney's assault upon *Patriarcha* was peculiar to him among that text's opponents. It was also deeply personal, so much so that Filmer's very title made Algernon see red. As the second son of the second earl of Leicester he could hardly have taken a dimmer view of the custom of primogeniture inheritance to which Sir Robert's argument committed him. Not only was it manifestly unjust that the oldest son should inherit the title: the individual in question, Philip, Lord Lisle, was in Algernon's opinion a dullard as well as a Cromwellian, and thus doubly unfit for purpose. Chapter Two, Section 4 of the *Discourses* carries the title: '*The Paternal Right devolves to, and is inherited by all the Children*'.

As a plethora of suits in Chancery plus related documents make clear, throughout his adult life Algernon waged a battle with Philip for what he considered an appropriate share of his inheritance. Thus when Sidney wrote in the quote above that, contrary to Filmer's opinion God 'did endow him, and those that came from him, as well the youngest as the eldest line, with understanding to provide for themselves' he was saying something as deeply personal as it was political. And when he added that 'a faculty as well as a liberty was left to everyone, and will be to the end of the world, to make use of his wit, industry, and experience, according to present exigencies, to invent and practise such things as seem convenient to himself', he was asserting the moral superiority of merit (wit, industry and experience) in matters of family inheritance as well as in government. Thus in 1656 Philip wrote to his father Leicester of my constant sorrow, to see that your Lordship never omits a oportunity of reproach to me; and in ernest I thinke, laying all other matters aside … [it] is very extraordinary, that the younger sonne should so domineer in your house [Penshurst Place] that … it is not only his chamber but the greate rooms of the house, and perhaps the whole, he commands. And I thinke I may most properly say it, that his extreamest vanity and want of judgement are so knowne that there will be some wonder at it.[8]

As this complaint suggests, Philip might indeed have had reason for worry, though Algernon's subsequent exile in Scandinavia, Italy, the United Provinces and France (1660–77) removed him from the immediate field of play. In fact, Leicester remained on bad terms with his eldest son for the rest of his life. The latter wrote to his father bitterly in 1672 that he had received nothing from him 'for thirty years' but one suit of clothes for his son.[9] The result was a final settlement of the Leicester estate, confirmed only three days before the earl's death (at which time he was attended by Algernon and Henry, but not by Philip) overwhelmingly favourable toward the younger sons. Moreover Algernon and Henry, but not Philip, were made executors of the will. Philip inherited the title of third earl of Leicester. But while Henry and Algernon received immediate lump sums of 10,000 pounds each, plus annuities of 150 pounds per year, Philip remained debarred from possession of any part of the estate until he had agreed to a development of the family's London properties which he had refused for almost a decade. When, following his father's death, he continued to refuse, Henry moved into Penshurst Place and Algernon into the family's London mansion Leicester House. Philip then challenged the will in Chancery, Algernon and Henry hired lawyers to resist the challenge, and the matter remained unsettled at the time of Algernon's execution six years later.

Thus we can see that Sidney resisted Filmer's advocacy of the 'government of one [man] over many' throughout his life, and in several ways. His adult existence was spent in multifaceted rebellion against both patriarchalism and primogeniture, in the public and private spheres. It is therefore not surprising that both the *Court Maxims* (unpublished in his lifetime) and the *Discourses* advocated such rebellion, in fact, on grounds that were religious (no man would govern Sidney's conscience), political (no one would govern him without his consent) and personal (the foundations of authority and power were reason and merit, not inheritance).

The other notable feature of the advocacy of these positions in the above quote was its defence of political and other change and development over time. Sidney thus resisted not only Filmer's attempt to collapse the elementary distinction traceable as far back as Aristotle, between the domestic and political government of fathers. He did so because the true, God-given sources of government lay elsewhere. He did so, further, because it was in the nature of those sources, in particular the right use of reason, that they would by experience lead to change and improvement over time. It was on these grounds that Sidney rejected not only the government of fathers, but any obligation to govern in the manner of our fathers: that is to say, adherence to political prescription in general.

Not only was it not the case that humankind's 'descendants were obliged not to add anything to what their forefathers practiced'. If this were the case, he said elsewhere in the same book, we would still be eating acorns and living in trees. But the 'invention of arts and sciences' showed that invention, innovation and improvement were natural effects of reason, industry and experience. Here too there is no reason to doubt that Algernon was speaking from experience, not only individual – Bishop Gilbert Burnet reporting that he 'had studied the history of government in all its branches beyond any man I ever knew'[10] – but political, the innovations of 1649–53 having transformed Britain from a military basket case into a superpower. And although this was what Machiavelli had said was usually the consequence of liberty, and Sidney's *Discourses* made constant and extensive use of this Florentine source (Machiavelli's *Discourses Concerning the First Ten Books of Titus Livy*), Sidney's defence of innovation and improvement, one of the most characteristic and important features of his work, also established a key distinction between them on this point. Like Sidney, Machiavelli had insisted upon the inescapability of change. The best change he could envisage, however, was to imitate the most successful (Roman) examples of the past. What Sidney argued was not only that change was inevitable, but that it should take the form of improvement.

> Such is the condition of mankind, that nothing can be so perfectly framed as not to … stand frequently in need of reparations and amendments … Some men observing this, have proposed a necessity of reducing every state, once in an age or two, to the integrity of its first principle: but they ought to have examined, whether that principle be good or evil, or so good that nothing can be added to it, which none ever was; and this being so, those who will admit of no change would … deprive … mankind of the benefits of wisdom, industry, experience, and the right use of reason.[11]

This was one of the more striking examples of a broader difference between Italian and Northern humanism. Sidney's political colleagues Marchamont Nedham and John Milton also defended the right of political societies to outgrow precedent and effect beneficial change. In his elaboration of this position, however ('he that should ... blame those that go out of that [way] in which their fathers had walked, when they find it necessary, does as far as in him lies, render the worst of errors perpetual' (173)), Sidney was indeed updating humanism for the Enlightenment. He was helping to prepare the ground for Thomas Paine who would make the point still more strenuously a century later: that it was a monstrosity for present generations to be bound by the customs of their ancestors; and that liberty entailed a freedom, not simply to form the best possible government, but in order to do so a freedom within time.

Locke's *Some Thoughts Concerning Education* (1693): Fathers and Conversational Friendship

J. K. Numao

I imagine every one will judge it reasonable, that their Children, when little, should look upon their Parents as their Lords, their Absolute Governors; and, as such, stand in awe of them: And that, when they come to riper Years, they should look on them as their best, as their only sure Friends; and as such, love and reverence them. The Way I have mentioned, if I mistake not, is the only one to obtain this. We must look upon our Children, when grown up, to be like our selves; with the same Passions, the same Desires. We would be thought Rational Creatures, and have our Freedom; we love not to be uneasie, under constant Rebukes and Brow-beatings; nor can we bear severe Humours, and great Distance in those we converse with. Whoever has such Treatment when he is a Man, will look out other Company, other Friends, other Conversation, with whom, he can be at Ease. If therefore a strict Hand be kept over Children from the Beginning, they will in that Age be tractable, and quietly submit to it, as never having known any other: And if, as they grow up to the Use of Reason, the Rigour of Government be, as they deserve it, gently relaxed, the Father's Brow more smooth'd to them, and the Distance by Degrees abated; his former Restraints will increase their Love, when they find it was only a Kindness to them, and a Care to make them capable to deserve the Favour of their Parents, and the Esteem of every Body else.[1]

For John Locke (1632–1704), life is like a pilgrimage. We were created and placed in this world to go about God's business. We each have a particular calling, such as to be a farmer or a scholar, but we also have a more general calling or duty as human beings, namely to worship God and to preserve ourselves and the rest of humankind to the best of our ability. The knowledge of this general calling is in principle available to each and every one of us if we would take the care to use our natural faculties of sense and reason to study God's will revealed through natural law. While we are all adequately equipped to perform this task, we can benefit greatly from having friends accompanying us on this life's journey. As the passage selected above and others suggest, a child might eventually become to a father, and the father to his child, one, if not the best, of these friends.

The passage appears in Locke's *Some Thoughts Concerning Education* (1693), which was, according to the author, a modest treatise on the education of children ('The Epistle Dedicatory'). The book developed out of a series of private letters sent to his friends, Mr and Mrs Edward Clarke, who had sought advice from Locke on how best to raise and educate their son. While the main concern of this book is pedagogic, it has implications beyond, and as such sheds light on the nature and extent of fatherly authority. However, in discussions of paternal power within Locke scholarship, modern commentators typically focus on the *Two Treatises of Government* (1689),[2] while tending to turn to *Some Thoughts* only in passing to reinforce or to add small details to the points made in the former work. Historically though in the case of America, *Some Thoughts* rather than the *Two Treatises* seems to have left a clearer imprint on its eighteenth-century anti-patriarchal revolutionary culture.[3] This essay therefore casts the spotlight on *Some Thoughts* in an attempt to draw attention to its unique contribution in this field, particularly on how it illuminates the father's role after the child matures, a subject that tends to be passed over in the scholarship. To see the significance of *Some Thoughts*, however, we first need to turn to the *Two Treatises* to set the stage.

Locke's main point in bringing up the discussion about paternal power in the *Two Treatises* was to show its irrelevance as a means of deriving political power. By contrast, paternal power had a different role to play in God's great design for humankind, namely to prepare one's offspring physically and mentally to undertake their natural duties. Locke's adversary in the *Two Treatises*, the Kentish gentleman Sir Robert Filmer, thought just the opposite: political power, indeed, absolute political power, was derived from paternal power. According to Locke, Filmer maintained that children were born in subjection to their parents, the act of begetting granting the begetter dominion over the begotten (I.50). This dominion – 'regal' or 'royal' power – is unlimited, and by this, fathers have power over the lives, liberties and estates of their children (I.9). Adam, by virtue of being the *first* father, together with God's blessing, was unique in this respect, enjoying paramount lordship over *all* his posterity, that is, the whole of humankind. This sovereign right enjoyed by Adam was then passed down to his heirs (how exactly it was transferred is less clear), who are the present-day absolute monarchs. Thus, while enjoying absolute power over their offspring, fathers are nevertheless subject to absolute monarchs who are heirs to Adam's supreme power. But the key point stands: fatherhood gives birth to political power.[4]

Not only did Filmer hold that fathers derive political power from fatherhood, but furthermore, Locke notes, he and his followers suggested that a father's activity resembles that of God's. For 'even the power which God himself exerciseth over mankind is by right of fatherhood' (I.53). As God, the maker, created and ruled over mankind, so too fathers give life and exercise dominion over their offspring.

In his response to Filmer in the 'First Treatise', Locke begins by denying that there is a parallel between God and fathers, and so denies that fathers have the same sort of power as God. In the first instance, Locke rejects that fathers 'make' children in the sense that God does (I.52–54). In other words, God's creative work is different from our producing children, and so too the rights that follow from these respective acts. The former implies making something *ex nihilo* and fixing its nature, whereas the latter simply involves moving about pre-existing things. Creation gives the creator the rights concerning how the created should be treated. Fathers are not creators but merely the occasion, and so cannot determine how their children ought to be treated without reference to God's law. Thus fathers do not resemble God in act, and consequently, in power.[5]

Even if we do grant that parents make their children and so have absolute power over them, Locke notes that this would only mean that fathers have a conjoint right with mothers, and so would not warrant an exclusive power over their children (I.55). This point has been taken up by feminist scholars, leading to a vast debate over gender equality within Locke's thought. This essay, however, will focus not on this discussion but on the significance of Locke's job description of fathers.[6]

While the 'First Treatise' tells us what fatherly authority is not, the 'Second Treatise' gives a more positive account of what it is and what its extent is. Locke argues that the father's authority over his children is determined by the law of nature (II.56), and this law shows that he is not given power specifically by being the biological father (II.65). According to natural law, fathers conjointly with mothers are '*under an obligation to preserve, nourish, and educate the Children, they had begotten*' (II.56). This obligation arises from children being not the workmanship of the parents, but of God who wills His creation be preserved. Although children are born *to* a state of equality of natural freedom, being yet imperfect in body and mind, they are not born *in* it, and so parents must take care of them until they develop the strength and rational capacity to subsist and subject themselves to the government of the law of nature (I.55–8). Thus parents' authority over their children during their minority originates from its being used for the children's good (II.63). The act of begetting itself does so little to establish any fatherly authority that should fathers not exercise guardianship over their children, they would quickly lose their power over them (II.65). Moreover, the power fathers have is only 'temporary' and so once his child comes into possession of reason, the father's empire ceases: the child becomes a fellow equal over whom the father as such has no power (I.65).

Thus there comes a time when the son leaves his parents and cleaves to his wife; but he is not thereby exempt from paying respect to his parents who have played a crucial part in God's great design. Children have a perpetual duty to honour their parents, inwardly in esteem, and outwardly in action, negatively by not compromising their parents' happiness and more positively by providing assistance and comfort (II.66). Parents, on the other hand, have a right to respect and support in proportion to their effort to raise their child (II.67). But as Locke tirelessly notes, the right to receive respect must not be confounded with a right to demand absolute obedience and submission from the child. At no time, does the father's power extend to the child's life or property.

Once the child grows up and leaves the care of his parents, that is to say, once he becomes the father's equal, other than the object of respect, what role is there for the father? The existing literature tends to be somewhat silent about this question, and it is here we should turn to *Some Thoughts* for insight. As the passage selected and others (§40–4, 95–7) show, Locke recommends that the father–son relationship in adulthood make a shift towards friendship: fathers should look upon their son not as a servant but as a friend, and the son upon his father not as a lord but as a friend, if not his best friend (§41).

What is it to be a friend in Locke's sense, then? What does friendship entail? For one, the relation is more than the friendship between George and 'innocent' Lennie we see in something like John Steinbeck's novel *Of Mice and Men* (1937).[7] While at times the relationship between the two characters seems to be that of 'guardianship', we may say it is also that of 'companionship', both characters benefiting from the fact that they give 'a damn about' each other and have each other to 'look after'. On the other hand, Locke's idea of friendship involves more than filling in loneliness, more than keeping each other in company. His is first and foremost a relationship between equals (§97). Thus, for fathers to treat their grown-up children as friends is to treat them 'to be like ourselves', that is 'Rational Creatures' (§41). Therefore, children who do not achieve a certain threshold of rationality must not leave the government of their parents (II.60). As rational creatures, people share a range of natural duties; and it is here that we see what the prime benefit of friendship is. A defining feature of friendship is 'love' and people's love of one's friends is often directed to 'those good things which they do love and which they cannot have without them [sc. friends]', and this is the 'conversation' they provide.[8] To say one enjoys the conversation of friends in the early modern period could mean that one enjoys discoursing with others, rather like the modern sense, and also to enjoy the company of others. Locke seems to use it predominantly in the former sense, often adopting the separate term 'company' to express the latter (although the two concepts are closely related in his mind). Conversation in this first sense between friends is important because it gives a chance for one to re-examine one's thoughts, beliefs and prejudices. It often happens that we hold beliefs without having ever examined them, but with 'the assistance of a serious and sober friend' we might hope to question and examine these, and thereby serve the cause of truth. There is no reason why a conversation with a stranger cannot yield similar results, but a friend, the best of friends, is someone whom we can truly confide in, someone who takes us seriously (§96). While Locke warns against closing the circle to one kind of friends, intimacy might be helpful to bring the really important issues on the table, being a 'sure' friend he who we can 'freely Consult on Occasion' (§96, and also §41). Thus, while we are in general capable of attaining the necessary knowledge to perform our natural duties, we are not infallible. To this extent, we are equally inquirers, and so the conversation with a friend on this godly intellectual pilgrimage would be reassuring.[9]

The father's role as the best friend of his grown-up child has a theological uniqueness to it as well. As part of his effort to distinguish between political and paternal power, Locke, as we have seen, rejects that there is a resemblance between God's creation of humankind and fathers' participation in procreation. Locke further distinguishes divine power, which is the source of our moral, political and religious obligations, from paternal power, which is subservient to the former's ends, by making friendship uniquely an inter-human relationship as opposed also to a divine–human relationship. In the seventeenth century, it was not uncommon to list 'friend' as one of the Christian God's attributes and talk about having a friendship with God. Isaac Barrow, a mathematician and theologian, even suggests that this relationship with God should be familiar and conversational:

> It is frequency of Devotion also which maintaineth that Friendship with God, which is the soul of Piety. As familiar conversation (wherein men do express their minds and affections mutually) breedeth acquaintance, and cherisheth good will

of men to one another … so is it in respect to God; it is frequent converse with him which begetteth a particular acquaintance with him.

Moreover, friendship could exist in unequal conditions. For example, Robert Sanderson, bishop of Lincoln, defines friendship as faithfulness, 'faith and obedience' being 'those very things that qualifie us for [God's] friendship', and argues that friendship can exist between unequals, such as between God and man or father and child. The act of chastising or punishing by the superior, insofar as it was for the good of the inferior, could be understood as an act of love of a friend.[10]

By contrast, Locke's idea of friendship presupposes conversation between equals. Thus consistently, friendship does not figure greatly in Locke's idea of God. When Locke describes God's attributes, while we find words such as 'superior', 'supreme', 'creator', 'maker', 'omnipotent', 'omniscient', 'just', 'eternal', 'infinite', 'sovereign' and perhaps 'father', we do not find him mentioning 'friend'.[11] And in the handful of cases when Locke touches on biblical verses that suggest a friendship between God and men, in one case he does not make great play of the verse, while in another makes the application of the term 'friendship' to God indeterminate. Otherwise, if friendship is used at all to describe the relationship between God and men, the idea of familiarity and conversation is stripped away.[12] While fathers and children might eventually become friends, God always remains sovereign over us. God's character and role can encompass and overlap with fathers (*'he chasten'd them as a Man chastens his Son'* (II.67)) and the human race as a whole (*'Let us make Men in our Image'* (I.30, 40)), but it does not follow that fathers can thereby enjoy the same rights as God. Familiar and conversational friendship exists uniquely between human beings, and is particularly suitable in a father–son relationship.

Locke, we may say, is a man of distinction by virtue of his distinction-making ability. Famously, in his defence of toleration, he distinguished between the purpose of the state and that of the church. Likewise, in his rejection of absolutism, he distinguished between the nature of paternal and political power; between the nature of divine and paternal power; and in his description of paternal power, between the treatment of one's offspring in childhood and adulthood. For Locke, God is sovereign, and we are subject to His incomparable power and wisdom. We exist to undertake his business in this world. In God's scheme, the father's authority in the child's early years ought to be used to prepare and to send the child out into the world, so that he can do what God has planned for him; and in the later years when he grows up, the father's rule would ideally change to friendship – to a relationship that is appropriate between equals, and perhaps to the best of its kind, intimate and familiar, thanks to the trust gained through the years spent together – whereby they can seek through exchanging insights what exactly God desires of them to do. Life is a godly journey. There may be 'trials'; we may feel 'weak and heavy laden'. But thank God, what a friend we have in our earthly fathers.[13]

'Nothing Pleases Like an Intire Subjection'[1]: Mary Astell Reflects on the Politics of Marriage (1700)

Brett D. Wilson

[I]f Absolute Sovereignty be not necessary in a State, how comes it to be so in a Family? or if in a Family, why not in a State; since no Reason can be alledg'd for the one that will not hold more strongly for the other? If the Authority of the Husband so far as it extends, is sacred and inalienable, why not of the Prince? The Domestic Sovereign is without Dispute Elected, and the Stipulations and Contracts are mutual, is it not then partial in Men to the last degree, to contend for, and practise that Arbitrary Dominion in their Families, which they abhor and exclaim against in the State? For if Arbitrary Power is evil in itself, and an improper Method of Governing Rational and Free Agents it ought not to be Practis'd any where; Nor is it less, but rather more mischievous in Families than in Kingdoms, by how much 100000 Tyrants are worse than one. What tho' a Husband can't deprive a Wife of Life without being responsible to the Law, he may however do what is much more grievous to a generous Mind, render Life miserable, for which she has no Redress, scarce Pity which is afforded to every other Complainant. It being thought a Wife's Duty to suffer everything without Complaint. If all Men are born free, *how is it that all* Women are born slaves? *as they must be if the being subjected to the* inconstant, uncertain, unknown, arbitrary Will *of Men, be the* perfect Condition of Slavery? *and if the Essence of Freedom consists, as our Masters say it does, in having a* standing Rule to live by? *And why is Slavery so much condemn'd and strove against in one Case, and so highly applauded and held so necessary and so sacred in another?*[2]

Near the outset of her career, Mary Astell (1666–1731) challenged critics who 'would perhaps remit me to the Distaff or the Kitchin [sic], or at least to the Glass and the Needle, the proper Employments as they fancy of a Woman's Life'.[3] Grasping the quill, she would vindicate herself adeptly. Often credited as the first English feminist, Astell produced treatises and occasional pieces on matters of state, church and civil society. *Some Reflections on Marriage, Occasion'd by the Duke and Dutchess [sic] of Mazarine's Case*, first published in 1700, with further editions appearing in 1706 and 1730, is a milestone in Anglophone feminism that comes into sharper focus when also read as the work of a significant political thinker.

Astell's depiction in *Reflections* of the position of women, especially wives, draws on *au courant* philosophies of political allegiance. In decades marked by what contemporary essayists called a 'Rage of Party', partisans clashed over the proper relationship between subject and sovereign. Tories, by and large, subscribed to doctrines of hereditary right, believing that political authority was rightfully vested in a monarch who had succeeded another in an orderly generational transition, and that the subject's place was to extend obedience in exchange for paternalistic protection. Whigs, their opponents, saw civil government as a compact that a sovereign could breach with outrageous acts, and defended the people's right to resist an oppressive ruler who overstepped his rightful bounds. Denying the existence of this right to resist, Tories professed twin precepts of passive obedience and non-resistance: if the sovereign commanded a subject to an unconscionable deed, the subject could at most refuse to perform it, accepting both the sovereign's authority and the consequences of inaction. Party wrangling on these matters surged in the aftermath of the Revolution Settlement of 1688–9. Their views somewhat confounded by the deposition of James II and consequent ascension to the throne of William and Mary, many Whig enthusiasts for the new reign tempered their endorsements of the right to resist. In turn, stalwart proponents of passive obedience under Charles II and James II refined their logic so that they might conscientiously withhold support for a new regime whose legitimacy they questioned – if not plot against it actively, as some Jacobites did.

Astell was a deep-dyed Tory. In other political writings contemporaneous with *Reflections*, she maintains that 'Order is a Sacred Thing', that 'Subordination is a necessary consequence of Order', and, since 'there is not any thing that tends more to Confusion than Equality', the people must 'humbly … observe where God has Delegated his Power, and submit to it'.[4] *Reflections*, which probes the parameters of the subordination of wives to husbands, is also a salvo in an ongoing battle about the nature of sovereign power and political obligation. The philosophical dialogue joined by such canonical figures as Thomas Hobbes, Robert Filmer and John Locke was itself shaped by analogical reasoning about the similarities between states and families: rulers (elected and hereditary), fathers and husbands. As we will see, Astell's figure of wifely submission embodies a distinctly Tory outlook on how passive obedience translates from the political to the personal realm – from one patriarchalism to another – to bespeak a concealed but conscientious resisting non-resistance.

In *Reflections on Marriage*, Astell takes as a point of departure, the Duchess of Mazarin, a well-connected socialite whose tempestuous marriage was a *cause célèbre*. Thwarted by a possessive, unstable husband, she had abandoned him and her young children to become a globetrotting *bonne vivante*; on her death in 1699, diarist John Evelyn remembered her as 'dissolute and impatient of matrimonial restraint'.[5] Astell begins *Reflections* by sympathizing with the notorious Duchess's frustrations, characterizing the Duke as an 'absolute Lord and Master' (34). However, she insists that his abuses do not 'Authorize a Woman's ... breaking from the strongest Bands' (35). Even if provoked, the Duchess ought to have endured the marriage in a spirit of 'Discretion' and 'Vertue [sic]' (34, 35).

Astell proceeds from the Mazarin case to expound the nature of contemporary marriage and alert women to its hazards. Kept ignorant of the world and fed on 'unreasonable Desires and Expectations' (60), imprudent women fall prey to designing men. Once under the 'Matrimonial Yoke' (59), Astell explains, 'the Woman has in truth no security but the Man's Honour and Good-nature, a Security that in this present Age no wise Person would venture much upon' (51). Free to inflict misery, domineering husbands consign wives to materially and spiritually unfulfilling lives. Sometimes neglect is the best outcome, because it affords women 'Silence and Solitude' (40). Astell concedes that 'if a Wife's case be as it is here represented, it is not good for a Woman to Marry, and so there's an end of [the] Human Race' (77–8). Forewarned by Astell's alarums, an informed woman could 'duly examine and weigh all the Circumstances, the Good and Evil of a Married State ... and either never consent to be a Wife, or make a good one when she does' (75).

Astell's treatise on marriage is rife with tropes of government. In the 1706 preface, she wryly remarks that *Reflections* has been 'accus'd of being so destructive to the Government, of the Men I mean' (8) because it exposes their 'Arcana Imperii', state secrets – a phrase she repeats in the treatise proper (78).

Astell describes a patriarchate comprised of artful and exacting despots. She maintains that modern beaus contrive 'to get the poor Woman into their Power, to govern her according to their Discretion' (66). Even when the wife is her husband's social superior before marriage, he demands a docile subject 'whom he can intirely Govern' (51). Marriage grants husbands 'an absolute Power over' wives' desires (48–9). Assurances are unreliable and unenforceable: Astell deplores that 'Covenants betwixt Husband and Wife, like Laws in an Arbitrary Government, are of little Force, the Will of the Sovereign is all in all' (52).

Because patriarchal dominion is absolute and often arbitrary, Astell equates women's social position to that of slaves – not to the chattel slavery of colonial plantations but to the political slavery of the radically unfree subject. The purposes of her famous analogy, however, are as much ironic as polemical. One instance of the comparison occurs as the crescendo of her 1706 preface:

> If all Men are born free, how is it that all Women are born Slaves? ... And why is Slavery so much condemn'd and strove against in one Case, and so highly applauded and held so necessary and so sacred in another? (18–19)

The outcry is eloquent. But being born free and equal was a Whig tenet, not a Tory one. Neither Astell nor her Tory fellow-travellers subscribed to the ideas of natural liberty articulated by philosophers like Locke, Gilbert Burnet and Benjamin Hoadly. Throughout *Reflections*, Astell means to make champions of resistance doctrine squirm by turning their own maxims against them. She taunts Whig contractualists for being covert supporters of the passive obedience they purport to revile – for wives, at least:

> how much soever Arbitrary Power may be dislik'd on a Throne, not Milton himself wou'd cry up Liberty to poor Female Slaves, or plead for the Lawfulness of Resisting a Private Tyranny. (46–7)

With a waspish desire to puncture Whig orthodoxy, Astell castigates those who, she alleges, 'practise that Arbitrary Dominion in their Families, which they abhor and exclaim against in the State', for 'if Absolute Sovereignty be not necessary in a State, how comes it to be so in a Family?' (17).

The intensity and expressiveness of Astell's critiques of marriage as practised – a zone of subjugation and unfreedom – raises the question of her views on marriage in theory. As much as Astell decries the desperate position to which wives have been relegated, her conjugal model might nonetheless aptly be characterized as patriarchal. For Astell as much as for contemporary anti-feminist writers, the married state grants the husband the place of authority, and the wife is obliged to accept it. She has willingly subjected herself, and hence her agency is tightly constrained. But in *Reflections* obligation does not license oppression. A good husband, like a good ruler, moderates his temperament: he self-governs as much as he governs (48–9). Husbands *ought not* flaunt their supremacy or exercise it cruelly: to do so 'provokes the Oppress'd' (78). They should 'sweeten' the authority they exercise: 'to give evidence that he has a Right to those Prerogatives he assumes, [a man] shou'd treat Women with a little more Humanity and Regard than is usually paid them' (58). To display benevolence demonstrates the rightfulness of their authority; severity makes it appear dubious. Extending her insights from the marital to the governmental, Astell argues that 'Authority may be preserv'd and Government kept inviolable, without…nauseous Ostentation of Power' (54), and hence it will never 'be well…even from the Throne to every Private Family, till those in Authority look on themselves as plac'd in that Station for the good and improvement of their Subjects' (56). As subjects will their sovereigns, ruled rightly, wives will honour and heed their husbands' dominion:

> A peaceable Woman indeed will…neither question her Husband's Right nor his Fitness to Govern; but how? Not as an absolute Lord and Master, with an Arbitrary and Tyrannical sway, but as Reason Governs and Conducts a man, by proposing what is Just and Fit. (79)

Astell rues that husbandly authority as practised seldom resembles her prescriptions, but avers that it is not the wife's place to challenge an imperious husband. In the event the marriage is malign, the 'peaceable' wife, like the Tory subject, nonetheless patiently perseveres.

Astell, like her cohort of Tory thinkers, anathematizes revolt. The spectre of female rebellion haunts the text, but its threat is consistently minimized. Responding to her initial critical reception in the 1706 preface, she insists that she cannot 'imagine how she any way undermines the Masculine Empire, or blows the Trumpet of Rebellion'; 'she did not in any manner prompt them to Resist' (8, 9). Having made 'Resisting a Private Tyranny' a sardonic joke, Astell acknowledges that 'women are not so well united as to form an Insurrection' (29). She adds that the notion that women might be 'Strong enough to break the Yoke, to Depose and Abdicate…[will] not be allow'd of here' (46). Not for her the rhetorical flourishes of Mary Wollstonecraft, who less than a century later would call for a 'Revolution in female manners.'[6] Astell instead contends that 'Patience and Submission are the only Comforts that are left to a poor People, who groan under Tyranny' (46). The same wisdom applies in the household as in the nation. When a woman marries, even when her husband proves himself to be foolish, despotic, or violent, it has to be her 'indisputable Maxim, that her Husband must govern absolutely and intirely, and that she has nothing else to do but to Please and Obey' (62), for 'she who Elects a Monarch for Life ... gives him an Authority she cannot recall however he misapply it' (48).

In Astell's account the task for women who self-subject by opting into the married state is to submit, but not unthinkingly. Wives supply not 'Blind Obedience' (61, 75) but a clear-sighted variant: resigned, reasoned, or, better still, 'Chearful' (54, 56). Astell's call is for a *virtuous* submission in keeping with the seamless garment of Tory passive obedience: 'A Woman ... that cannot patiently submit even when Reason suffers with her, who does not practice Passive Obedience to the utmost, will never be acceptable to such an absolute Sovereign as a Husband' (61). Astell avows that 'She who can't do this is no way fit to be a Wife' (62), and in an earlier treatise she outlined another option: a haven for unmarried women, part academy and part Protestant monastic community, where dedication to the *vita contemplativa* could produce a 'Beneficence [that] moves in the largest Sphere' and secure 'the Glory of Reforming this Prophane and Profligate Age'.[7] (Astell herself never married.)

Bleak as the conjugal state may appear, for Astell it is through acts of submission that wives achieve a sort of moral power. Marriage becomes a trial of, and staging ground for, beliefs both religious and political. While active rebellion is prohibited, conjugal dissidents can withdraw into a world of conscience that is even, after a fashion, liberating: 'the Mind is free, nothing but Reason can oblige it, 'tis out of the reach of the most absolute Tyrant' (56). Astell also allows the possibility of a 'meer Obedience' (50) produced only by discipline – a coerced subjection that calls attention to its own incompleteness. Even in the midst of patriarchal oppression, the submissive wife shines:

> When a Superior does a Mean and unjust Thing ... and yet this does not provoke his Inferiors to refuse that Observance which their Stations in the World require, they cannot but have an inward Sense of their own real Superiority, the other having no pretence to it, at the same time that they pay him an outward Respect and Deference, which is such a flagrant Testimony of the sincerest Love of Order as proves their Souls to be of the highest and noblest Rank. (58)

Even as her compliance in the face of injustice registers outwardly, the patient and principled wife exudes a glorious righteousness that upholds a larger social and political hierarchy.

This disposition, for Astell, is expressly *heroic*. Women's inferior social position may not be enough 'to make a Noise ... to found or overturn Empires, yet it qualifies them for what is infinitely better, a Kingdom that cannot be mov'd' where 'her Soul shall shine as bright as the greatest Heroes' (76, 75). In Heaven, gender inequities cease. Moving from the equal to the comparative and superlative, Astell soon represents this feminine mode of passive heroism as unparalleled: to discharge an

> intire Submission for Life, to one whom she cannot be sure will always deserve it, does certainly perform a more Heroic Action than all the famous Masculine Heroes can boast of[.] (78)

Even Cato, whose love of liberty led him to commit suicide rather than kowtow to Julius Caesar (63), is bested by the iconic wife, who by enduring 'continual Martyrdom' (78) maintains a luminous and indomitable integrity that shames the power that looms over her. This is her recourse; her 'consolation' (75); her 'Remedy in reserve' (80). 'Subjection ... is not over easie', Astell affirms. Only a 'sound Understanding, and Grace' can 'heartily reconcile us to Obedience' (54). Outward self-abnegation thus masks inward self-assertion.

The end of the 1706 preface to *Reflections* offers an alternative iconography: Queen Anne, an indisputable example of female authority whose accession postdates the original treatise. Practically daring men to withhold their allegiance and prove themselves both misogynists and rebels, Astell lauds the Queen as a defender of liberty whose auspicious reign will lead to 'Halcyon, or if you will Millennium Days,' when 'a Tyrannous Domination which Nature never meant, shall no longer render useless if not hurtful, the Industry and Understandings of half Mankind!' (31). Astell's detractors are Anne's, she insinuates, and threaten the golden age Anne would otherwise inaugurate for England and for women. If the icon within the *Reflections* proper is the steadfast wife accommodating her husband's power while exercising her contemplative conscience, the new preface enfolds the wifely martyr's perseverance into a triumphant, even triumphalist, scene of sovereign splendour.

Astell's feminism in *Reflections* is thoroughly enmeshed with her Tory views on state power. Her rebuff to classic patriarchalism is most discernible in the way she aligns the relation of wife to husband and that between subject and sovereign *de facto* rather than *de jure*. For Astell it is not the nature of things but 'the Custom of the World [that] has put Women, generally speaking, into a State of Subjection' (10). As with other post-1688 Tory political thinkers, passive obedience and non-resistance prevail as moral duties. Wives must defer to husbands, and subjects to their sovereigns, not because of their inherent superiority or the authority they have inherited since Adam, but simply because they happen to be in place at present. Astell's bad husband must be obeyed no less, and no more, than King William III, who (at the time of *Reflections'* first publication) occupies the throne irrespective of its rightfulness.

Cannily switching between figure and ground in likening family to state, Astell uses arguments about marriage to ridicule her ideological opponents as champions of political resistance who nonetheless cling to patriarchal privileges in their home lives. This is the context for the statements about slavery and liberty for which Astell is most remembered. Passive obedience underpins Astell's thinking about both subjects and wives. But in the interstices of *Reflections* is a kind of principled noncompliance located inwardly in the conscience, rather than outwardly in the temporal world. In a different vein, her prefatory encomium to Queen Anne imagines a female sovereignty that overthrows notions of natural womanly obedience and gives at least one woman a new way forward extrinsic to the family. *Reflections* exposes the abuses of patriarchal authority while also carving out a space for women both to withstand and ultimately overcome them. For in marriage as in the state, Astell's passive obedience may evince quietism – but not complicity.

Ants, Bees, Fathers, Sons: Pope's *Essay on Man* (1734) and the Natural History of Patriarchy

Paul Baines

Great *Nature* spoke; observant Men obey'd;
Cities were built, Societies were made:
Here rose one little *State*; Another near
Grew by like means, and join'd, thro' *Love* or *Fear*.
Did here the Trees with ruddier Burdens bend,
And there the Streams in purer Rills descend?
What *War* could ravish, *Commerce* could bestow,
And he return'd a Friend, who came a Foe.
Thus *States* were form'd; the name of *King* unknown,
'Till common Int'rest plac'd the Sway in One.
Then VIRTUE ONLY (or in Arts, or Arms,
Diffusing Blessings, or averting Harms)
The *same* which in a *Sire* the *Sons* obey'd,
A *Prince* the Father of a *People* made.
'Till then, by Nature crown'd, each Patriarch sate,
King, *Priest*, and *Parent* of his growing State;
On him, their second Providence, they hung,
Their Law, his Eye; their Oracle, his Tongue.
He, from the wondring Furrow call'd their Food,
Taught to command the Fire, controul the Flood,
Draw forth the Monsters of th' *Abyss* profound,
Or fetch th' Aerial Eagle to the Ground.
Till drooping, sick'ning, dying, they began
Whom they rever'd as *God*, to mourn as *Man*.
Then, looking up from Sire to Sire, explor'd
One Great First Father, and that *first* Ador'd.
Or plain Tradition that this All *begun*,

Convey'd unbroken Faith from Sire to Son,
The Workman from the Work distinct was known,
And *simple Reason* never sought but *One*:
E're *Wit* oblique had *broke* that steady Light,
Man, like his Maker, *saw*, that *all was right*,
To Virtue in the Paths of Pleasure, trod,
And own'd a *Father* when he own'd a *God*.
Love all the Faith, and all th' Allegiance then;
For Nature knew no *Right Divine* in *Men*,
No *Ill* could fear in *God*; and understood
A *Sovereign Being* but a *Sovereign Good*.[1]

Alexander Pope was born in the year of the 'Glorious Revolution' (1688), an obvious test case for the contest between patriarchal or divine-right and social-contract theories of sovereignty, as it was played out during Pope's childhood. Alongside Robert Filmer's *Patriarcha* and John Locke's *Of Civil Government*, the main ideas were notably dramatized in poetry in John Dryden's royalist *Absalom and Achitophel* (1681), an enormously influential satiric model. Dryden became a Catholic on the accession of James II in 1685 and remained so on his removal from the throne in 1688, necessarily thereby sacrificing his state appointments. In the course of his career Pope, a Catholic by birth and permanently excluded from public office, university education and the franchise, would self-consciously model himself on the independent satiric commentator in a voice sometimes closely echoing Dryden's later mode. As a young man, Pope read widely in religious and political controversy, finding himself strongly swayed by successive arguments, and he attempted an ecumenical, centrist position in early works like the *Essay on Criticism* (1711). But, as party lines between Whig and Tory hardened towards the end of the reign of Anne, bringing with it the prospect of a desacralized monarchy whose claim to sovereignty obviously lay with Parliament rather than divine right, Pope launched a kind of elegiac Tory myth of a Stuart golden age in *Windsor-Forest* (1713), and was thereafter always suspected of High Tory, if not Jacobite, sympathies. His mock-epic *Dunciad* (1728), together with his verse *Epistles to Several Persons* and series of *Imitations* of the Roman poet Horace, in the 1730s, were laced with anti-Hanoverian innuendo. The Whig regime of Sir Robert Walpole was fairly solid for the majority of Pope's later career, and Pope derived much poetic energy and material from his oppositional stance. He was courted by and attracted to the cluster of opposition politicians around the Prince of Wales, but was too independent of mind to become their official laureate, preferring to present himself as outside party divisions.

Pope's *An Essay on Man* is normally considered as a single poem, but the four constituent epistles, composed somewhere around 1730–1, were originally published separately, at intervals of a few months between the first (20 February 1733) and the last (24 January 1734), with the composite sequence coming out in April 1734. The poems were also published anonymously, and not through Pope's usual publisher; until his *Works* of 1735, the *Essay on Man* was not acknowledged as his at all. The speaker of the *Essay* has a notional observer-companion, originally named 'Lælius'. This figure was later identified as Pope's close friend Henry St. John, Viscount Bolingbroke, who had returned from his Jacobite exile in 1723 but was still regarded by some as a freethinking troublemaker, making disguise necessary in Pope's deliberate strategy to wrongfoot his opponents, ever ready to damn him as a potential traitor. The poem was originally intended as the first volume of a four-part sequence of 'ethic epistles', and was initially received warmly as a non-party poem of moderate rationalism, with some unwitting praise from Pope's political and literary enemies. Latterly it was regarded by continental theologians, using a poor translation, as heretical, and it was at times accused of deism: the poem has indeed nothing to say of revelation, the redemptive role of Christ, or the functions of religious practice. It was defended with a heavy hand of commentary by a rising Anglican clergyman, William Warburton, soon a close associate of Pope's.

An *Essay on Man* adopts, in theory, something of the ethical middle way of *An Essay on Criticism*: in 'The Design' prefixed to the first edition of the whole poem, Pope describes it as 'steering betwixt the extremes of doctrines seemingly opposite … forming a *temperate* yet not *inconsistent*, and a *short* yet not *imperfect* system of Ethics'. Though the ostensible field of the *Essay* is thus ethics rather than politics, much of it is open to a political reading. The first Epistle, setting out the 'order' of the universe, suggests that everything, including 'Man', has its correct place in a 'Vast Chain of Being' (237), resistance to which is characterized as pride of the kind John Milton explored in his epic of rebellion against God, *Paradise Lost* (1667). As the 'Argument' to the Epistle declares, 'Absolute Submission' to Providence is required, and it might be possible to read that requirement as analogous to a worldly doctrine of Passive Obedience. The second Epistle, however, models the universe, and the mind of Man, horizontally, as a set of mixed, contrasting and balanced parts, a self-governing system in which the appetitive thrust of self-love is countered by reason, vice by virtue, the 'Ruling Passion' (a dominant emotional drive, a sort of monarch within an individual psychological 'commonwealth'), by internal opposition and external contrary forces. This could be read as an image of a constitution functioning by means of competing but balanced interests, as the British one was supposed to do. Pope's couplet art is very good at analysing and holding in tension opposite qualities, which are themselves writ large over the four contrasting Epistles; with the first two Pope has set up one essentially hierarchical system and one more laterally balanced, each contributing to the overall stability (and immutability) of the cosmos.

In Epistle III, from which the extract is taken, Pope sets out a narrative theory of the origins of government, in which these and other contrasting ideas are explored in explicitly political terms. It is worth noting that the biblical story of Adam and Eve, from which the grant of patriarchal sovereignty is supposed by Filmer to take its narrative shape and explanatory origin, plays no part whatever in Pope's conception: there is no acid Lockean refutation of its validity, it is simply not there at all. Since Pope's concern is to 'vindicate' a structure in which all dynamism ultimately results in replication of the *status quo*, narrative is itself problematic, since history implies that things have been otherwise and therefore could be otherwise again; but theories of government often sought some historical or mythic point of origin, supposedly granting explanatory authority, and Pope gingerly follows this model. The 'Argument' added to later printings of Epistle III gives the relevant sequence as: 'Origin of Political Societies. Origin of Monarchy. Origin of Patriarchal Government', which implies a bald kind of logic. The actual narrative is more complicated and much less clear-cut.

Pope initially suggests that cosmic structure shows co-operation and mutuality down to the inanimate and atomic level (7–14). He next takes us through the collaborative instincts of plants, then animals, which naturally conspire to 'Eternal ORDER' (113). From 150 to 201 Pope gives an account of the State of Nature: not Hobbes's reign of terror but an Edenic 'reign of God', in which self-love and social instinct simply cohere and balance, and no one has mastery over anyone else. During this passage, 'Nature' (a sort of divine apostle of rationality) instructs early humans to study the instinctive self-organization of miniature animal states, particularly '*The Ants* Republic, *and the* Realm *of Bees*'. These represent two alternate models, both valid within an overall providential system, in one case communitarian ('*How those in common all their Stores bestow,* | *And* Anarchy without Confusion *know*'), in the other, a monarchy which nonetheless guarantees the 'liberties of the subject' ('*And these for ever, tho'* a Monarch *reign,* | *Their sep'rate Cells and Properties maintain*'; III. 187–191). (Pope does not mention female dominion of the hive. John Geddie's *The English Apiary* (1721) discusses the role of the queen bee; but Pope follows the model of Bernard Mandeville's *Fable of the Bees* (1714), a political analysis which ignores the issue of a visible matriarchy). These political alternatives are offered to mankind in some exemplary couplets which appear to balance their claims to attention equally. The excerpted section then follows.

Some examples of Pope's 'steering' across a spectrum of political argument mark the narrative, and there are several areas of ambiguity and slippage. 'Men' follow the instructions of Nature to build cities and found societies, which then combine 'thro' *Love* or *Fear*'; Pope does not determine which, but in the ensuing lines he privileges the mutual friendship borne of commerce, over the enmity of war, as the developing force in social intercourse, later adding further lines to strengthen the image of an antediluvian golden age of benign natural law. 'The name of *King* unknown' indicates a self-governing organization, of the ant kind; until the unknown point in history at which 'common Int'rest plac'd the Sway in One'. That 'one' is (inevitably) male, already eminent for 'Virtue' – whether in 'Arts, or Arms' Pope diplomatically leaves undecided. This apparently contractual or elective origin of kingship is at once mapped directly and seamlessly onto a 'natural' origin for the patriarchal authority of a head of state, which is found in the reverence of male children for their father. This brings us to Pope's almost sole use of the word 'Patriarch' in poetry. Though Pope mentions the biblical patriarchs in the notes to his translations from Homer, and lightly in passing in the *Essay on Criticism*, this is his only use of it in a serious political context. In his correspondence he often uses the word in a jocular sense to praise, or tease, men at the head of a family, and on occasion to joke about his own status as a (childless) 'patriarch' of hospitality; these references, always at least a little ironic, nonetheless suggest an image of benign and natural authority, compatible with the narrative through which patriarchalism comes to the fore here.

> 'Till then, by Nature crown'd, each Patriarch sate,
> *King*, *Priest*, and *Parent* of his growing State;

The force of 'Till then' is odd, in that it seems to point to a definite moment in time which is not actually given: as if Pope is saying 'Until the point at which, by Nature crown'd . . .'. We have patriarchal authority because sons worship their fathers, and that is the 'natural' law. There is nothing to show the process by which the father of one *particular* family becomes king, priest and parent of the state: the extrapolation from domestic to political unit is magical and opaque, and if Nature is God's surrogate there is nonetheless no visible mandate from God.

Avoiding the issue of the succession of another which might emerge at this point, and therefore simply ignoring the question of how hereditary right becomes a normal model, Pope redirects attention upwards; the 'sons' now require a better explanation for power than the godlike nature of their own father, soon locating it in 'One Great, First Father', or God, who thus appears to be deduced rather than self-evidently present or revealed. Alternatively, in an equally unhistoricized invention, a 'plain Tradition' of God's work perhaps 'Convey'd unbroken Faith from Sire to Son'. Again Pope aligns two complementary possibilities, the authority of a quasi-scriptural tradition and the light of reason deducing an uber-patriarch on the basis of the local father-son model. Most shades of contemporary opinion, from the deistical proponents of 'natural religion', to Catholic followers of orthodox church doctrine, could probably find something to agree with (and to dissent from) here. Pope does however make one point clear: in this still Edenic state of Nature, 'LOVE all the *Faith*, and all th' *Allegiance* then; | For Nature knew no *Right Divine* in *Men*'. The historical existence of patriarchs is the natural thing, even the best thing, but it does *not* entail a divine grant of power which can be cited in favour of divine right theory. (Nor, however, did anyone require any state oaths of 'Allegiance', so troublesome to Catholics like Pope, in this golden age of patriarchy.)

The point at which having a '*Sovereign Being*' might be other than a '*Sovereign Good*' is also not specified, as Pope goes on to obfuscate that shift as well. He asks 'Who first taught Souls enslav'd, and Realms undone | Th' enormous Faith of *Many made for one*' (242–3), much as Milton asks, rhetorically, who caused the Fall in the early lines of *Paradise Lost*; but whereas Milton has an identifiable narrative villain in Satan, Pope's answer for the development of tyranny out of his ideal patriarchal community is merely this: 'Force first made *Conquest*, and that Conquest *Law*' (246). The subsequent emergence of 'Superstition' and 'Fear' wraps 'Tyranny' in some effective ideological mysticism, but, as narrative, it conspicuously avoids causation. While the obvious historical tyrannies of the world are characterized as malign parody of a beneficent patriarchalism, the only way Pope finds to link the two is through an abstract and unexplained 'Force'. Milton and other republican Whigs often identified the biblical hunter Nimrod as the first patriarchal ruler by conquest (or usurpation). Pope had indeed cited Nimrod as a vicious tyrant in his own early tribute to Stuart paradise, *Windsor-Forest*, finding Nimrod's methods replicated in the Norman Conqueror (and by implication in the methods of William III, the military prince who had displaced James II); but here he eschews the opportunity to give his 'Force' any quasi-historical identity. It is a sort of Fall, with no apparent cause, though with grim results (242–69).

Redemption from the tyrannical perversion of patriarchalist rule takes the form not of some Christic sacrifice (the prophetic Christian story of Milton's *Paradise Regained* is also completely absent) but of some conveniently emerging 'Friend of Humankind', whether 'Poet or Patriot', to 'restore' the 'ancient Light' of nature by teaching 'Pow'rs due Use to *People* and to *Kings*' (290). This is a political lesson the poem itself seeks to embody, just as its addressee, Bolingbroke, would contrastingly develop the ideal of a 'Patriot King' of disinterested civic virtue, through the 1730s and 1740s. All of which brings us optimistically to 'Th' according Musick of a *well-mix'd State*', the 'WORLD's *great Harmony*': a mixed constitution of checks and balances which was supposedly the guarantee of British 'liberty'. Beyond that, non-partisan Pope declares:

For *Forms* of *Government* let Fools contest;
Whate'ere is best administer'd, is best. (304–5)

After all narrative exploration, Pope appears not to want to foreground any particular identifiable system, patriarchal or otherwise. Epistle IV, on happiness, sounds in summary like a set of instructions for conformity to a general system of order Pope feels he has proved to be valid, immutable and nurturing, never mind particular local variants.

Pope's poem is sometimes referred to as a theodicy, a form of argument which, being a defence of God's authority, might seem patriarchal by definition, though it is important to remember that the poetic model of theodicy towards which Pope's poem nods, in seeking to 'vindicate the ways of God to Man' (I. 16), is *Paradise Lost*, written by the most outspoken regicide of them all. But in place of Milton's apocalyptic mode, centred vividly on the fatal failings of Eve and Adam in relation to the authority of God, Pope presents the universe as a providential mechanism which reconciles all seemingly contrary dynamics – individual, internal and political. It is a compromise model, drawing on elements of both Filmer and Locke; but while in one sense Pope sees the appetite for social organization as prior to monarchy, his narrative also presents patriarchal government as a 'natural' and in principle right and fundamental human development. As Howard Erskine-Hill summarizes the matter, Pope indeed has 'something for the contractualists, and something more for the patriarchalists'.[2]

Moreover, a poem calling itself *An Essay on Man* is likely to be masculine in focus, despite the assumed inclusiveness of the title term. It is easy to find an inherent gender imbalance underlying the term 'Man', skewing the poem towards patriarchal thinking: the patrilineal pronouns 'he' or 'his' dominate, and gendered nouns are typically androcentric, 'son' or 'father'. 'Nature' and other such abstractions (such as 'Superstition') are feminine, in a grammatically traditional way which grants a quasi-female figure a 'power' so diffuse as to be ineffable, and wholly fictional. Human female presence is largely confined to roles as nurses, wives, mothers and mistresses, with the occasional errant queen. That Pope as an eighteenth-century male Catholic should tend to privilege a patriarchalist view of the operations of power, and of language, is not very surprising. However, Pope's particular situation is interesting. As Catholicism was effectively proscribed in Britain he was able to use it as a label of alienation without actually having to submit to much by way of religious authority. He could not really practise Catholicism, and sometimes went out of his way to criticize the power of his Church, loyal as he was to English Catholics as an oppressed social group. He is happy here to take a swipe at '*Pope* or *Council*' as irrelevant sources of authority when compared to natural instinct (III. 88). His religious identity prevented him from assuming official kinds of authority; it gave a paradoxical freedom to exercise other kinds of power.

The final Epistle is one of interesting cracks, in that Pope's normal voice as satiric censor is easier to find here, and among his targets are the *actual* monarchs of his world. After the death in 1714 of Queen Anne, last of the Stuarts and the only sovereign for whom he was prepared to express much warmth, Pope had been routinely disrespectful towards kings and queens. Granted, the reigning British examples were the despised Hanoverians, but there is much anecdotal evidence to suggest that Pope had little time even for earlier Stuarts like Charles II, the all-too-potent parent-king of Dryden's poetry. The opening of the poem called the addressee away from the 'low Ambition, and the Pride of Kings' (I. 2), and in revised versions Pope targeted several aggressive male leaders; Julius Caesar and Alexander the Great are not among the heroes of the finished poem. The final Epistle repeatedly expresses contempt (and little else) for monarchs as a class. While he was from a legal point of view a 'quiet' subject, Pope was no more able than Milton to align his work with the authority of a court in the way his model Dryden could: however natural patriarchal monarchy might once have been, implicitly as the poem draws to a close there is a shift in authority towards the independent power of the pen. That this has a patriarchal aspect of its own is another story.

Rousseau's *Emile* (1762): The Patriarchal Family and the Education of the Republican Citizen

Sandrine Parageau

It also makes a great difference for the good order of the marriage whether the man makes an alliance above or below himself. The former case is entirely contrary to reason; the latter is more conformable to it. Since the family is connected with society only by its head, the position of the head determines that of the entire family. When he makes an alliance in a lower rank, he does not descend, he raises up his wife. On the other hand, by taking a woman above him, he lowers her without raising himself. Thus, in the first case there is good without bad, and in the second bad without good. Moreover, it is part of the order of nature that the woman obey the man. Therefore, when he takes her from a lower rank, the natural and the civil order agree, and everything goes well. The contrary is the case when the man allies himself with a woman above him and thereby faces the alternative of curbing either his rights or his gratitude and of being either ungrateful or despised. Then, the woman, pretending to authority, acts as a tyrant toward the head of the house, and the master becomes a slave and finds himself the most ridiculous and most miserable of creatures. Such are those unfortunate favorites whom the Asian kings honor and torment by marrying them to their daughters, and who are said to dare to approach only from the foot of the bed in order to sleep with their wives. I expect many readers, remembering that I ascribe to woman a natural talent for governing man, will accuse me of a contradiction here. They will, however, be mistaken. There is quite a difference between arrogating to oneself the right to command and governing him who commands.[1]

In book V of *Emile or On Education*, the eighteenth-century French *philosophe* Jean-Jacques Rousseau (1712–78) presents his patriarchal conception of the family. While the first four books focus on the early years of Emile and his progressive transformation into a man under the guidance of his governor, the last book of Rousseau's treatise on education introduces a new character, Sophie, 'or the Woman', who is destined to be Emile's wife. The book narrates how they meet, fall in love and are then separated, while Emile, following his governor's advice, travels around the world to get better knowledge of foreign political cultures, before they are eventually reunited and married. The final book of *Emile* appears therefore both as a romantic novel, in which the progression of Emile and Sophie's love story is described with much detail, *and* a political treatise. Indeed, Emile is now ready to enter society and become a citizen. The issue of the best political system is also at stake in this book, which includes a summary of the *Social Contract* (published the same year as *Emile*, in 1762), a treatise conceived as an 'appendix' to *Emile*, according to Rousseau himself. Finally, book V should be read as a political treatise because Rousseau uses the relationship between Emile and Sophie to illustrate his conception of the family.

The extract above reveals two important aspects regarding Rousseau's patriarchalism. First, it explicitly states that the man is the sole head of the family, and that, therefore, a woman ought to obey her husband; the man is presented as the master, the one who commands. The social inferiority of the woman to her husband agrees with her natural submission. Secondly, in the extract, Rousseau mentions the link between family and society, or the role of men in the civil and the natural orders: as citizens and fathers, they are the connection between the state and the family, women being submitted to them in the natural order and merely absent from the civil order. The subordination of women is presented in book V of *Emile* as a natural principle: it is 'part of the order of nature', or, as the governor tells Sophie: 'It is for you to obey, just as nature wanted it' (478). The patriarchal dimension of family life is also praised by the governor, who advises Emile, on their coming back from their travels throughout Europe, to adopt 'the patriarchal and rustic life, man's first life' because it is the most natural 'and the sweetest life for anyone who does not have a corrupt heart' (474). In his *Discourse on Political Economy*, which was first published as an article on '(Moral and political) Economy' in the *Encyclopedia* (volume V, 1755), Rousseau explains why a woman should obey her husband: first, he says that there must be only one final authority in the family so that decisions can be made when opinions are divided, and, given that women are sometimes incapacitated by their reproductive functions, this authority must be given to the man; secondly, Rousseau repeatedly emphasizes the necessity for a man to know for sure that the children are his own, and, for paternity to be ascertained, absolute control of the husband over his wife is required.[2]

Book V of *Emile* opens with an anthropology of the sexes and a description of Sophie's education, which serve as a basis and justification for the establishment of patriarchal principles in the family. Rousseau first insists on the similarities between the sexes: 'In everything not connected with sex, woman is man. She has the same organs, the same needs, the same faculties. The machine is constructed in the same way; its parts are the same' (357). One would therefore expect Sophie's education to be the same as Emile's, but, on the contrary, education is strongly 'gendered' in Rousseau's treatise, as it reflects men's and women's distinct roles in family and society. Man and woman are identical in so far as they belong to the same species, but '[i]n everything connected with sex, woman and man are in every respect related and in every respect different' (357). Rousseau brushes aside all discourses on the superiority of one sex over the other because, he says, '[i]n what [man and woman] have in common, they are equal. Where they differ, they are not comparable' (358). Therefore, both sexes contribute to the same aim, but in different ways. On this assertion is premised the first and main difference between man and woman: the latter is 'passive and weak', while the former is 'active and strong'. This is the law of nature, which entails two very different educations for boys and girls. Contrary to Emile, an isolated child whose only parent and social contact is his governor, Sophie grows up in a family, she is taught to get used to authority, she must pay attention to the opinion of others and she is encouraged to care about appearances: 'in her conduct woman is enslaved by public opinion, in her belief she is enslaved by authority' (377). It seems that Rousseau first assumes what women's role should be in society, from which he deduces the capacities that are required from them to fit their proper function.[3] The education they are given is therefore based on what is expected from them. In other words, woman's natural weakness is not the cause of her subordination to the man in the family, but rather the consequence of it. The education of girls that Rousseau advocated was in keeping with the general, traditional conception of the time; as such, it was a step backward from more progressive conceptions, such as Fénelon's in *De l'éducation des filles* (1687).

Many feminist critics have denounced Rousseau's definition of woman's place in the family and his arguments in favour of a sex-roled society. Soon after the publication of *Emile*, at the end of the eighteenth century, Mary Wollstonecraft expressed her strong disagreement with the philosopher's patriarchal principles and insisted on the necessity of giving the same education to boys and girls: 'women, considered not only as moral but rational creatures, ought to endeavour to acquire human virtues (or perfections) by the *same* means as men, instead of being educated like a fanciful kind of *half* being – one of Rousseau's wild chimeras'[4] More recently, feminist critics have underlined the surprising contradiction between Rousseau's emphasis on equality and freedom on the one hand, and his defence of the subordination of women on the other; indeed, his patriarchal principles – and the submission of women they entail – seem to contradict his egalitarian political theory, as it is presented in the *Social Contract* and the *Second Discourse* (*Discourse on the Origin of Inequality*, 1755) in particular. Moreover, no satisfactory explanation for the emergence of the patriarchal family can be found in Rousseau's theory of the state of nature. Indeed, in the 'original state of nature', all individuals are free and equal; women are perfectly capable of rearing their children on their own, which is necessary anyway since sexual relations are random and therefore the identity of the father of a child is usually unknown. However, with the division of labour and the emergence of private property, universal equality is suddenly – and without justification – replaced with 'the golden age' of the patriarchal family and the subordination of women. When it comes to the roles of the sexes and the relations of man and woman, it seems that Rousseau makes inconsistent use of the concept of nature: whereas the 'natural man' is man in the original state of nature, the 'natural' woman is defined in reference to the age of patriarchal families.

Other interpreters have endeavoured to reconcile the family and the state in Rousseau's political theory, either by arguing that the family should be seen as a retreat from corrupted modern governments, or by insisting on the pivotal role that the family plays in the formation of good citizens, showing the link between pedagogical and political ideas in Rousseau's thought.[5] Moreover, in an attempt to play down the impact of Rousseau's patriarchal principles, it has often been argued that the power of the husband over his wife and that of the father over his children are far from absolute in Rousseau's conception of the family. There are actually two limits to the power of the father: first, a man should not use tyrannical force against his wife and children, and secondly, the power of the father over his children is limited in time – once they become independent adults, children are no longer expected to obey their fathers, but only to respect them and be grateful to them. In book V of *Emile*, Rousseau suggests that there might be another limit to the power of the husband in the patriarchal family: if women are cunning enough, a balance of power might be established between husband and wife because 'woman [has] a natural talent for governing man', as the extract above states. Indeed, even though the man is the one who commands, the woman, as 'the arbiter of his pleasures' (478), might eventually govern him if she learns how to manipulate his sexual needs. In book V, the governor says that the woman should learn how to use 'the modesty and the shame with which nature armed the weak in order to enslave the strong' (358). However, Rousseau fears that the woman might become a 'tyrant' and turn the master into a slave (see extract above), which is probably one of the reasons why he insists so much on the importance of patriarchal principles in *Emile*.

If the French *philosophe* adopts a patriarchal conception of the family, which is clearly expressed in *Emile*, he strongly and explicitly refutes 'the odious system which Sir Filmer tried to establish in a work entitled *Patriarcha*', adding that John Locke and Algernon Sidney should not have dignified Robert Filmer with a response.[6] Yet Rousseau's own refutation of Filmer's doctrine is even more radical than that of the English philosophers as he refuses to make any concessions to political patriarchalism. In his *Discourse on Political Economy*, Rousseau states that the power of the father over his family is in no way identical with that of the magistrate over his subjects, contrary to Filmer's contention in *Patriarcha* (published in 1680). Emphasizing the distinction between political and domestic economy,[7] Rousseau shows that the state and the family cannot be administered in the same way, the main reason being that the state is much larger than a family – Rousseau explains that the father can watch all that happens at home but the magistrate will only ever see part of what happens in the state. Rousseau adds another fundamental distinction, which he borrows from Locke: the power of the father in the family is natural, whereas political authority is based on conventions, which is why the father will act according to his heart, while the magistrate should have no rule but the law. Moreover, in the family, the children do not own anything but what they eventually inherit from their fathers; conversely, the general administration of the state is established to protect private property, which precedes it. In a further attempt to refute Filmer's doctrine of Adamic patriarchy, Rousseau states in the *Social Contract* that Adam governed the world merely because he was the first and sole inhabitant of the earth, like Robinson Crusoe on his island, not because he had been given divine power, as Filmer had argued. Rousseau adds with much irony:

> I have said nothing about King Adam, or about emperor Noah, father of three great monarchs who among themselves divided the universe, as did the children of Saturn, whom some believed they recognized in them ... since I am a direct

descendant from one of these Princes, and perhaps from the elder branch, for all I know, I might, upon verification of titles, find I am the legitimate King of humankind.[8]

The only similarity between state and family, according to Rousseau, is that they should both aim at happiness.

In mid-eighteenth-century France, when Rousseau was writing *Emile*, patriarchalism was being questioned, and the consensus on the legitimacy of the paternal image of monarchy was challenged.[9] The reflection on the role and power of the father and on the reform of education was fuelled by ideas inherited from seventeenth-century English authors, whose works were translated into French, commented upon and published in the first half of the eighteenth century. Rousseau was strongly influenced by Locke's ideas on education as they are presented in his treatise entitled *Some Thoughts concerning Education* (translated into French by Coste in 1695, only two years after its publication in England) and he had read the summary of Locke's *First Treatise of Government* by Jean Le Clerc (1690). Rousseau had also read Algernon Sidney, whose *Discourses concerning Government* (1698) were translated into French in 1702. Although no translation of Filmer's *Patriarcha* was available in France before the twentieth century (and Rousseau could not read English), the author of *Emile* could have knowledge of Filmerian patriarchalism thanks to its detractors, such as Jean Barbeyrac in his translation of Pufendorf's *Droit de la nature et des gens* (1706). It appears that Rousseau had second-hand knowledge of Filmer's doctrine. The refutation of Filmerian patriarchalism by English authors was appropriated and developed by French philosophers of the mid-eighteenth century, before being widely spread in the pre-revolutionary context. In the years before 1789, it was fairly common for political thinkers to insist on the absurdity of 'a father who has twenty million children'.[10]

The influence of Rousseau's ideas on the actors of the Revolution cannot be doubted. *Emile* was regularly reprinted in the second half of the century, and it was mentioned in political and pedagogical debates in the context of the Revolution. The relevance of *Emile* to the revolutionaries could also be found in the prospective dimension of Rousseau's treatise on education as it explicitly heralded the end of monarchy in Europe. Indeed, in a note to book III, Rousseau writes: 'I hold it to be impossible that the great monarchies of Europe still have long to last' (194). Moreover, the definition of the good father, the good husband and the good citizen was a major focus of political thinkers in pre-revolutionary France, underlining the relation between political ideas and pedagogical principles, between the state and the family. Rousseau explains in the *Discourse on Political Economy* and in the 'Considerations on the Government of Poland' (1772) that public education should be preferred to private education because education first aims at making citizens. Yet, Emile is educated at home by a governor – the reason for the choice of private education in this case is that the state in mid-eighteenth-century France had become too large, according to Rousseau, and therefore no effective system of public education could be implemented in this context. Rousseau's idea that love of the family is what brings love of the state was also of interest to the actors of the Revolution; in particular, a passage from *Emile* may have inspired the authors of Article 4 of the Declaration of Rights and Duties of Man and Citizen, Constitution of the Year III (1795): 'as though it were not by means of the small fatherland which is the family that the heart attaches itself to the large one; as though it were not the good son, the good husband, and the good father who make the good citizen!' (363). In other words, the family is the place where public virtues are learnt: if mothers do nurse their children, a reformed public and private morality can be expected, maternal love being the first step towards patriotic citizenship. This passage also shows that, despite the criticism of patriarchalism, the family remained a model for political authority, or rather it was the place from which a new public and private order could emerge, with members loving one another as 'brothers'. Indeed, the paternal image of the king was progressively replaced with ideas of 'fraternity' (which triumphed in the Revolution) and representations of the republic as a mother figure.

To conclude, the publication and reception of Rousseau's *Emile* in pre-revolutionary France can be seen as a 'patriarchal moment' for two apparently contradictory reasons: first, *Emile* strongly reaffirmed traditional conceptions of the subordination of women in the family, but secondly, by giving women an essential role in the formation of citizens and by contesting political patriarchalism, it contributed to the transformation of the paternal representation of political power and the emergence of the image of the nation as a mother.

Patriarchy and Enlightenment in Immanuel Kant (1784)

Jordan Pascoe

Enlightenment is the human being's emancipation from its self-incurred immaturity. Immaturity is the inability to make use of one's intellect without the direction of another. This immaturity is self-incurred when its cause does not lie in a lack of intellect, but rather in a lack of resolve and courage to make use of one's intellect without the direction of another. 'Sapere aude! Have the courage to make use of your own intellect!' is hence the motto of enlightenment.

Idleness and cowardice are reasons why such a large segment of humankind, even after nature has long since set it free from foreign direction (naturaliter maiorennes)*, is nonetheless content to remain immature for life; and these are also the reasons why it is so easy for others to set themselves up as their guardians. It is so comfortable to be immature. If I have a book that reasons for me, a pastor who acts as my conscience, a physician who determines my diet for me, etc., then I need not make any effort myself. It is not necessary that I think if I can just pay; others will take such irksome business upon themselves for me. The guardians who have kindly assumed supervisory responsibility have ensured that the largest part of humanity (including the entirety of the fairer sex) understands progress toward maturity to be not only arduous, but also dangerous…. It is thus difficult for any individual to work himself out of the immaturity that has become almost second nature to him. He has even become fond of it, and is, for the time being, truly unable to make use of his own reason, because he has never been allowed to try it.*[1]

In this passage from the beginning of *What is Enlightenment?* Kant defines 'enlightenment' as the courage and capacity to think for oneself. For Kant, the central question is: why do we hold ourselves back from enlightenment?

In Kant's nod to the 'the entirety of the fairer sex', the only direct reference to women that Kant makes in this essay, he intimates that women, in particular, see enlightenment as both dangerous and difficult. Women are not alone in this: Kant critiques many men, too, for failing to claim their intellectual maturity. Nevertheless, the reference is striking: *all* women find themselves in a condition of intellectual immaturity, dependent upon others for guidance and uniformly failing to undertake the arduous task of working towards enlightenment.

There are two ways we might read this claim. Either Kant is making a rather insulting assumption that all women are by nature immature, or he is issuing a call to arms: a call for women to overthrow the guardians and institutions holding them back, and to develop their capacities for independent thought and autonomous action. My question is whether this latter reading squares with Kant's patriarchalist tendencies elsewhere in his moral and political philosophy. Kant's call for women to seek liberation rests on the premise that women are holding *themselves* back from enlightenment, and that they have the power to overthrow the 'guardians' that stand in their way.

Who are these 'guardians'? Kant seems to be using this term in two ways: on the one hand, there are persons (like the pastor and the physician) who perform this role, and on the other, there are institutions and statutes that do this work. For women, these 'guardians' are specific and unmistakable: they are husbands, of course, as well as the institution of marriage itself, which positions women as wives, and therefore as legal minors under the protection of their husbands. Kant is quite specific about the nature of this dependency: in the *Anthropology* he argues, 'woman regardless of age is declared to be immature in civil matters; her husband is her natural curator.'[2] If she has no husband and owns her own property, he goes on to say, 'then another person is the curator'.

This assumption about women's immaturity is borne out in the *Doctrine of Right*, where Kant argues that men ought to have dominance over their wives, based on the 'natural superiority of the husband to the wife in his capacity to promote the common interest of the household'.[3] In these passages, husbands are explicitly the guardians of wives, and their right to guardianship seems to be grounded in an assumption of the 'natural inferiority' of women to their husbands.

Kant is famous for making these sorts of disparaging remarks about women, particularly in his anthropological works and popular essays. Many scholars argue that these comments should be taken with a grain of salt, and distinguished from Kant's more rigorous philosophical claims that all persons are ends in themselves, with an innate right to freedom and equality. Of course, Kant is also guilty of defending and justifying women's legal inequality in his political philosophy. This poses a bit of a chicken-and-egg problem for Kant scholars, since it is not always clear whether Kant thinks that the legal inequality of women is justified because of the natural inferiority of women, or whether the inferiority of women is simply a reflection of their limited legal rights and opportunities. So, to understand the passage above, we need to ask: are women *naturally* inclined to be immature and unenlightened, or does their lack of legal rights force them into a life of immaturity?

In order to answer this question, I want to connect Kant's fuzzier claims about enlightenment and intellectual maturity in *What is Enlightenment?* to the more concrete political arguments he makes about independence, since both are concerned with the ability to think and act for oneself. In both *Theory and Practice* and the *Doctrine of Right*, Kant ties this idea of independence to a distinction between *active* and *passive* citizens. Active citizens, he argues, are those who have achieved political independence, and thus find themselves in a position where they can think for themselves (1996: 314). This qualifies them, he argues, to vote. Passive citizens, on the other hand, are those who find themselves dependent on others for their existence, and who therefore cannot be relied upon to think independently.

As in *What is Enlightenment?* the emphasis is on the capacity to think for oneself, although in the citizenship arguments, Kant seems concerned not only with intellectual maturity, but also with the material conditions that make independence possible. Kant claims that the central requirement for active citizenship is to 'be his own master', and argues that those who support themselves with 'any skill, trade, fine art, or science' qualify, whereas those who can earn a living only by 'allowing others to make use of him' would not (2006A: 295). On these grounds, Kant argues in the *Doctrine of Right* that passive citizens include 'an apprentice in the service of a merchant or artisan; a domestic servant (as distinguished from a civil servant); a minor (*naturaliter vel civiliter*); all women and, in general, anyone whose preservation in existence (his being fed and protected) depends not on his management of his own business but on arrangements made by another (except the state)' (1996: 314). Once again, we find Kant making the sweeping assumption that *all* women find themselves in a condition of dependency, although the reasons for this are not entirely clear. And so we must return to the question posed above: do women find themselves in positions of dependency by nature, or by law?

First, let's explore the evidence that Kant thought women were simply *naturally* inferior, particularly when it came to intellectual capacities. In an early text, the 1764 *Observations on the Beautiful and Sublime*, he argues that 'laborious learning or painful grubbing, even if a woman could get very far with them, destroy the merits that are proper to her sex, and on account of their rarity may well make her into an object of cold admiration, but at the same time they will weaken the charms by means of which she exercises her great power over the opposite sex'.[4] In one of his latest published texts, the 1798 *Anthropology from a Practical Point of View* he adds, 'as concerns scholarly women: they use their *books* somewhat like their *watch*, that is, they carry one so that it will be seen that they have one; though it is usually not running or not set by the sun' (2006b: 307). These comments suggest that, whatever Kant hints at in *What is Enlightenment?* intellectual maturity is not a natural state for women, and those women who strive for intellectual independence deserve only mockery for their efforts.

But it need not follow from this that Kant thought women were naturally submissive and dependent. In his anthropological texts, Kant maps a story of gender relations in which each sex dominates the other in different domains. He argues that, because 'nature entrusted to woman's womb its dearest pledge', women tend to experience fear and timidity in their desire to provide safety and stability for their young, an urge that pushes them to seek male protection, to entreat men to behave 'sociably and with propriety' and to establish marriage and the household, those two key civilizing features of social life. Women are not *naturally* inferior to men, but a civilized condition and, as we will see, a *rightful* condition, will mean that women will find themselves in conditions of dependency, confined to a life within the household, where 'woman should dominate and the man should govern'.[5] The domestic sphere is her domain, as the public sphere is his (2006b: 309).

In the anthropological texts, then, Kant does seem to be making essentialist claims about gender difference and women's nature. Kant's story is not one of simply domination and submission, however, but something akin to Rousseau's ideal of separate spheres. Nonetheless, a pattern emerges in these arguments that will echo in Kant's political arguments: men's and women's natures require the existence of institutionally produced separate spheres organized so that men may indeed become women's legal guardians. These separate spheres may complement and balance one another, but they do not grant equal access to the conditions of enlightenment.

Before we attribute a simplistic patriarchalism to Kant, let us explore one more passage that seems to support the progressive imperative from *What is Enlightenment?* – namely, that women ought to throw off their tutelage and seek maturity and independence. In the *Doctrine of Right*, he argues that all passive citizens (a category that includes women) ought to have the right to 'work their way up' towards active citizenship (1996: 315). A state is just, he says, only if every subject of that state could potentially work towards full political independence. And this suggests to many contemporary Kantians that Kant was far more progressive than we give him credit for, and that he envisioned a future in which men and women had full and equal political rights – and thus, an equal shot at achieving enlightenment.

Of course, in the same text in which Kant opens the door to women's political equality, he also defends women's inequality in marriage, pointing to the natural superiority of the husband. This does not conflict with the 'natural equality of the partners', he says, but it is necessary because of the duty of unity that marriage requires (1996: 279). This suggests that the problem is not that *women* are necessarily unequal to men, but that *wives* are necessarily unequal to their husbands – and this inequality is a necessary feature of the rightful state. Wives, after all, have the domestic sphere as their domain, while husbands participate in politics and public discourse.

If this is so, then we might argue that Kant's account of gender inequality is merely an institutional inequality, created and maintained by law, such that wives are placed under the guardianship of their husbands, the better to 'rule' in the domestic sphere. And if this is so, then we can imagine that if a woman were to find herself in a position of independence – as a wealthy widow, perhaps, who owned her own property – then nothing would hold her back from working her way up to full citizenship, overthrowing her dependency and attaining full maturity. Thus, *wives* are barred from political equality for Kant, but *women* are indeed free to 'work their way up' to full participation in the public realm.

There is a catch, of course: Kant repeatedly assumes that all women have the political status of wives. He refers to 'women' and 'wives' more or less interchangeably in his political works, and assumes that even unmarried women find themselves under the guardianship of a man. In the *Anthropology*, recall, he argued that 'woman regardless of age is declared to be immature in civil matters; her husband is her natural curator' (2006b: 209).[6] Women need not be naturally unequal: in a rightful political condition, women will be 'declared to be' legally unequal to men, placed in positions of dependency and tutelage by the normative requirements of law. And this is perhaps because, as Kant himself admits, his observations about women's nature are necessarily shaped by the conditions in which he finds them – which, in late eighteenth-century Konigsberg, were generally conditions of dependency.[7] So, if Kant found women to be more emotional and less rational than men, or preoccupied with silly, domestic problems and thus unfit for public discourse,[8] this may indeed be the result of women's status as legal dependents. Women's dependency has 'become second nature' to her; her legal status has shaped her identity and sense of self. And if this is the case, then women, indeed, might be called to overthrow their guardians and fight for independence, equality and enlightenment, since it is the system of guardianship, rather than her own nature, that holds her back.

Kant's references to women in *What is Enlightenment?* suggest that whatever his anthropological views about women's nature, he leaves open the possibility that women, too, must achieve enlightenment, working their way out of dependence and immaturity. However, Kant's own account of the rightful civil condition poses significant challenges to this imperative. First, he explicitly argues that women ought to be *declared* legal minors as wives, and sets up significant obstacles to women gaining the status of active citizenship and the intellectual maturity it implies.

Second, he systematically constructs a social and legal structure in which it would be nearly impossible for *all* women – or even most women – to gain legal independence and equality. And this means that even if we can take Kant at his word that 'anyone' – including women – 'ought to be able to work their way up' (1996: 315) and envision cases in which individual women (like the wealthy widow) might achieve this status, it is virtually impossible that women *as a class* could obtain political and legal equality with men. This is so because of the structure of marriage and the family, the distribution of labour and its role in determining active citizenship, and Kant's own insistence that women's roles as mothers and breeders make them better suited to dominate the domestic realm than to participate in public discourse. Whatever his claims about the capacities of women to 'work their way up', Kant actively defends a patriarchal model of the state and consistently justifies the legal immaturity and political exclusion of women, and thus presents significant barriers to the fairer sex's access to enlightenment.

Of course, Kant was writing in the late eighteenth century, and so we might ask to what degree we can hold him responsible for this patriarchalism, and to what degree he is simply reflecting the norms and values of his time. We might also argue that we should take into account his more progressive moments – as in *What is Enlightenment?* – when he resists his own tendency towards patriarchalism.

I think we might have reason to excuse Kant's sexist remarks in his anthropological writings, where he is explicitly reflecting the state of gender relations as he saw them. But we will have a much harder time excusing the arguments in his philosophical texts, where he is making normative claims about what a rightful world ought to look like. When Kant penned his most extended account of marriage in the *Doctrine of Right*, he was responding in part to a broad social debate about the nature and purpose of marriage, and about the place of women in society. His friend and frequent dinner companion Theodor von Hippel had anonymously written books arguing for the moral and legal emancipation of women, and a radical restructuring of marriage to make this emancipation possible.[9] By comparison, Kant's arguments about women and marriage are quite reactionary, and suggest that he thought there was normative value in upholding patriarchal marriage and the legal minority of women.

Thus, despite Kant's promising 'feminist moments' including his suggestion in *What is Enlightenment?* that women have a duty to free themselves from their dependence and work their way towards enlightenment, he remains a staunch patriarchalist in both his anthropological works and in his more rigorous philosophical texts. This suggests a troubling answer to the question I originally posed. While there is evidence in the anthropological texts to suggest that Kant thought women's natures prevent them from achieving intellectual maturity, there is a more troubling sense in which Kant's own vision of the rightful political state is responsible for holding women back from enlightenment. Women find themselves in a condition of dependency not by choice, but because of the systemic and institutional order of the rightful Kantian state.

In 'Her Father's House'[1]: Women as Property in Wollstonecraft's *Mary* (1788)

Michelle Faubert

NEAR to her father's house was a range of mountains; ... [and] an old castle, a haunted one, as the story went; it was situated on the brow of one of the mountains, and commanded a view of the sea. This castle had been inhabited by some of her ancestors; and many tales had the old house-keeper told her of the worthies who had resided there.

When her mother frowned, and her friend looked cool, she would steal to this retirement, where human foot seldom trod – gaze on the sea, observe the grey clouds, or listen to the wind which struggled to free itself from the only thing that impeded its course. When more cheerful, she admired the various dispositions of light and shade, the beautiful tints the gleams of sunshine gave to the distant hills; then she rejoiced in existence, and darted into futurity.

One way home was through the cavity of a rock covered with a thin layer of earth, just sufficient to afford nourishment to a few stunted shrubs and wild plants, which grew on its sides, and nodded over the summit.... In this retreat she read Thomson's Seasons, Young's *Night-Thoughts, and* Paradise Lost.[2]

Mary, the autobiographical protagonist of Mary Wollstonecraft's first novella, *Mary, A Fiction* (1788), is homeless. Both Chapters III and IV begin with the almost identical phrase, 'Near ... her father's house' (86),[3] a somewhat awkward construction that reminds us that Mary does not live in her own house. Rather, she lives in 'her father's house'. This distinction, though minute, is far from nugatory; it represents the major source of Mary's grief and main driver of the novella's plot, as I will show. What might at first appear to be an editorial slip emphasizes a hitherto unrecognized theme of *Mary*: that of the relationship between women and the patriarchal laws and customs surrounding property and ownership in Romantic-era England.

Wollstonecraft's repeated phrase 'her father's house' draws attention to the fact that the autobiographical protagonist, Mary, does not own property – does not own *a* property, such as a house, and, in broader terms, she does not have *any property* of any kind, for whatever wealth exists for the taking in this patriarchal society is available only to men. The description of the 'castle [that] had been inhabited by some of her ancestors' raises the issues of inheritance and property, and reminds us that, in the Romantic period, the eldest sons inherited all of the family wealth under the laws of primogeniture. The patriarchal attitudes upon which such laws were based were also reflected in English custom, which dictated that upper-class women were not permitted to hold jobs in order to gain their own money and property. As a result of such misogynistic laws and customs, women were forced into what Wollstonecraft would label 'legal prostitution' in *A Vindication of the Rights of Woman* (1792), marriages based on economic concerns rather than love. Moreover, daughters were essentially owned by their fathers until they were 'given away', to use the still-common term, in marriage. The husbands would thereafter own this female chattel, a legal fact enshrined in the wife's adoption of her husband's surname. As historian Carol Blum argues in 'Of Women and the Land: Legitimizing Husbandry', the historical development of the term 'husbandry' demonstrates the links between the ownership of land and women. Blum notes that

> In the eighteenth century and up to our own time, defining property generates major questions ... : who could be a legitimate person, what justified ownership, and whether women were things, a form of property, or persons, proprietors in their own right? (161)

As an inmate in 'her father's house', Mary is no proprietor, but mere property – a 'thing to be possessed' – and would remain so to her husband through what Wollstonecraft terms her 'forced' marriage (95).

All of these issues regarding women and property plague the heroine of Wollstonecraft's novella and become the driving forces of the plot. Mary only becomes an 'heiress' when her older brother – to whom her mother had shown marked 'partiality' – dies suddenly, but Mary's new-found power lasts for only two sentences before her father decides to marry her off to settle a property dispute between the two families, since 'part of the estate she was to inherit had been litigated' (84, 92). Mary recognizes her identity as property to be traded: 'Her cheeks flushed with indignation, so strongly did she feel an emotion of contempt at having been thrown away – given in with an estate' (113). Mary considers such a marriage to be 'slave[ry]', for it positions her as the property of her husband (131). The remedy for slavery is freedom, including the liberty to find paid work, which Mary attempts to obtain. She boldly defies her interlocutors, who wonder 'how [she] will ... live' apart from her husband: 'I will work, she cried, do any thing rather than be a slave' by allowing her husband to support her (131). The notion of human beings as property was challenged in the period's abolition debates, to which John Locke's statements about human freedom from the late seventeenth century were essential. In *Two Treatises of Government* (1689), Locke writes, 'it is evident, that ... man ... [is] master of himself, and proprietor of his own person, and the actions or labour of it' (225). In this context, the patriarchal system that treats women as property and denies their ability to gain their own property through paid work casts them as slaves. As I will show, connected to the notion of women as property is that they are not independent persons in English law, nor are they subjects, philosophically speaking. The selected passage explores these implications of the patriarchal system through references to Mary's genius and (frustrated) desire to develop it through a Rousseauvian education.

This passage contains several elements that address how Jean-Jacques Rousseau's philosophy acts as both the inspiration and foil for Wollstonecraft's broad message in *Mary*. The period's debates about slavery and democracy responded to and helped to form the celebration of the autonomous individual that we recognize as part of the Romantic *zeitgeist*, and Rousseau was one of the most influential definers of these topics in the eighteenth century. His works on education emphasize fostering one's unique character, type of intelligence and inclinations – called 'genius' in the period – through education in nature and the development of sensibility. As I note in the Broadview edition of *Mary*, the novella's epigraph in French – from the Genevan philosophe's *Julie, ou, La Nouvelle Héloïse* (1761) – indicates Wollstonecraft's most obvious concerns in the novella: the development of female natural genius through education and the 'sublime virtue[]' that is true sensibility (73). Roughly translated as 'The exercise of the most sublime virtues raises and nourishes genius', the epigraph also prepares the reader to recognize the significance of several additional aspects of the selected passage. For example, Mary's genius is nourished through her solitary and self-guided education: 'she would steal to this retirement, where human foot seldom trod' to read poetry by James Thomson, Edward Young and John Milton – works that would refine her sensibility, build her sense of the sublime and confirm her quintessentially Romantic genius. As if these qualities were not enough to authenticate her genius in Rousseauvian terms, she learns from nature itself: she would 'gaze on the sea, observe the grey clouds, or listen to the wind'. Nature also develops Mary's aesthetic appreciation: 'she admired the various dispositions of light and shade, the beautiful tints the gleams of sunshine gave to the distant hills'. What solitary walker could do more? This passage suggests that Mary's highly individual genius is nourished through Rousseauvian principles of education – at least those he outlines for male education.

However, Rousseau's theory of *female* education fell far short of developing women's minds to the extent that he denied their very claim to being autonomous selves. Wollstonecraft was acutely aware of this failing. In *A Vindication of the Rights of Men* (1790), Wollstonecraft quotes Rousseau in a way that summarizes his patriarchal views on women succinctly: 'As they are not in a capacity to judge for themselves, they ought to abide by the decision of their fathers and husbands' (210). According to Rousseau, women's intelligence is essentially different from that of men – deficient to the degree that women must submit their opinions to those of their male family members. Rousseau's theory of male education is the pattern for the development of Romantic genius, and, significantly, he denies the possibility of *female* genius. Rousseau's directive that a female should acquiesce to the authority of her patriarchal masters expresses the English laws of coverture in the language of education, genius and Romantic individualism. As outlined in the eighteenth century by the great English legal commentator William Blackstone, the laws of coverture state, 'By marriage, the husband and wife are one person in law: that is, the very being or legal existence of the woman is suspended during the marriage, or at least is incorporated and consolidated into that of the husband'.[4] The laws of England confirmed that married women were not individual persons under English law, and Rousseau, the most influential educational philosopher in eighteenth-century Europe, agreed that women are devoid of the intellect needed to establish them as legal subjects – as anything but the property of men.

The selected passage describes Mary's innate attraction to self-education and, notably, to texts that promise to develop her intellect, sensibility and sense of the sublime. With respect to Rousseau's texts on education, then, she has everything she needs to be an ideal Romantic genius, except for a penis. Wollstonecraft foreshadows that Mary's innate genius will be stifled in the ensuing narrative by developing two natural metaphors in the selected passage. She describes the 'retreat' where Mary reads as containing a 'few stunted shrubs and wild plants' that are 'afford[ed] nourishment' 'just sufficient' to survive. Similarly, Mary has only enough support to begin to nurture her genius, and not nearly enough to thrive. She is also very like 'the wind which struggled to free itself from the only thing that impeded its course'; for this child of nature, misogynistic social rules 'impede' her 'course' of education and independence. The selected passage confirms that, when in nature, Mary 'rejoiced in existence, and darted into futurity'. Left to develop her innate abilities, this Romantic flower would bloom. However, her development is halted by the perverse laws and customs of her society that cast women as devoid of legal and philosophical subjecthood – as unthinking property to be traded among members of the patriarchy.

The vehicle of Wollstonecraft's natural metaphors draws attention to the *unnatural* character of patriarchal laws. Like those of slaves, women's natural rights as autonomous human beings are crushed by a legal system and the attendant customs and attitudes that deny basic human liberty. In a response to Edmund Burke's defence of the patriarchal system, *Reflections on the Revolution in France* (1790), Thomas Paine would call the period's inheritance laws, which favour the eldest son, a predatory and cannibalistic relationship 'against every law of nature', and he assures his reader that 'Nature herself calls for its destruction'.[5] Six years previous to Paine's publication, Wollstonecraft similarly represents the world ruled by such patriarchal laws as an unnatural, hostile environment that kills some creatures doomed to it.[6] The final sentences of *Mary* reveal that, fully cognizant of her role as patriarchal property, the protagonist no longer 'rejoice[s] ... in existence, and dart[s] ... into futurity', as she does in the selected passage. By the tale's end, she can only hope for death:

> Her delicate state of health did not promise long life. In moments of solitary sadness, a gleam of joy would dart across her mind – She thought she was hastening to that world where there is neither marrying, nor giving in marriage. (148)

Having been betrayed by this world, Mary dreams of an unnatural space, a genderless realm of spiritual being, where the body with which she was born will not identify her as property to be traded in marriage.

Indeed, given the focus on nature and naturalness in the period, perhaps just as significant as the phrase 'her father's house' in the selected passage is the great attention it devotes to nature. Notably, Wollstonecraft does not describe the physical appearance of Mary's 'father's house' at all; nor does she provide a glimpse of our heroine in it. Rather, she immediately moves to a meticulous delineation of the natural environment *around* the house: it is 'near' 'a range of mountains', 'cloud-capt' and with 'sides [featuring] ... little bubbling cascades', as well as 'straggling trees and bushes [through which] the wind whistled'. Nature is Mary's proper home, it seems, since she flees to this 'retreat' '[w]hen her mother frown[s]' – or, in short, when her family fails to provide the support she needs to thrive. By establishing Mary's link with nature in the selected passage from the novella's first pages, Wollstonecraft shields her heroine from the accusations of perversity that Mary's later refashioning of the patriarchal family structure may invite.

The novella's main theme of genius – that is, natural intelligence and innate ability – also helps to defend Mary against the charge of unnaturalness. Arguably, Mary's native intelligence necessitates that she rebel against the social conventions that identify her as the property of familial patriarchs. Given her innate genius, it follows that Mary should defend her independence by reforming the traditional family structure. Mary does not respect the males to whom she belongs; she does not recognize the authority of her father, whom she considers immoral (98), and her husband inspires no feelings but abhorrence in her: 'her marriage appeared a dreadful misfortune.... An extreme dislike took root in her mind; the sound of his name made her turn sick' (97). Precisely because of her genius, which is synonymous with her intelligence and independence, Mary comprehends well her humiliating situation as the property of such males. She, therefore, tries to change it by casting *herself* as a husband and property owner. When that plan fails, she chooses a new father/brother/husband – one who is devoid of patriarchal power.

Wollstonecraft's protagonist marries not to be united to Charles, her groom, but to be united to Ann, her best friend and true beloved. In a passage of free indirect discourse that is typical of *Mary* (although it is more often associated with Jane Austen's later works), the narrator informs the reader,

> She loved Ann better than any one in the world – to snatch her from the very jaws of destruction – she would have encountered a lion. To have this friend constantly with her ... would it not be superlative bliss? (95)

If her desire to save the proverbial 'damsel in distress' does not demonstrate clearly enough Mary's thirst for masculine power, then her wish to support Ann and have her 'constantly with her' confirms Mary's attempt to adopt the role of husband.[7] Mary's patriarchal desires are partially the result of her 'extreme horror at taking – at being forced to take, such a hasty step' as marrying to settle her father's litigation suit (95). To survive the 'horror' of patriarchy, Mary attempts to infiltrate it.

Unfortunately for Mary, her patriarchal reign does not last long. Fulfilling the duties of good husbandry, she takes her infirm charge to Lisbon in the hope that the warmer climate will heal Ann, but the latter dies, nevertheless. While Mary is there, however, she meets the gentle and infirm Henry and devises a novel plan for a reformed family relationship with him that, like her relationship with Ann, will position Mary as the one who is in control. Mary's initial attraction to Henry is bound up with the pleasure she takes in his fragility: 'Henry's illness was not alarming, it was rather pleasing, as it gave Mary an excuse to herself for shewing him how much she was interested about him' (113). Mary's love for Henry is intimately bound up with her perception of his weakness and, given her relative health and strength, her ability to care for him – a task usually reserved for the more powerful male, such as a husband, in a traditional romantic relationship.

The familial resonances of their relationship become even more bizarre as the novella continues. In several passages, Wollstonecraft presents Henry as the father-figure: he calls her his 'child' (121) and asks, 'If she would rely on him as if he was her father; and [says] that the tenderest father could not more anxiously interest himself in the fate of a darling child, than he did in her's' [sic] (117). Nor is Mary ignorant of the familial relationship his words signify. She thinks,

> My child! His child, what an association of ideas! If I had had a father, such a father! – She could not dwell on the thoughts, the wishes which obtruded themselves. Her mind was unhinged, and passion unperceived filled her whole soul. (117)

Mary is at once enchanted with the notion of Henry's fatherly relation to her and overwhelmed with 'passion' at the mere thought of it. Mary and Henry's amorous relationship is incestuous in another way, too: they are, Wollstonecraft suggests, like brother and sister. Thinking of Henry's impending death, his mother asks Mary to confirm her acceptance of this new familial structure, which has been suggested by Henry: 'If I am to lose the support of my age, and be again a widow – may I call her Child whom my Henry wishes me to adopt?' (144)[8] Wollstonecraft provides several instances of familial reimagining in this novella. In the context of the theme of Mary's patriarchal power-struggle, these apparently odd references to Mary as a husband/wife/sister/daughter to Henry accrue great significance. He is her dream-man: a husband/father/brother without power and without proprietary rights over her.

Initially, the selected passage from *Mary* may seem to be a relatively insignificant description of setting in a novella about education and female genius, as these main themes are identified in the Advertisement: Wollstonecraft claims *Mary* 'artless[ly]' displays 'the mind of a woman, who has thinking powers' (76). However, alerted to the patriarchal implications of the repeated phrase 'her father's house' in the first sentence of two consecutive chapters early in the novella, the reader becomes aware of a connected theme here: that of the relationship between women, property and patriarchy. In this light, the apparently haphazard plot of the novella appears, rather, to illustrate aptly the trials experienced by an intelligent, critical woman – a female genius – in the early Romantic era. The major points of the plot and both of her romantic relationships illustrate her role as the property of various patriarchal figures, her rebellious responses to this situation and her attempts to rewrite her identity through the invention of novel familial structures. Yet, all of Mary's attempts to assert her independence fail. The protagonist we find so full of promise in the selected passage hopes, by the end of the novel, only for escape – into her Divine father's house (136).

Father Enfantin, the Saint-Simonians and the 'Call to Woman' (1831)

Daniel Laqua

Woman is still enslaved; we need to liberate her. Before she passes to the state of equality with man, she needs to have her liberty. We must therefore realize, for the Saint-Simonian women, this state of liberty, by destroying the hierarchy that has hitherto existed for both them and for the men, and by making them [the Saint-Simonian women] return to the state of equality among themselves. THERE ARE NO MORE WOMEN IN THE DIFFERENT DEGREES OF THE HIERARCHY [OF OUR CHURCH]. Our apostolate, which is the call to woman, is an apostolate of men. Man can today be classified because he has had for a long time his complete liberty in relation to woman; but woman cannot be classified because she has not yet revealed herself.

Thus goes our new position with regard to women … This state of confused equality *will undoubtedly present some great inconveniences; but it will have an immense advantage over the* faulty hierarchy *that we have erected until now, because without woman having revealed herself as free, each classification of her was done by man's law and badly done.*

Women will no longer appear on the podium, at the sermon. Women will no longer … be part of the Saint-Simonian family; they will … be in the state of the call, like all women of the world around us. [Points at the empty armchair next to him.] *This is the symbol of the call …*

Woman lacks a doctrine, she has not revealed herself, she is still in the state of slavery, she will enter into the state of confused equality; *she needs to exit from it, we will wait for her, she needs to speak; she will speak, because she has been called upon.*[1]

By the late 1820s, Saint-Simonism had emerged as 'the most striking social movement of the day'.[2] The extract above is taken from the record of two Saint-Simonian meetings in November 1831, marking a crisis in which issues of sex, gender, morality and personality intersected. The statement's central premise certainly invites bafflement. The speaker advocates the liberation of women from the 'state of slavery' and yet announces their exclusion from his organization. The source of these paradoxical remarks was no peripheral figure: Prosper Enfantin (1796–1864) was worshipped as the 'Father' of a movement that cast itself both as a family and a church. Pamela Pilbeam has described him as a man full of 'magnetic, hypnotic charm and irrepressible confidence', with an appeal that derived from 'his intelligence, his seductively compelling personality and his handsome presence'.[3]

If Enfantin stood at the head of Saint-Simonism, his remarks demonstrate the place of women at the very heart of Saint-Simonian debates. In the above speech, Enfantin redefined Saint-Simonism as an all-male movement – 'an apostolate of man' – that was preoccupied with one central quest: to find the maternal figure who would heed 'the call'. Yet, even prior to this episode, Saint-Simonians had engaged with issues of gender as part of their commitment to social and moral change. It is therefore necessary to start by outlining the origins of Saint-Simonism and the role of women within the movement. This chapter subsequently summarizes the events of November 1831 and considers the aftermath of women's exclusion from the Saint-Simonian hierarchy. As the discussion will show, Saint-Simonism was both patriarchal and anti-patriarchal – and while this may sound contradictory, such contradictions were intrinsic to the movement itself.

The Saint-Simonians were named after Henri de Saint-Simon (1760–1825), a French aristocrat whom some praised as a genius and others dismissed as an eccentric. He was undoubtedly a prolific writer, drawing up plans on a variety of questions – from economic progress to the future peace of Europe. His ideas did not amount to a uniform system of thought: it was only after his death that his followers developed them into a doctrine, both through their editorial work and their practical efforts. In doing so, they not only created Saint-Simonism but also shaped the posthumous image of Saint-Simon himself. According to Christophe Prochasson, 'the Saint-Simonians did not altogether invent Saint-Simon, but they did much to make him exist'.[4]

Three overarching ideas connected the work of the Saint-Simonians to their late master. The first was his critique of those who lived idly off their landed property. Saint-Simon viewed *les oisifs* (the idlers) as obstacles to cooperation and industry, the forces to which he accorded prime importance. The Saint-Simonians sought to live by these principles, launching cooperative ventures and developing considerable business acumen. The second major aspect was Saint-Simon's belief in the rule of experts. He argued that the social machinery should be designed and administered by well-trained individuals. Such ideas appealed to his highly educated disciples: many of them had attended the *École Polytechnique*, the Parisian élite institution for aspiring engineers. The third strand was his call for a new religion that would cure the social and moral ills that Saint-Simon had diagnosed. He outlined the features of this religion in his last major work, *Le Nouveau Christianisme* (1825). This line of thought explains why the Saint-Simonians came to describe themselves as members of a 'church' – even if this step also had a practical advantage, as it circumvented restrictions on the formation of political associations. The Saint-Simonians strove to build on Saint-Simon's ideas, even when venturing far beyond them. Robert Carlisle has therefore criticized accounts that interpret the 'later developments of the doctrine as an Enfantinian revolution, a Saint-Simonian heresy', deeming such views 'simply astigmatic'.[5]

Olinde Rodrigues (1795–1851) embodied the personal connection between Saint-Simon and the Saint-Simonians. A gifted mathematician whose Jewish background had limited his academic career opportunities, he became the director of a mortgage bank, the *Caisse Hypothécaire*, in 1823.[6] In the final two years of Saint-Simon's life, Rodrigues was his closet associate and was even present at his master's deathbed. He was also responsible for bringing his former tutee Enfantin into the fold. From 1825, Rodrigues and Enfantin cooperated with like-minded individuals to preserve Saint-Simon's legacy. Saint-Amand Bazard (1791–1832) was a key figure in this undertaking. He represented the political wing of Saint-Simonism, having previously co-founded the *Charbonnerie*, a republican underground society. In December 1828, the development of Saint-Simonian doctrine culminated in its proclamation as a religion, initially led by the trinity of Enfantin, Bazard and Rodrigues.

The Saint-Simonians undertook extensive publishing activities, from print editions of their master's writings to the periodicals *Le Producteur* (1825–6) and *L'Organisateur* (1829–31). In 1830, *Le Globe* – a well-established liberal newspaper – converted to the Saint-Simonian cause. Shortly before this, the Saint-Simonians had moved into premises that hosted its editorial offices. Located near the Palais Royal, the building became a home for the family and served as a venue for ceremonies, assemblies and public events. Because of their efforts on behalf of workers and artisans, the Saint-Simonians usually feature in accounts

of early socialism. Although the Saint-Simonian family was numerically small –
a few hundred faithful in Paris – it reached out to wider segments of society. Its
Parisian district sections educated artisans, organized cooperative workshops,
dispensed charity and ran two hostels whose services extended to non-residents.
The Saint-Simonians also ventured beyond Paris, as exemplified by their active
section in Lyon and large audiences for public lectures in several cities.[7]

The Saint-Simonian concern for artisans and workers extended to working
women. Many of them were recipients of practical aid, yet some also joined
the family. Claire Moses has noted that around 110 women from working-
class backgrounds were registered as 'faithful', with a similar number of female
followers in Lyon.[8] As Naomi Anderson has argued, women's and workers' rights
were treated as interrelated issues during the 1830s, with constructions of the
social having 'a distinctly gendered connotation'.[9] Enfantin himself stressed the
need for the joint emancipation of women and workers (4–5). The focus on such
connections was not confined to the Saint-Simonians, as the writings of Charles
Fourier and Flora Tristan testify.

At a practical level, women made significant contributions to the family's
activities. Indeed, Enfantin's proclamation that there would be 'no more
women in the hierarchy' (55) implicitly acknowledges the role that they
had hitherto played. Female involvement covered a range of Saint-Simonian
efforts, from their workshops and hostels to their educational work. Each
of the twelve district sections in Paris was jointly headed by a 'father' and a
'mother', with Claire Bazard (1794–1883), wife of Saint-Amand, being tasked
with proselytizing among women. Another leading activist, Eugénie Niboyet
(1796–1883), made around fifty visits per week to dispense charity to families
in need.[10]

In one respect, the role of women within Saint-Simonism may seem
striking: Saint-Simon himself had barely mentioned them. Even *Le Nouveau
Christianisme*, his ambitious blueprint for a moral and spiritual reorganization
of society, did not address gender relations explicitly. This silence evidently
contrasted with Enfantin's 'call to woman'. How are we to make sense of this
development? A key element was the Saint-Simonians' belief that God was
androgynous – an idea that they embraced from 1828 onwards. Based on
this conviction, they championed the collaboration between man and woman.
This principle manifested itself in the Saint-Simonians' practical work, yet
it did not extend to the church hierarchy. Despite theoretically being open
to both sexes, no woman was appointed to a Saint-Simonian priesthood,
and women were mostly excluded from the elaboration of Saint-Simonian

doctrine. In claiming that woman had not yet 'revealed herself as free' (56), Enfantin suggested that no female Saint-Simonian had gained the level of understanding that he attributed to himself. This conclusion was a particular blow to Claire Bazard, who had been expected to take up a role as spiritual leader. In the autumn of 1831, she was pushed aside shortly before the two meetings from which the extract is taken.

The opening extract highlights the centrality of women for Saint-Simonian doctrine. Yet, it also relates to specific events, namely a major rift within the movement – far from the only one in its history, but certainly the most dramatic. In the Saint-Simonian assemblies of 19 and 21 November, Enfantin denounced the 'hostile passions' (3) of the absent Saint-Amand Bazard. In turn, he met with protests from followers of the man who had served as the church's Supreme Father alongside him. Both meetings featured long speeches by Enfantin as well as emotional, quasi-confessional statements by members of the Saint-Simonian family. Jeremy Jennings has claimed that 'it is hard not to conclude that many of the meetings held by the Saint-Simonians were characterized by collective hysteria'.[11] While the term 'hysteria' may not entirely capture the atmosphere of the November discussions, their highly personal tone revealed how far the private, religious and social worlds of the Saint-Simonians had merged into one another. As a result of their disagreements, Bazard's followers left the Saint-Simonian fold. Their departure contrasted with the stance of Rodrigues who had remained a key member despite his resignation as one of the Supreme Fathers nearly two years earlier. At the close of the meeting on 21 November, he lauded Enfantin as 'the most moral man of my time' (58).

The rupture was not simply due to a clash of personalities: it reflected wildly diverging views on morality. On 17 October 1831, Rodrigues had presented a 'note on marriage and divorce' that outlined Enfantin's new moral doctrine. The statement formed part of wider French debates about legalizing divorce, which had been prohibited in 1816. To Enfantin, divorce was not a political issue: it was one element in the recasting of gender relations. In a new society, man and woman would enter into 'successive unions' (12), with divorce allowing them to pass from one state to the next. To many people, such views smacked of sexual libertinism. They were also rejected by Bazard, who deemed them a distraction from Saint-Simonism's political and social objectives.

How did Enfantin come to adopt this controversial stance? Seen from one angle, the attack on conventional marriage built upon Saint-Simon's dislike of 'idlers' who lived off their inherited wealth. By challenging traditional family relations, the Saint-Simonians targeted the institution through which property was passed on. Yet, during the November meetings, Enfantin went further. He suggested that the new doctrine reflected an attempt to overcome fundamental binaries. On the one side, he claimed, stood the flesh, which, by itself, bore the threat of violence. On the other side was the spirit whose Christian manifestation had sought to control the flesh but gave rise to dishonesty. The law of love would help to overcome this dichotomy and result in the 'rehabilitation of the flesh' (7–9). Thus, marriage and divorce were part of a wider desire for harmony: the union between flesh and spirit, between woman and man, between father and mother.

As the extract indicates, Enfantin did not believe the time to be ripe for such unions: woman first needed to 'reveal herself as free' (56). Until woman had become truly liberated, any attempt to include men and women within the same organization would produce a 'faulty hierarchy' (55) in which man would remain dominant. The exclusion of women from the Saint-Simonian church exposed its underlying patriarchal features. At the same time, it inaugurated a peculiar form of patriarchy: an apostolate characterized by the absence of women. Yet, how exactly was woman to overcome the state of 'confused equality' (55)? On this question, Enfantin ventured into the sphere of the mythical: his 'call to woman' was based on the anticipation of a female messiah who would join him as pope of the Saint-Simonian church. As shown by the extract, an empty chair symbolized this quest. Thus, the search for the Woman turned into the overarching concern of the Saint-Simonians.

These ideas cannot be detached from Enfantin's patriarchal role. Many Saint-Simonians lived in a state of close emotional dependency on Father Enfantin – a situation that he fostered by taking (and breaching) confession and by inviting professions of love. These interpersonal bonds extended to Enfantin's relationships with Saint-Simonian women. Alongside various other liaisons, the unmarried pontiff of the Saint-Simonian church had a longstanding mistress who gave birth to his son Arthur in 1828. The latter's existence was only acknowledged in 1832, when Enfantin made him the focus of an elaborate ceremony. These blurred boundaries between life and doctrine meant that private matters were far from peripheral to Saint-Simonism.

After the departure of Bazard's followers and the removal of women, Enfantin continued to elaborate his doctrine. In April 1832, he retreated to his family estate in Ménilmontant, taking forty disciples with him. The group members adopted a celibate communal lifestyle in an all-male environment, attracting curiosity and ridicule for their extravagant ceremonies, their lavish costumes and their pursuit of domestic activities. In the meantime, Rodrigues too had left the fold: while affirming his support for the liberation of women, he questioned Enfantin's moral pronouncements, instead making 'radical claims concerning women's political and social rights'.[12]

The most serious problem, however, was the fact that the Saint-Simonians had become a target of the public authorities. An initial police raid in January 1832 was followed by charges of running a political organization and of being a threat to public morality. The subsequent trial gave Enfantin further opportunities to challenge convention, for instance when he unsuccessfully insisted on being represented by female legal counsels. In the end, Enfantin and his close associate Michel Chevalier received prison sentences, while Rodrigues – despite his break with the organization – was ordered to pay a fine.

Enfantin resumed the quest for the Woman after his release in 1833. He gathered his declining band of followers in the *Compagnonnage de la Femme*, which looked for the female Messiah in Egypt. The pilgrimage implied that the union between man and woman would be paralleled by the union between Occident and Orient. Yet, alongside this quixotic mission, Saint-Simonians addressed more practical concerns. During the 1830s and 1840s, they developed various infrastructural schemes, remaining faithful to Saint-Simon's focus on industry. The most eye-catching project was their contribution to plans for the Suez Canal, promoted by Enfantin's *Société d'Études du Canal de Suez* (1846).

What, however, did the events of November 1831 mean for Saint-Simonian women? Some of them sought to live according to Enfantin's new moral law, in several cases with unhappy outcomes. Even for those who rejected Enfantin's ideas, his controversial pronouncements caused problems: by association, female Saint-Simonians had been tainted with the brush of immorality. Several of them abandoned the movement, embarking on other forms of activism. For instance, Jeanne Deroin (1805–94), a former Saint-Simonian seamstress, moved towards Fourierism and emerged as a pioneering figure in the history of French feminism.

More generally, their exclusion from the Saint-Simonian church forced the Saint-Simonian women to launch alternative projects. One tangible outcome was their foundation of the *Tribune des Femmes* (1832), the first feminist newspaper in France. Edited by Jeanne-Désirée Veret (1810–91), Marie-Reine Guindorf (1812–37) and Suzanne Voilquin (1801–77), the periodical initially debated Enfantin's moral doctrine. However, as Claire Moses had noted, 'radical sexual opinion' soon disappeared from its pages, and its authors concentrated on the legal and economic position of women.[13] Such examples illustrate how Saint-Simonism could provide an inspiration to women – even if their response to the 'call' differed from Enfantin's ideas.

On the whole, Saint-Simonism provides us with an ambivalent picture. Seen from one angle, it involved a challenge to patriarchy. Enfantin placed a maternal figure at the centre of his church's spiritual quest. He also acknowledged that the existing moral order prevented genuine equality between the sexes. In this respect, the exclusion of women from the Saint-Simonian hierarchy went hand in hand with a critique of existing social relations. At the same time, the patriarchal elements of his church were self-evident. In November 1831, Enfantin asserted his authority as father of the Saint-Simonian family and pontiff of the Saint-Simonian church. Even before these events, the movement had been hierarchically organized and led by Supreme Fathers. Women could engage in practical activities, but had little power to shape the doctrine.

As Claire Moses' work has shown, Saint-Simonism rose to prominence shortly before the emergence of a separate women's movement in France. These two phenomena were interconnected. Both the Saint-Simonians and the followers of Charles Fourier (1772–1837) sought to address the position of women in society and the moral issues that underpinned it. These movements provided stimuli for further activism. They thus did not only form part of the history of early socialism, but also of feminism – even if the events of November 1831 ultimately highlighted the persistence of patriarchal discourses and structures.

Leo Tolstoy, *The Kreutzer Sonata* (1889)

Charlotte Alston

'You know,' he began while packing the tea and sugar into his bag. 'The domination of women from which the world suffers all arises from this.'

'What "domination of women"?' I asked. 'The rights, the legal privileges, are on the man's side.'

'Yes, yes! That's just it,' he interrupted me. 'That's just what I want to say. It explains the extraordinary phenomenon that on the one hand woman is reduced to the lowest stage of humiliation, while on the other she dominates. Just like the Jews: as they pay us back from their oppression by a financial domination, so it is with women. "Ah, you want us to be traders only, – all right, as traders we will dominate you!" say the Jews. "Ah, you want us to be mere objects of sensuality – all right, as objects of sensuality we will enslave you," say the women. Woman's lack of rights arises not from the fact that she must not vote or be a judge – to be occupied with such affairs is no privilege – but from the fact that she is not man's equal in sexual intercourse and has not the right to use a man or abstain from him as she likes – is not allowed to choose a man at her pleasure instead of being chosen by him. You say that is monstrous. Very well! Then a man must not have those rights either. As it is at present, a woman is deprived of that right while a man has it. And to make up for that right she acts on man's sensuality, and through his sensuality subdues him so that he chooses only formally, while in reality it is she who chooses. And once she has obtained these means, she abuses them and acquires a terrible power over people.'

'Shall I go to her?' I asked myself, and immediately decided that I must go to her. Probably it is always done, when a husband has killed his wife, as I had – he must certainly go to her. 'If that is what is done, then I must go,' I said to myself. 'If necessary I shall always have time,' I reflected, referring to the

shooting of myself, and I went to her. 'Now we shall have phrases, grimaces,
but I will not yield to them,' I thought. 'Wait,' I said to her sister, 'it is silly
without boots; let me at least put on slippers'.[1]

Tolstoy completed *The Kreutzer Sonata* in 1889. His novella offers a frank
critique of the state of late nineteenth-century marriage and the relationship
between the sexes. The story begins on a long train journey. A female passenger
and her companion, a lawyer, allude to a recent scandalous case of divorce in
their social circle. This prompts a discussion among a wider group of passengers
about the incidence of divorce in Europe, whether it is reasonable and how it
might be prevented. A tradesman opines that a wife ought to fear her husband,
and through fear love him: this would prevent her from straying. The female
passenger, horrified at this reactionary stance, argues that marriage can only
be based on 'real' love, and a community of ideals. A woman should not be
forced into a marriage in which there is no love. This declaration prompts an
intervention by Pozdnyshev, a short, fiery-eyed passenger who until this point
has avoided conversation. In the course of the impassioned discussion, he reveals
that 'love' led him to kill his wife. As other passengers make their excuses to leave
the carriage, the narrator and Pozdnyshev drink tea together and Pozdnyshev tells
the story of his marriage, which is presented as typical of the modern marriage.

The views Tolstoy put forward in this novella reflected the Christian anarchist
philosophy that he espoused from the late 1870s onwards. His beliefs extended
to the realm of sexual relations. They were frequently and perhaps inevitably
interpreted against the widely known backdrop of Tolstoy's own marital
situation: by the 1880s his relationship with his wife, who had borne him thirteen
children, had become increasingly turbulent. The clandestine circulation and
later publication of *The Kreutzer Sonata* prompted an outpouring of discussion
and criticism, both in public and private, that fed into and fuelled wider debates
on sex and marriage in late nineteenth-century Russia, Europe and America. As
readers and critics agreed with, disagreed with or dismissed the text, or used it
as a starting point for the articulation of their own views, *The Kreutzer Sonata*
allowed for both critiques and reinforcement of nineteenth-century patriarchy,
from sometimes predictable and sometimes surprising quarters.

As Pozdnyshev tells his story, he explains that, before his marriage, he
lived 'as everyone does, that is, dissolutely', and 'practiced debauchery in a
steady, decent way, for health's sake', avoiding women who might tie his hands
by having children or developing an attachment to him (123–4). He made
sure to deal with any potential moral or emotional ties by paying the women

appropriately. Here Tolstoy critiqued his own past behaviour, the attitudes of his class (for example, the pursuit of these debauched men as worthy husbands for their daughters), of doctors, who advocated extra-marital sex for good health, and of the government, which licensed and regulated brothels.

After the age of thirty, Pozdnyshev began to look for a woman who was fit to be his wife. A woman who was attractive, he believed, surely must also be intelligent and deeply moral; he was convinced that his chosen bride understood all he thought and felt, when in reality 'it was only that the jersey and the curls were particularly becoming to her' (129–30). He opined that this focus on outward appearances was not simply the responsibility of men, but also of women, and their mothers, who were aware that 'we are continually lying about high sentiments, but really only want her body and will therefore forgive any abomination except an ugly, tasteless costume that is in bad style' (132). The inequalities in this relationship and the ways in which they were manipulated by both sides are highlighted in the introductory quote above. On the one hand, the woman was 'reduced to the lowest stage of humiliation', while 'on the other she dominate[d]' (136).

After marriage, the Pozdnyshevs' relationship developed from the anti-climax of the honeymoon, through to dullness, irritation and eventually hostility. Their five children were only the source of more jealousy, quarrels and torment about their health and well-being. While *The Kreutzer Sonata* ends with the protagonist killing his wife, Pozdnyshev speaks about having killed her much earlier. Within marriage, he asserts, women become 'mentally diseased, hysterical, unhappy, and lacking capacity for spiritual development'. This could not be altered through 'equality', or education, but only 'by a change in men's outlook on women and women's way of regarding themselves' (152). Things came to a head for the couple after doctors instructed Pozdnyshev's wife not to have any more children, and taught her how to prevent this – a practice that Pozdnyshev found repellent. She became healthier and handsomer, and began to attract attention from other men, in particular a violinist named Trukhachevksy, with whom she played the piano, evidently enjoying both his company and the music. Their proximity and shared passion were displayed in a public performance of Beethoven's *Kreutzer Sonata*. Pozdnyshev admits that his wife's actual relations with this man, as they developed on his increasingly frequent visits to their house, were immaterial – what mattered was Pozdnyshev's own 'swinishness', and jealousy. When he returned from a trip to Moscow and found them together, Pozdnyshev stabbed his wife to death, and Trukhachevsky fled. The unnatural conventions of society imposed themselves even here, as Pozdnyshev considered running after Trukhachevsky, but remembered 'that it is ridiculous to run after one's wife's lover in one's socks: and I did not wish to be ridiculous but terrible' (202). He remembered to 'put on slippers at least' before going to see his dying wife (206–7).

What was the answer to all this misery generated by marriage? For Pozdnyshev, and for Tolstoy, the answer was clear. No good could come from marriage, which was simply a means of licensing the sexual exploitation of women by men. The 'Christian' ideal of marriage was effectively no better than the debauchery of unmarried men. It would be better for all men and women to strive for chastity. When Pozdnyshev describes his physical relationship with his wife after marriage as unnatural, the narrator responds that, if everyone thought along such lines, the human race would cease to exist. Pozdnyshev counters that if life has any meaning, it is that it should be lived through selfless brotherhood and love. If the realization of this ideal eventually brought the world to an end, it would be no bad thing. Tolstoy clarified these points in an 'epilogue' to *The Kreutzer Sonata* completed in 1890. The Christian ideal, in his view, was chastity. There could therefore be no such thing as a 'Christian marriage'. However, true Christian teaching did not dictate codes of behaviour; it pointed towards an ideal that should be aimed at, but would not always be met.

The Kreutzer Sonata was not the first vehicle for the expression of Tolstoy's opinions on the role of women, sex and marriage. In the last thirty years of his life he devoted himself to the articulation of his newfound Christian anarchist faith. In a series of key texts he outlined his rejection of the church, the state, private property and money, and his commitment to absolute pacifism, vegetarianism, temperance and chastity. The novels, plays and short stories he wrote in this period were brought into the service of this philosophy. However, Tolstoy's biographers routinely note that, despite the dramatic change he describes in *My Confession* (1884), elements of Tolstoy's struggle with life and faith inhabited his life and work from a much earlier period. In the later sections of *Anna Karenina* (1877) particularly, the traces of Tolstoy's disillusionment with contemporary society and his idealization of the simple life are visible. This is true also of the author's attitudes to women, family life, and the relationship between the sexes. *Anna Karenina* highlights the hypocrisy of society's attitudes to adultery and debauchery on the part of men and women. While Vronsky's affair with a married woman is accepted as routine, and only frowned upon because he takes it so seriously, Anna is ostracized by high society for her decision to leave her husband. *Anna*

Karenina also offers a broader critique of marital and other relationships. The 'true love' that Anna pursues cannot ultimately make her or anyone else happy. Even Levin and Kitty, who represent purity, hard work and family happiness, by the end of the novel are potentially divided by Levin's faith.[2] Some of the themes developed here – the corruption and worthlessness of high society, and the importance for family life of simplicity and hard work – built on those evident in Tolstoy's much earlier *Family Happiness* (1859).

After the onset of his spiritual crisis, the first clear articulation of Tolstoy's views on the role of women can be found in *What Then Must We Do?* completed in 1886. Here Tolstoy railed against the inequality inherent in a society where some men worked while others profited from their labour. Just as he exhorted men to return to the land and earn their bread by labour, he demanded that women embrace their traditional roles as mothers and bearers of children. The nonsense called 'women's rights', he maintained, came from a realization by women that men had abandoned their real work, and a desire likewise to 'make a pretence of labour … to avail ourselves of other people's work and to live only to satisfy our lusts'.[3] The Tolstoyan philosophy was radical but also retrogressive: it was about the observation of duties, not a demand for rights. In 1894 Tolstoy told Ernest Howard Crosby that

> women do much harm because they use their liberty to neglect their duties of caring for their children, etc. In old times they were forced to keep in their place which was wrong; but all will be well when at least they use their liberty to accept their old domestic position.[4]

The Kreutzer Sonata, with its rejection of education as a step towards equality, its presentation of marriage as an institution fundamentally based on coercion and its promotion of chastity as the ideal, built on all of these themes.

Steps were taken to censor *The Kreutzer Sonata* almost immediately. This included a ban on discussion of the book in print. In 1891 Tolstoy's wife, Sofia, requested an audience with the Tsar in order to (successfully) protest the censorship of the text. Sofia confessed the motivation for this trip to her diary shortly afterwards:

> I wanted to show that I wasn't a victim at all; I wanted people to say my visit to St Petersburg was something I had done instinctively … If that story had been about me and my relations with Lyovochka, I would hardly have begged him to let it be published.[5]

In any case, even before the censorship was rescinded, *The Kreutzer Sonata* circulated at evening gatherings, where one or more individuals would read the text to avid listeners. Its first reading, at the house of Tatiana Kuzminskaia and Alexander Kuzminski (Sofia's sister and brother-in-law), was of a penultimate draft. The story was read again at the Tolstoyan publishing house *Posrednik* a few days later, and within a week 300 lithographed copies had been produced.[6] This means of dissemination, and Tolstoy's continuing efforts to put the final touches to the story, resulted in the circulation of a number of versions in Russian society.

In England, the enthusiasm for publishing Tolstoy meant that four different editions of *The Kreutzer Sonata* appeared in 1890 alone. In Germany also, a *Kreutzer Sonata* fever took hold. Some publishers, translators and critics refused however to take any part in the promotion of the book, on moral grounds. While W. T. Stead told readers of the *Review of Reviews* that he refused to print it, because he found Tolstoy's prose coarse and brutal, and he fundamentally disagreed with the direction of his teachings, Isabel Hapgood, a prominent but unsympathetic translator of Tolstoy in America, refused to translate the work. In fact, the U.S. post office took steps to ban conveyance of the novel by mail, under a law about the distribution of immoral content.[7] As in Russia, it is unlikely that steps taken to prevent distribution of the novel did anything to prevent its circulation, or to hinder its popularity – the reputation of the book as illicit reading probably only added to Tolstoy's appeal and to his readership.

The debate on *The Kreutzer Sonata* can be traced in reviews and responses in print, through counter-literature that directly engaged with the story, and through the personal responses that readers wrote to Tolstoy. The author's high profile conversion and his controversial but appealing philosophy meant he was inundated with correspondence in the 1880s and 1890s. Letters streamed in from readers asking for advice, agonizing over their own personal dilemmas, adding their perspective, recommending their own work or the work of others, admonishing or correcting him. In the aftermath of *The Kreutzer Sonata* many of these letters described the correspondents' own marriages or relationships, asked for clarification of Tolstoy's views, or described the relief or revulsion they had felt upon reading his novella.[8]

Perhaps ironically, one of the first to break the ban on discussion of *The Kreutzer Sonata* in print was a senior figure in the Orthodox Church, Archbishop Nikanor of Kherson. Nikanor regarded censorship of Tolstoy as largely pointless, and preferred a robust and public defence of the Church's position. His *Conversation on Christian Marriage* refuted the idea that Pozdnyshev's marriage was typical, and asserted that good, Christian marriage was widely practised in Russia. He used the royal family as the ultimate example. Peter Ulf Møller identifies three main strands in the Russian debate: firstly those, like Nikanor, who launched a defence of the 'Christian marriage', and saw Pozdnyshev's marriage (or Pozdnyshev himself) as unusual or unnatural; secondly, those liberals and progressives who used *The Kreutzer Sonata* to argue for equality in marriage, for equal status and education for women, and for marriage based on a community of ideas and interests; and thirdly, those who argued for chastity before marriage. Some engaged with Tolstoy's advocacy of chastity, principally to refute it, but many simply used the story as a starting point for their own opinions on sex, marriage and the relationship between the sexes. This was also true abroad. The publication of an article by Tolstoy 'On Marriage' in the British Christian journal *The New Age* in 1897 generated a storm of correspondence from clergymen and laymen and women alike, defending or critiquing the institution of marriage, noting the value of Tolstoy's contribution, but rarely agreeing with all his conclusions.[9]

The Kreutzer Sonata generated a range of counter-literature, in Russia and abroad. While many of these texts were polemics, others simply used the story's popularity as a means of generating sales. There were many attempts to end the story differently, or to tell it from the wife's point of view. In one instance Pozdnyshev's wife survives and flees to a nunnery in England, where she confesses all to a monk who turns out to be her ex-lover Trukhachevsky. Some stories missed the point entirely: in D. N. Goltizin's *Thou Shalt Not Kill*, the author contests what he understands to be Tolstoy's assertion that a man has the right to kill his adulterous wife.[10] Mrs James Gregor, in *Whose Was the Blame? A Woman's Version of the Kreutzer Sonata*, cast the Trukhachevsky character as a good and moral man, where Pozdnyshev was small-minded and jealous: the principal character points out how different her story might look if her husband were to have written it.[11] Gerhardt von Amyntor's *Ciss-Moll Sonata*, published in Leipzig in 1891, sought to demonstrate the damaging impact of Tolstoy's work. In this tale, a reading of *The Kreutzer Sonata* persuades the husband to remain chaste towards his wife, against her wishes. The story ends with him killing her would-be lover, a scenario that could have been avoided were it not for the malign influence of Tolstoy's book. The Tolstoy family also contributed their own additions to the counter-literature: Sofia through her unpublished manuscript *Who is to Blame: A Woman's Story*, based heavily on the Tolstoys' marriage, in which a self-absorbed, womanizing husband neglects his beautiful and hard-working wife, not realizing her value until he has killed her in a fit of jealousy; and their son Lev L'vovich in his *Chopin's Prelude* (1900), which both of his parents dismissed as talentless, if sincere.[12]

Because of its notoriety, *The Kreutzer Sonata* provided a focus for discussion of established and developing attitudes to sex, marriage and gender relations. However, at a time when demands for political and social equality were gathering momentum across Europe, Tolstoy's attitude to patriarchy was a curious combination of the radical and the retrograde. He condemned marriage as an institution that licensed the sexual exploitation of women. Yet he encouraged women to embrace domestic duties rather than seeking to be liberated from them. Tolstoy's writings on sex and marriage were just one dimension of a wider series of Christian anarchist polemics, in which he advocated a return to manual labour, and denounced all forms of coercion. Even among Tolstoy's Christian anarchist followers, the author's attitudes to women, sex and marriage were controversial. Their refusal to acknowledge church or state meant that many Tolstoyans rejected marriage ceremonies and entered into 'free unions' instead. The making and breaking of these unsanctioned arrangements led critics outside and within the movement to accuse them of being dissolute rather than chaste. For female followers of Tolstoy, his rejection of the women's movement was a source of great frustration.[13] In society more widely, few commentators took *The Kreutzer Sonata*'s central message – the ideal of chastity – seriously. The novella became the centre of a debate in which many points of view were articulated, but Tolstoy's key concerns were often lost. Tolstoy's blunt exposure of the inequalities inherent in marriage proved a powerful source of fuel for these discussions, but his emphasis on duties, rather than rights, sat uncomfortably within contemporary debates about patriarchy.

Henrik Ibsen's *Hedda Gabler* (1890) as 'Patriarchal Moment'

Arnold Weinstein

(Then she goes over to the writing table, takes out the envelope with the manuscript, glances inside, pulls some of the sheets half out and looks at them. She then goes over to the armchair by the stove and sits, with the envelope in her lap. After a moment, she opens the stove door, then brings out the manuscript.)

HEDDA (throwing some of the sheets into the fire and whispering to herself). *Now I'm burning your child, Thea! You, with your curly hair!* (Throwing another sheaf in the stove.) *Your child and Eilert Løvborg's.* (Throwing in the rest.) *Now I'm burning – I'm burning the child.*[1]

This passage – stage directions and all – comes at the close of the fourth act of Henrik Ibsen's (1828–1906) domestic tragedy *Hedda Gabler* (1890), and it constitutes step one of an unfurling action that is completed at the play's end, with step two, when Hedda shoots herself. These two gestures – burning someone's manuscript and committing suicide – would seem to be as desperate, destructive and end-oriented as human actions can be. But they are also luminous, and the purpose of this essay is to unpack their contestatory power, so as to gauge the profound ideological charge that fuels them; and to see in them some possible vision of the future.

Let us, first, back up. To examine *Hedda Gabler* as a 'patriarchal moment' is to run a number of gauntlets: (1) the challenge of enlisting literature itself as a lens for gauging patriarchal power, and (2) the question of assessing – ideologically – a work of art that is diabolically twisted and 'knotty' in its representation of gender in late nineteenth-century Norwegian (European) cultural arrangements. Complicating matters still further is Ibsen's own (vexing) claim that he was not a feminist in any specific sense, but that his concerns were instead universal, regarding 'human rights' at large.

It might well be thought that Ibsen's earlier, trailblazing *A Doll's House* (1879) – with its epochal representation of a woman walking out of a bad marriage, leaving her two children as well, as a defiant act of emancipation that shocked bourgeois pieties throughout Europe and America – would be a better choice for this volume on patriarchy. But, unlike Nora, who famously exits, Hedda remains caught in the marriage trap (as did millions of real women), and her only liberation is through suicide. Suicide-as-option stamps some of the most famous literary depictions of entrapped nineteenth-century women: Emma Bovary, Anna Karenina, Miss Julie. Yet, Hedda is different. As Joan Templeton has remarked, Hedda 'does not destroy herself because she has failed to satisfy a patriarchal norm, but because she refuses to'.[2] That refusal is the subject of this chapter; in it, in its remarkable complexity and colouration, we can discern something of the surprising dimensions of literary utterance as barometer of the times.

If you have not read the play, the book-burning passage will be puzzling, even if arresting. Who are Thea and Løvborg? Why burn a manuscript? Why call it a 'child'? If you know the play, it starts to make at least some sense. Thea, Hedda's former school friend, has left her older husband (whom she despises), due to her liaison with their 'tutor', the wild man of the story, Eilert Løvborg. Their relationship seems as much writerly as sexual, inasmuch as Thea has helped the dissolute Løvborg regain discipline, and she has been his indispensable 'helpmeet' in actualizing his talents, inspiring him to write this portentous manuscript, said to be a 'History of the Future'. That is what Hedda is burning.

Why? The obvious answer is: jealousy. In an earlier scene, figuring an almost Proustian recollection of the past, we learn of the crucial prior romantic attachment between Hedda and Løvborg. Each was infatuated with the other. The 'Dionysian' young man would come courting the proper Hedda Gabler, and the two young people would sit together on the sofa, in the presence of the imposing (now dead) grand patriarch of the play, General Gabler. Their courtship consisted of feverishly whispered confessions on the part of the young man (regarding both sexual and drinking exploits), as the young woman egged him ever more insistently on, all the while pretending to be examining an illustrated magazine. Why did she do it? he asks even now. To get, she says, a glimpse – a vicarious experience – of male freedoms and appetites strictly 'off limits' to her as proper young lady. Løvborg, we realize, was Hedda's virtual taste of passion, and it remained virtual. Right through to the bitter, tragic end, when she will urge the utterly distraught Løvborg – become outright suicidal because he is (wrongly) convinced he has 'lost' his manuscript for good, at a brothel – to go ahead and off himself, but to do it 'beautifully', with 'vine leaves in his hair'. Crafting, like an artist, her fantasy-lover's exit, she will even offer him one of her father's (notably phallic) pistols to do the deed with. Løvborg is never to know that Hedda had the manuscript all along, but elected to burn it; she knowingly sends him off to his death. What kind of act is this?

Løvborg signifies for Hedda the *vicarious* experience of passion, beauty and even agency, in a world that is suffocatingly ugly, bourgeois, coercive and sterile. That Thea (who has had the courage to abandon her husband) could think herself Løvborg's mate or even 'colleague', that the two of them could 'sire' together the manuscript: this is more than enough to motivate the burning of the book, the burning of their 'baby' – all to be followed, by the end of the next act, by her own suicide. *Life* does not seem to stand a chance in this manic text about virtuality and denial that yields only a burned book and a cadaver at its close. Why?

Critics and audiences have been asking that question since 1890. The play was thought, like so many of Ibsen's works when they first appeared, to be incomprehensible; as if Ibsen knew that is how they would react, the work's last line is 'People don't *do* such things!' (778). It is passing odd that our modern view of Ibsen goes just the other way: his plays seem altogether too cogent, too spelled out in their meanings. But this one continues to puzzle. Above all, its female protagonist has come in for much invective: monstrous, frigid, neurotic, destructive, vicious, evil. It is worth noting that scholars of both genders have gone after Hedda. Failure to love, failure to act: these are the basic indictments, both then and now.

But if we invoke Lucifer's *Non serviam*, if we replace 'failure' with 'refusal', we then make room for a wider-angled view of the play, and patriarchy is exactly the right lens for understanding the larger scheme as well as the world view that Hedda understands in her very bones, and therefore rejects. Joan Templeton, Ross Shideler and Gail Finney are among the recent commentators who take the measure of the play's carceral arrangements, its stifling definitions of appropriate womanhood.[3] Ibsen himself stressed that the conservative forces of order (aunts, maid, community values) are aligned against Hedda from the get-go. Likewise, Thea's commitment to a role as 'helpmeet' to a more powerful male is cut from the same ideological fabric as Aunt Juliana's cult of self-effacement and maternal duties. Is this a life, the play seems to ask? Hedda Gabler – destroyer and denier, but scarcely spokesperson for any form of liberation – has exacerbated critics forever. Might we understand her better today?

Many readers and critics have lamented the fact that Hedda has not had the courage for a full-blooded passional affair with Løvborg: back then when they were younger, even now when they meet again. But Løvborg is shown as reckless and dissolute from the outset, and his quick relapse into drunkenness and rashness during the events of the play makes any genuine Dionysian comparisons seem rather a long stretch. In fact, *all* of the males in the play border on caricature. No one has ever doubted that Hedda's husband, George Tesman, is ridiculous. His verbal tics, his sterile pedantry, his glaring inadequacies in the love department, make us (as well as others in the play itself) wonder why on earth the ravishing Hedda Gabler could have married such a sorry figure. She had run out of time, she says, when the play's third male, the shrewd and phallic Judge Brack (former companion, out to be the 'cock of the walk' in setting up a comfortable little sexual triangle now that Hedda has returned) poses that same question to her about Tesman.

There is an early painting of Edvard Munch's 'Sphinx', and it pictures three distinct kinds of women (as Munch and his culture fantasized them): the angelic in white who yearns for the infinite, the naked one who thrusts her pelvis frontally at the viewer and the one in black who figures death; next to them, almost invisible, poor bleeding Edvard is shown to be negotiating such a maze. If we flip, gender-wise, Munch's painting, we get a fix on women's choices in 1890. The trio of Løvborg, Tesman and Brack constitutes a similar triptych of hieratic, quasi-caricatural male postures; and the play makes us realize that this masculine grouping – dissolute writer, fatally boring husband, oily cocksman – is a distinctly unsavoury proposition, ultimately not worth living with, or for. Hedda wants more.

Ibsen titled his play *Hedda Gabler* rather than *Hedda Tesman* to indicate that his protagonist is to be understood as the patriarch's daughter, not the historian's wife. The General's crucial loaded pistols parse the play. Hedda aimed one at Løvborg in the past, aims one at Brack in the present, hands one to Løvborg for killing himself and uses one to commit suicide. She is, in ways we need to understand, the play's actor, indeed the play's 'male'. But how to assert oneself when patriarchy is choking you? One solution is to control and script others; this she attempts with Løvborg. As for Tesman, living with him would be a terminal disease, and divorce is not much of an option either. Brack is the one who thinks he has corralled her at the play's end – he knows the pistol that killed Løvborg was hers; he will stay mum only if she agrees to the triangle – but she goes him one step better and uses the pistol herself.

I do not want to glorify Hedda. Ibsen presents her as a timorous person, afraid to dive into life, more content to direct – even manipulate – others, critical of her culture yet *of* that culture, thus all too sensitive to the social proprieties that still regulate human affairs. Yet one might argue that theatre exists in order to show that 'fear of acting' can be a vibrant spectacle, full of a special 'sound and fury', casting its light on the repressive world in a way that 'doing' and 'deeds' cannot show. *Hamlet* toiled in this vineyard. Further, Ibsen's play might well have been titled *Huis Clos* (*No Exit*) which was to be Sartre's term for the existential and relational prisons we inhabit in both life and death. We are not born knowing about these prisons, but the apprenticeship for women comes quickly. Hedda resembles Emma Bovary in as much as they both experience life as a cheat, inasmuch as both discover *ennui* to be the residue of living. Whatever beliefs she may have had earlier, none survives the actions of the play. Love is a fool's errand. (She is surrounded by fools.) No social avenue exists for her. Haughty, cutting, yet fearful, she is indeed monstrous in 1890. And it is frankly not easy to see in her suicide much of a vision for repudiating or transcending patriarchy.

But literature has never believed all that much in either repudiation or transcendence. Such things are trumpeted in political manifestoes; in literature we find, instead, the story of how culture actually *feels*, how it goes poisonously inside, how it constructs subjectivity, and finally how we might make knowledge of all that. Literature shines its light on the actual fabric of human interiority: dread, desire, want, joy, all those inner pulsions for which there is no empirical measure, no historical or documentable metric. As Hamlet said, this inner world is precisely that which 'passes show'. And, in this regard, Hedda Gabler is a stunning creation. All her responses to the cages she inhabits – contempt (sometimes gentle, sometimes withering) for the sorry Tesman; seesaw of attraction/distance, of adrenalin/irony with 'genius' Løvborg; familiar yet diffident entente with the ominous Brack; overall sardonic and abrasive treatment of those who come her way, who get in her way – testify to a portrait of uncommon depth and reach. Her 'condition' speaks volumes about the nineteenth-century ideological binds that coerced women. Hedda Gabler can be seen as Exhibit A for what patriarchy does to female subjectivity.

Nowhere can we better see this than in the bristling passage cited earlier, when Hedda burns Løvborg's manuscript. Hedda's exclamation, 'I'm burning your child, Thea', announces the jealousy/revenge theme of the play. In calling the manuscript the *child* that Løvborg and Thea created together – a notion that is emphasized repeatedly in the text, so much so that Løvborg will construe the loss of his book in a whorehouse (sic) as the bringing of one's own innocent baby into a brothel – Ibsen is hammering home a dear male fantasy, one that looms large in a number of his plays, namely the conceit that *writing* is the male's form of *engendering*, that writing is the male's way of rivalling women who bear children. This construct has its nineteenth-century history, but I would argue that it remains alive and well in today's academy, where the writing of books is not only required, but where it may indeed compete with any and all domestic agendas. 'One's book as one's child' is a potent formula for creativity in general, but perhaps especially for male doing, for male priorities. In a brilliant later play, *Little Eyolf* (1894), Ibsen will show precisely how this competition produces tragedy, since the man who subscribes to it must realize that he has been blind to his own flesh-and-blood child; at that play's end, there will be neither book nor child.

But 'I'm burning your child, Thea' is, in addition to being a psychological truth for Hedda, also a biological prophecy that has the dark power of a curse. The child that is to be destroyed in this play is not only the figurative manuscript, but Hedda's own unborn infant, the foetus she carries inside her. Hedda's coming suicide is an infanticide. And it is cogent. Among the patriarchal prisons at work in this play is the one closest to home: the woman's body. And even a nincompoop such as George Tesman is capable, by dint of his marriage rights, of impregnating Hedda Gabler. The entire play is cued to this pregnancy: Aunt Juliana, from the moment she enters the stage, is fixated on this inevitable marital outcome, this 'blessed event'; Judge Brack teases Hedda about this new regime which he fully expects her to enter and respect; Tesman, benighted as always, can scarcely believe his great good fortune in knowing that he has seeded his wife. At each mention of this topic, Hedda writhes in pain, grits her teeth, discovers all over again the idiotic bondage that is her lot. For all these reasons, Hedda's suicide expresses a double bid for freedom: to exit her ideological prison, to undo marriage's biological trap. An entire maternal narrative of bliss and fulfilment – patriarchy's (concocted) libidinal script for women – is being turned on its head.

Patriarchy's libidinal script. One wonders what Ibsen actually thought of that grand History of the Future (yes, that is its title) that Eilert Løvborg has delivered himself of, only to have it burned by Hedda Gabler. Given Ibsen's predilection for 'universals' as opposed to 'particulars', it is quite feasible that he regarded the destroyed manuscript as a 'genderless' beacon of light; hence its burning should constitute a ponderous loss for human well-being. For culture at large. For us. But the play he wrote allows us to feel otherwise. How can we not consider Løvborg's work as male-authored, as permeated by male vision, male aspirations, male appropriations? Men have written our histories. This was certainly the case in 1890. Maybe Ibsen's own genius whispered to him that this 'History of the Future' might well need to be rescued from male hands and male minds. That its burning might indeed be a possibility for rebirth, for rewriting. Perhaps even that Løvborg's grasp of the social might be biased, cyclopic, unattuned to some of patriarchy's human costs; that it might, in fact, be a lesser vessel, a more dubious testimony, than the shimmering experience of both life and death chosen and suffered by Hedda Gabler. Perhaps *her* story is a history-in-the-making.

Must Hedda's suicide be defeat? Using General Gabler's pistol, her final gesture seems richly ambiguous to me: yes, the phallic weapon has killed her, but then she has taken control of it herself, used it to her own ends. One of Emily Dickinson's finest poems, 'My life had stood, a loaded gun', figures the feminine as lethal weapon, possessed of 'the power to kill, without the power to die'.[4] Is this not potency? Is this not a kind of futurity? A shot heard, as they say, 'around the world'? Could Hedda's two gestures be an opening, rather than a closing?

Let me close by revisiting, one final time, the key passage where Hedda burns the manuscript, burns the 'child'. I invoke yet another poet. Adrienne Rich, major counter-cultural lesbian poet, wrote in 1968 – surely a year for contestatory writing – a poem entitled *The Burning of Paper Instead of Children*. Rich acknowledges that 'book-burning' seems the very embodiment of dark reactionary forces, yet she wants to focus on the emancipatory possibilities to be found in it. One of her references is Joan of Arc: female actor/victim who could not read, but who did indeed burn. Her poem challenges the sacrosanct status of language, calling it 'a map of our failures', and it ends with a mention of real burning happening in 1968, in Vietnam. Here are the final lines: 'The burning of a book arouses no sensation in me. I know it hurts to burn. There are flames of napalm in Catonsville, Maryland. I know it hurts to burn. The typewriter is overheated, my mouth is burning, I cannot touch you and this is the oppressor's language'.[5]

Hedda Gabler has none of the overt political thrust found in Rich's poem, but it nonetheless stages the burning of the oppressor's language as it appeared in 1890 in a bourgeois salon. And one act later, after taking the full measure of the wreckage around her and the hopeless prospects facing her, Hedda shoots herself. No political theory in sight, just a play, yet this is a patriarchal moment.

Account of a Fight against Paternal Authority: Franz Kafka's *Letter to his Father* (1919)

Oliver Jahraus

There is only one episode in the early years of which I have a direct memory. You may remember it, too. One night I kept on whimpering for water, not, I am certain, because I was thirsty, but probably partly to be annoying, partly to amuse myself. After several vigorous threats had failed to have any effect, you took me out of bed, carried me out onto the pavlatche[1] *and left me there alone for a while in my nightshirt, outside the shut door. I am not going to say that this was wrong – perhaps there was really no other way of getting peace and quiet that night – but I mention it as typical of your methods of bringing up a child and their effect on me. I dare say I was quite obedient afterward at that period, but it did me inner harm. What was for me a matter of course, that senseless asking for water, and then the extraordinary terror of being carried outside were two things that I, my nature being what it was, could never properly connect with each other. Even years afterward I suffered from the tormenting fancy that the huge man, my father, the ultimate authority, would come almost for no reason at all and take me out of bed in the night and carry me out onto the* pavlatche, *and that consequently I meant absolutely nothing as far as he was concerned.*

That was only a small beginning, but this feeling of being nothing that often dominates me (a feeling that is in another respect, admittedly, also a noble and fruitful one) comes largely from your influence. What I would have needed was a little encouragement, a little friendliness, a little keeping open of my road, instead of which you blocked it for me, though of course with the good intention of making me take another road. But I was not fit for that.[2]

Franz Kafka (1883–1924) was and is an extraordinary author, but his struggle against his father was not. It was rather typical for this epoch and for the literary trend in German expressionism around the turn of the century in 1900.[3] These struggles took place in particular in literature, and young intellectuals and authors like Kafka found in their fathers all they wanted to overcome, or imagined father figures onto whom they could project their resistance against old and rigid social structures. The fatherly image drawn by this generation of young men was a symptom of a special state of society after the very long nineteenth century, which lasted until the (end of) the First World War and beyond, as in the case of Kafka, who wrote his famous letter a year after the war.

Until the end of the war, the two big countries at the heart of Europe, Germany and Austria-Hungary, were ruled by emperors. The possibility of a double throne anniversary of the German Emperor Wilhelm II (thirty years) and the Austrian Emperor and Hungarian King Franz Joseph I (seventy years) is described as the so-called 'Parallelaktion' (which never took place) in Robert Musil's (1880–1942) big novel *Der Mann ohne Eigenschaften/The Man without Qualities*. The two emperors embodied two different kinds of men and different types of male and paternal authority, the one acting like a young and strong-willed soldier with catastrophic consequences, the other appearing as an old and seemingly benevolent father and symptom of patriarchal and paternalistic backwardness. These caricatures recalled the three dimensions of patriarchal ideology known since the time of Goethe and Schiller, and depicted in the latter's drama *Die Räuber/The Robbers* (1781/2), in which the father is God, regent and biological father. Thus the father figure had a central function in all systems that constituted a society – fathers were physicians as well as judges, and administration was a paternal concept to be found not only in society but also in governance, in schools and universities, in prisons and in barracks and, above all, in families.

The war had not only ended these two monarchies, but also brought new dynamics into social structures. Thus, female labour during the war both led to new impulses for emancipation and other cultural, political and legal transformations. Female characters in their struggle for social recognition became a subject of literature as in the famous novel *Das kunstseidene Mädchen/The Artificial Silk Girl* (1932) by Irmgard Keun (1905–82). Thus literature became in itself a symptom of these structures, an awareness that the time of these father figures and even the generation of fathers in politics and society had come to an end.

This loss of authority was especially noticeable where fathers tried to keep it. The case of Otto Gross serves as a radical example.[4] Otto Gross was born in 1877 as the son of the famous Austrian jurist Hans Gross (1847–1915). Otto studied zoology but, at his father's request, turned to medicine. He married in

1903 and later came into close contact with radical movements and had to fight against drug addiction. Several illegitimate children made his social standing unsustainable – at least in the eyes of his father. Using his judicial authority Hans Gross had his son declared insane, and Otto spent time in several mental institutions before a reappraisal set him free again. Otto Gross died in 1920.

In the relationship between Otto and his father we find the fault line of different discourses: jurisprudence on the part of the father, psychoanalysis on the part of the son. Psychoanalysis delivered insights into the sexual conflicts which might undermine the civic society of the fathers. While Sigmund Freud described these conflicts on the one hand, he himself was such a father figure on the other. Even Kafka would notice in his diary after the writing of his first successful novel *Das Urteil/The judgement* as an experience of his readings: 'Gedanken an Freud natürlich' ('Of course, thinking about Freud').[5]

Otto Gross meanwhile had a different understanding of psychoanalysis. His sexual promiscuity was closely related to his way of thinking about sexual affairs as conflicts with the rigid and paternal structure of society. Freud described the son's fight against his father in the 'Oedipus complex'. Later, in the 1950s, Jacques Lacan invented the conception of the *non/nom du père*, which plays which the homonymity of the French *non/nom*, 'no' and 'name' of the father and is the goal in the process of constituting a subject. The subject enters the state of the symbolic order when it learns to follow the law and the signification of the father. The conflict between Otto Gross's sexual promiscuity and his father's judicial power seems to be an early display of Lacanian psychoanalysis.

At the turn of the century these social structures were so stable and unquestioned that they were at the same time exhausted and an object of psychological theories as well as literary and aesthetic challenges. A process of erosion had begun, and literature and art were fields which both reacted with and promoted this process. Otto Gross himself was turned into a literary character in several of Franz Werfel's works and in the expressionist drama, *Der Sohn/The son* (1914) by Walter Hasenclever (1855–1934). In this play a son cannot stand paternal expectations any longer; he has failed his exam, thinks about suicide, becomes a member of a youth movement, makes first sexual experiences, gets himself arrested and is finally brought to face his father. Self-confident, he does not want to hear the paternal judgement (as in Kafka's novel of the same name), but demands his freedom. The father would have his son institutionalized to protect society, but the son is prepared and determined to kill his father, when the latter suddenly dies from a heart attack.

Kafka's *Letter to his Father* is both a typical and a special case, generically poised between biographical conflict and literary document. It is a document of the loss of paternal authority and at the same time a very personal report of his own emancipation from the dominant figure of his father and his own understanding of himself as an author outside his middle-class career. The relationship between Kafka and his father is not easy to understand. The situation was difficult, and Kafka's own description of this relationship in his *Letter to his Father* is neither objective nor fair, which means we have to modify his perspective.[6] While the depiction of this fraught relationship was important for his own literary biography, not all of it was incorrect or wilfully misleading. Kafka's literary self-fashioning, and thus his description of his father, was part of his strategy to establish writing as his one and only acceptable principle of life. Thus, Kafka follows a double strategy. On the one hand, he reports how his father had judged him – with devastating psychological effects. On the other hand, Kafka also uses these reports to judge his father – mercilessly. His highly sophisticated letter thus follows a legal principle: *audiatur altera pars* ('hear the other side too'). His father is given the chance to express himself, but only to give his son, the author of the letter, the opportunity to respond and to reject the father's position even more powerfully. Kafka himself referred to his 'lawyer's tricks' ('advokatorischenKniffe') and calls his letter in a comment to Milena Jesenká a 'lawyer's letter' ('Advokatenbrief').[7] This son is no longer the object of his father's judgement. Instead, he has become a lawyer himself making his father an object of his judgement framed in a literary text.

These tricks meant that Kafka always linked the judgement of his own position with his father's judgement, and the judgement of his father with his admiration for his father. This strategy is independent from Kafka's real argument with his father. In the same way, his letter oscillates between biographical authenticity and literary fiction as Kafka's self-expression and his late fight against his father come closer together. His self-fashioning as an author, his identity and conception of literature, as well as his way of writing on the one hand, and his hatred of his father and even of himself on the other, are entangled in his letter.

This is how we may approach the beginning of the letter. The son picks up his father's question of why he, Franz Kafka, could claim to have been afraid of his father. This question remains unanswered – because of the son's fear. From this point on Kafka describes his relationship to his father as a relationship filled with fear in every aspect of family life. But he has no illusions. The letter does not and cannot lead to a better relationship, to a better understanding between father and son, or to mutual respect. Kafka knows that it is too late. The relationship cannot be modified or renewed. The family is broken. What he, the son, wants is a clarification of his own motives and of what the son assumes to be his father's motives. He does not want a final and definitive expression of the truth of this relationship but, as Kafka points out in the last sentence of the letter, something so close to this truth, 'that it might reassure us both a little and make our living and our dying easier' (167).

In the opening lines of his letter cited above, Kafka describes an archetypal scene from his relationship to his father, in which all ingredients of the later conflict are already present. Yet, more importantly, Kafka reconstructs the scene as symptomatic for his view of this relationship. The judgement of the father begins with a judgement of Kafka himself which may excuse the father: the child was noisy, and his father wanted to sleep. However, these opening lines only serve to make the subsequent judgement of the father even harsher. Kafka's accusations reach existential dimensions when he characterizes 'the methods of bringing up a child and their effect on me' ('die Erziehungsmittel und ihreWirkung auf mich') (119). Kafka stresses that his suffering results from this scene. As he styles his father, he styles himself. Yet, the two parts of his rhetorical figure aim in opposite directions. Kafka employs two techniques which he also uses in his literary texts, for example, the enlargement of body sizes and the use of legal terms as metaphors for social roles and relationships. The father appears as a huge man and at the same time is characterized as an almighty authority. The bigger and mightier the father appears the smaller and weaker Kafka himself becomes. Immediately after this first scene Kafka remembers a second one, which also operates with this aggrandizement. In the changing rooms of the public swimming baths Kafka was overwhelmed by his father's size: 'I was …weighed down by your mere physical presence [Körperlichkeit]. I remember …how we often undressed in the same bathing hut. There was I, skinny, weakly, slight; you strong, tall, broad' (120–1). The passage closes: 'this difference between us remains much the same to this very day' (121). Addressing his father as an institution and highest authority, Kafka becomes implicitly – and artfully – an accused about to receive the maximum penalty. The punishment of having to stay on the balcony all night turns into the father's attempt to destroy his own son. 'This feeling of being nothing' (120) would never leave the child. The letter then turns from physical to intellectual hegemony ('geistige Oberherrschaft'), especially concerning the father's authority to give orders in every practical and ideological aspect. Paradoxically, Kafka concedes this intellectual hegemony to his father within a text which is itself an example of intellectual hegemony. But this is also a part of his lawyer's tricks.

Throughout the letter the reader can follow this interplay between the accusation of Kafka himself and the accusation of his father. Kafka concedes his father's 'gift for bringing up children' ('Erziehungstalent') while insisting that this gift has had devastating effects on him. Yet, between the lines, Kafka delivers an accurate characterization of the man who was his father. Hermann Kafka was born in 1852 in Bohemia as the son of a Jewish butcher family of lower social rank. His only aim in life was to rise to become a member of civic society. This meant he had to earn money and assimilate to the dominant class in Prague: the German-speaking Christian upper class. He established rigid norms and standards for himself, his family, and especially for his children, including Franz and his social environment. He was the typical representative of his civically assimilated Jewish class and a typical father in the paternal society of the late nineteenth century. This was revealed when he accused his children of being 'too well off' (135). We have to see Kafka's failure in or aversion towards his father's business in this context. Kafka returns his father's reproach. He, the father, was responsible for Kafka's refusal to join his business. The son describes his father's behaviour as a tyranny. He himself would not follow the rules he expected others to follow.

Over the course of the letter several issues arise which were all crucial for Kafka's life, such as his relationship to his father, his (Kafka's) position in the family and in business, his father's educational methods, the father's tyranny over his family and employees, and the overall atmosphere of repression. Besides, Kafka mentions his own plans to choose a profession, his family's attitude towards sexual education, and finally the way the father and his family lived their Jewish faith.

Kafka's problems in getting married (for example, to his fiancée Felice Bauer), his relationships to women, and his reinforcement of his Judaism were attempts to escape his father. He shows that all these paths led nowhere, that his failure was inevitable as a result of his respect for his father. Conflict with his father was particularly strong in two areas, marred by misunderstandings and failed hopes of agreement: Judaism and sexuality.

> I found just as little escape from you in Judaism. Here some measure of escape would have been thinkable in principle, moreover, it would have been thinkable that we might both have found each other in Judaism or that we even might have begun from there in harmony. (145–6)

Kafka talks about rescue and escape, which also means salvation, and so he uses religious terms. Kafka starts an apotheosis of his father: he is not only the highest authority on all questions concerning the family but also a religious authority like a god ruling over his creation, his family. Yet, due to Kafka's negative characterization of their relationship, his struggle against his father assumes the character of a primal sin. Kafka bemoans that his Judaism has become a social mask, while also putting himself into the position of his father's judge in social and even religious questions. But Kafka himself could not claim to lead his life in accordance with the strict rules of an authentic Judaism. Only from 1911, when he met JichzakLöwy and his eastern Jewish theatre troop, did Kafka become seriously interested in religious questions. In these people he found the real authentic Judaism, and subsequently turned his own erratic behaviour against his father. His own father was sceptical towards his Judaism. Kafka notes in his diary that his father denigrated Löwy: 'If you lie down with dogs, you get up with fleas.' ('Wer sich mit Hunden zu Bett legt, steht mit Wanzen auf.')[8] The same denigration can be found in his letter, when Kafka describes his fight as a 'combat of vermin'. Kafka lets the reader understand that his father may accuse him, but these sentences can always be read as Kafka's own accusations of himself. As a central metaphor, bugs or vermin are part of his second novel *Die Verwandlung/The metamorphosis*.

The differences between Kafka and his father are even more radical in questions of sexuality and marriage. As he points out in a letter to his fiancée's friend Grete Bloch of 11 June 1914, marriage is for Kafka 'the most social action' ('sozialste Tat').[9] In his letter to his father he describes an embarrassing situation. The son speaks about his sexual education, even though the father has never taught his son about the facts of life. Instead he advised him to go to a prostitute, which strongly violated his son's sense of shame. Kafka was disgusted, if not by this advice. He visited prostitutes frequently, which was common at the time for an unmarried son of this class. Kafka indeed pursued a sexual snobbery ('Sexualsnobismus') as his biographer Klaus Wagenbach has shown.[10] However, he was disgusted by the fact that even an intimate conversation like this was overshadowed by alienation and a lack of love. For Kafka, the crucial point is his father's opposition to both his engagements, the earlier one to Felice Bauer and the later one to Julie Wohryzek. Kafka reports that his father assumed sexual motivations on his part, while Kafka himself describes these potential matches as marriages of convenience: 'The fundamental thought behind both attempts at marriage was ... to set up house, to become independent. An idea that does appeal to you ... '. The son's foundation of his own family would have led him out of the position of a son: 'I would be your equal; all old and even new shame and tyranny would be mere history' (162). Marriage would thus become an act of emancipation, and so Kafka delivers an argument which we can also find in his early novels: marriage is a rebellion against paternal power and punished with death. In his *Letter* Kafka concedes: 'It is too much; so much cannot be achieved.' His equality with his father becomes immediately dubious. Kafka could not stand this 'most acute form of self-liberation and independence' (162). Consequently, he never married, and he makes his father responsible for his own mental block. At that point in the *Letter* the son has turned the asymmetrical power relations between father and son into their opposite. Kafka explains that his father's mere existence meant that he could only be nothing. But at the same time he explains why his father could destroy the son so easily. The relationship between father and son is a relationship of mutual annihilation. The guilt (of being nothing) and the accusation (of annihilating the other) were far beyond a solution of this problem.

Kafka's *Letter* has often been read as a biographical document. This only makes sense if we do not read it as a historical document, but as a document of Kafka's writing. The son describes his father as accusing his son, as much as the son himself accuses his father. In the same way in which the son accuses his father he also needs his father as a force to fight against and a cause to write against. The description of the father's annihilation of his son is also an act of the son's self-constitution through the act of writing this letter. Thus Peter-André Alt takes Kafka's conception of being such a son as a principle which opens a perspective on Kafka's writings and biography. We do not know for certain if Kafka's father ever read this letter, nor does it matter. The most important thing is that Kafka wrote it. This letter is the document of a struggle of a son against his father. Perhaps this struggle was not so successful existentially, but it was very successful from a literary point of view. Thus, the *Letter* is not only a literary document of patriarchalism but also a document of its literary negotiation.

Federico García Lorca's *Blood Wedding* (1932): Patriarchy's Tragic Flaws[1]

Federico Bonaddio

[It's wedding day somewhere in rural Andalusia, and the mother of the groom and father of the bride are sharing a private conversation.]

MOTHER: *That's what I'm hoping for: grandchildren. (They sit.)*

FATHER: *I want them to have plenty. This land needs hands that aren't hired. You're forever battling weeds, thistles, stones that appear from nowhere. And those hands should be the owners' own, able to punish and master, to make the seed grow. You need a lot of sons.*

MOTHER: *And a daughter or two! Men come and go like the wind! It's in their nature to turn to knives and guns. Girls never venture out of the house.*

FATHER

(Happily): *I'm sure they'll have both.*

MOTHER: *My son will cover her well. He's of good stock. His father could have had plenty of children with me.*

FATHER: *I wish it could all happen in a day. That, just like that, they could add two or three men to the family.*

MOTHER: *But it's not so. It takes time. That's why [referring to the loss of her husband and another son in a murderous feud] it's so terrible to see one's own blood spilt on the ground. A fountain that spurts for a minute but that cost us years.*

[Later, during the wedding reception, the groom's mother happens upon her son who is, strangely, unaccompanied.]

MOTHER
[To her son]:   So where's your wife?
BRIDEGROOM: Resting a while. It's a bad day for brides!
MOTHER: A bad day? It's the only good day! For me it was like
                          coming into inheritance. [...] It's like ploughing new
                          fields, planting new trees.

[Eventually she finds a moment in the conversation to give her son some advice.]

Please, try to be affectionate with your wife. If ever you
find her to be cold or vain give her a caress that hurts
a little, a firm embrace, a bite and then a gentle kiss.
Nothing to upset her, but enough to remind her who's
the man, the master, the one in charge. That's what I
learnt from your father. And now you don't have him
anymore, it's me who has to teach you how to be strong.[2]

Lorca's *Blood Wedding*, first performed in 1933, presents a story of elopement, a jilted husband and revenge in the playwright's native Andalusia. The scene cited above takes place soon after the ill-fated nuptials have ended. The conversation between the unknowing Mother of the Bridegroom and Father of the Bride centres on the prospect of grandchildren. In this agricultural community, no one underestimates the value of having male heirs – and in numbers –, given the physical nature of the work required to extract profit from one's lands. Economic necessity rather than male pride is no doubt at the root of the preference to employ home-grown rather than hired hands. We know too, from an earlier conversation (Act I, scene ii), that the marriage joins not only two families but also their lands, affording them efficiencies as well as enhanced status in the community. If the Mother declares the benefits of having a daughter or two as well, it is not out of some loyalty to her gender but in recognition of the stability they afford the family because of their confinement to the home. 'As in the rest of the Mediterranean world', writes David D. Gilmore, 'in Andalusia the social space of the community is rigidly divided into discrete and bounded male and female spheres. Man's sphere is the space outside of the house: the public spaces. Women's realm is the inside of the house: the private spaces.'[3] 'Do you know what it means to get married, child?' the Mother asks the Bride. 'A man, some children and a wall that's two feet thick for everything else' (338–9). Her view has hardened, no doubt, due to the experience of losing both her husband and a son to a feud between clans, something which in her mind now characterizes the dangers lurking in the public sphere of men.

Of course, the Mother's view of women represents the patriarchal ideal, and in this tragedy – suffused with the inevitability characteristic of the genre – it is her earlier concerns about the suitability of her son's choice of woman (Act I, scene i) that win out over the commonplaces of her culture. That wall – some 'two feet thick' – is as much to keep women in as it is to keep the world out. But the problem is that, in their designated role as pillar of the family and upholder of its values, women can all too easily bring the home and its patriarchal head tumbling down. 'Masculine hono[u]r', explains Gilmore, 'depends upon feminine shame, or modesty, and a man therefore depends upon the good behaviour of his womenfolk as guarantee of his public esteem. In an important sense, his masculine esteem and image rest upon this weak link of female shame'.[4] Thus we can see that, beyond the warning signs represented in the play by the Mother's early sense of foreboding or by elements of the plot such as the Bride's previous engagement to Leonardo – the man with whom she elopes and a member of the Félix clan that murdered the Bridegroom's brother and father –, patriarchy contains its own tragic flaws. Moreover, while the Mother might pride herself on the virility of her son and, before him, on that of her husband, she knows all too well that an accident of fate can snatch a man from this life in a mere instant and bring his bloodline to the swiftest of ends.

Although she may harbour misgivings about her daughter-in-law, the Mother appears to have none about the institution of marriage itself: not a bad day, but a good day for brides! Her husband's death has left her as head of the family and as custodian of its laws and values. In the social order to which she is committed, sentiment is a secondary concern when it comes to betrothal, so it is no coincidence that she should mention marriage and inheritance in the same breath. The advice she gives to her son on controlling his wife is equally telling. It reaffirms the expectation that men should rule not only outdoors but indoors too. To this end, even a degree of violence, albeit softened with a kiss, is not only permitted but advisable. Above all, the Mother's advice reveals the process by which the Law of the Father is handed down: not only in the words of a mother to her son, but in the education she has received from her husband and according to which her outlook on life is structured. Yet it is this conformity to patriarchy – with all its flaws – that ensures a tragic outcome, both for the Mother and the Bridegroom, as well as the Bride and her lover, Leonardo.

The tragic potential in patriarchy resides in a combination of factors. First, if it is to function properly, patriarchy depends on both men and women submitting to its rules, values, rituals and beliefs; second, there is the fact that this submission cannot be guaranteed; third, there are the codes that make transgressions intolerable for families and their members; and fourth, there is the requirement in patriarchal culture that transgressions be punished. Because submission to the rules cannot be guaranteed, the relation in Andalusian culture between a man's honour and a woman's shame – between his reputation and her sexual purity, modesty and restraint – is always fraught with danger and conflict is always a possible outcome. The consequences of such conflict can even be fatal. The risks are compounded by the fact that while men are charged with protecting their women and their individual and family honour, their masculinity is also measured by their ability to seduce other women: a double standard inherent – another flaw – in the sexual culture of patriarchy.[5] The contradictory positions of men pit them against one another in what Gilmore calls 'the game of reputation by female proxy'.[6] Whether the catalyst is a man's reputation or his masculinity or a woman's conduct, an accident, if you like, is always waiting to happen, even more so if the notion of love is thrown into the equation, too.

In *Blood Wedding*, as it turns out, it is love and not reputation that inspires betrayal, this motive, because of its purity, acting as a counterpoint to the mixed messages of patriarchy's codes even though, as we shall see, there was cause to make the Bride's illegitimate suitor want to prove his worth by making her his conquest. Although love (or 'erotic love' as Reed Anderson puts it) looks likely to lead to adultery, it is not condemned but instead 'is represented as the liberating ideal which with energetic and rebellious force asserts its own life principles against all the alienating prohibitions of family, tradition and social class'.[7] At the start of Act III, three young woodcutters who, like Greek Fates, survey the scene in the woods to which at night time the eloping couple has fled, predict that Leonardo and the Bride will be caught; but they also acknowledge that their affair was inevitable and just and that not to have attended to their desire would have been an act of self-deception: 'You have to follow your calling; they were right to run away.... They were deceiving one another until their blood could no more' (387). That calling is not to the conventional scenario, legitimized by marriage, in which a wife submits dutifully to her husband and is resigned to her servitude. Instead, it is to love, pure and simple. This is what is meant when the Bride tells Leonardo 'I want neither a bed nor dinner with you, and there's not a minute in the day when I'd rather not be with you' (398–9).

The love between the Bride and Leonardo, therefore, is founded on an equality that is not recognized by the structures or interests of the patriarchal order. Arranged marriages, for example, made with the economic interest of the two families in mind and bound up with matters of inheritance and lineage, do not take into account affairs of the heart and, rather unwisely, underestimate their power to move individuals. The Bride's three-year relationship with Leonardo ended, we presume, because he was not deemed, or did not deem himself, to be good enough for her. 'Two oxen and a bad hut don't amount to much' (352) is Leonardo's bitter admission to her, and one wonders to what degree his desire for her is now bound up with the need to prove himself. By contrast, the Bridegroom seems to have no such problem and is able to offer the Bride considerable land to add to her own. The Father is not ashamed to admit that his future son-in-law's family is wealthier than his own. 'You are richer than me', he gladly concedes to the Mother. 'Your vineyards are worth a fortune. Each shoot, a silver coin' (335). From his perspective, his daughter is a means to an end, and love is less of a concern than the prospect of merging estates. His only regret is that their land is not adjacent. When the Mother asks him why he would want them to be, he replies: 'What is mine is hers and what is yours is his. That's why. To be able to see it all together, how wonderful that would be!' (335).

After his separation from the Bride, Leonardo went on to marry her cousin with whom he now has a child and another on the way. Whereas we only have the Mother's word for the virility that has been passed down from father to son, in this department Leonardo has more than proved himself. But clearly, for him, children are not enough, although by the time he decides to act on the feelings which he has harboured for the Bride since they separated, the situation has become irretrievable. If in the past it was his status that was the problem, the order now dictates that the Bride is entirely out of bounds: first, because he is both married and a father; second, because the object of his desire is betrothed. Here, as he was throughout his career, Lorca is concerned with the tension between freedom and limits, something which he conceived of, more often than not, in terms of the desire for self-expression and fulfilment in the face of either artistic or social constraints. Patriarchal culture, with all its flaws, provides a fitting arena to explore this tension, which manifests itself not only in the clash between society's precepts and the impulse of love, but also in the internal conflicts suffered by those who are structured according to patriarchy's conflictive, even impossible, demands. As Anderson argues, 'the principles that the characters hold as truths are shown through the conflicts produced by the action of the play to be flawed, even crucially deficient, both at the level of individual experience and at the level of community life.[8] These principles also condemn the characters to intense and inescapable suffering.

The Bride knows only too well the value that maintaining her decency holds for a woman in her community. So too does the Mother who, on learning of the Bride's disappearance, makes clear to the Father that his daughter is shameless. 'It can't be her', he pleads. 'Perhaps she has thrown herself down a well.' 'Only decent women, clean women, throw themselves into water', the Mother retorts. 'Not that one!' (382). When, in Act II, Leonardo comes riding to pay the Bride a visit, she responds to his tales of regret with caution and holds firm, at least on the surface, to what she knows is socially correct and her duty: 'A man with his horse knows a lot and can do much to take advantage of a woman lost in a desert. But I have my pride. That's why I am getting married. And I will shut myself in with my husband, whom I must love above all else' (354). Leonardo speaks on behalf of love and freedom and against convention, realizing that there are some passions that cannot be kept down: 'To burn within and not say anything is the greatest punishment we can heap on ourselves. What good did pride do me and not seeing you while knowing you were awake night after night? Nothing at all!' (354). The Bride's response makes clear the conflict within, caught as she is between her family duty and the immense force of her attraction to Leonardo: 'I can't listen to you anymore. I can't listen to your voice. It's as if I'd drunk a whole bottle of anisette and had fallen asleep wrapped in a quilt of roses. And it's dragging me down, and I know I'm drowning, but still I fall' (354).

It is perhaps no accident that in *Blood Wedding* the elopement takes place after the wedding ceremony and not before. Although the Bride was duty-bound even by her engagement and Leonardo, as a married man, stands to be an adulterer no matter what, that she should be breaking her wedding vows makes the eloping couple's transgression all the more forceful and the need for punishment an absolute certainty. The Bride knows this and says as much in the woods before the Moon, who appears in the form of a young white-faced woodcutter, finally seals their destiny by lighting up the way and revealing their whereabouts to the Bridegroom. Her caring words for Leonardo reveal a selflessness that belongs to the realm of love as opposed to that of social responsibility: 'I've abandoned a good man and all his people in the middle of a wedding and with my bride's crown still on. You're the one they'll punish and I don't want that to happen. Leave me here alone! Run away! No one will defend you!' (399).

The play ends with two deaths: those of the Bridegroom and Leonardo, each dying at the hands of the other in a struggle that repeats the violent history between their respective clans. The Bride's punishment is that she has now joined the company of women who have lost their men, whether it is their husband, lover or son. She is spared physical violence other than at the hands of the Mother who, in anger and despair, beats her to the ground, lamenting her son's lost honour and name. The Bride insists that she is still pure, but naturally cannot deny the charge of elopement. Her only defence is that her passion rendered her helpless, and would always have, despite the benefits she stood to gain from her marriage:

> I was a woman burning, wounded within and without, and your son was a drop of water that promised me children, land, good health; but the other man was a dark river filled with branches that brought to me the sound of its reeds and whispered me its song ... . Your son was right for me and I did not cheat on him, but the other's arm pulled me away with all the force of the sea ... and would have done so forever ... , even if I had grown old and all your son's children had held onto my hair!', (409–10)

Juxtaposed in her statement is the destiny she knew she should choose for herself – a husband, a family, a home – and the fate that her passions thrust upon her. In *Blood Wedding*, desire is set in opposition to the precepts of society, and tragedy is assured by patriarchy's intolerance and incoherence. The play exposes the flaws in a system marked by irreconcilable tensions: between the constraints of familial honour and the vagaries of masculine reputation; between the security and status associated with property and the personal fulfilment which love connotes; and, of course, between a woman's shame and the force of her desire. In the end, the Bride's inability to conform reveals the very folly of patriarchy's fixation with the principles of female modesty and restraint.

'His Peremptory Prick': The Failure of the Phallic in Angela Carter's *The Passion of New Eve* (1977)

Ruth Charnock

Then the loudspeaker crackled again, to attract my attention: a gong sounded and a crisp voice with the intonations of an East Coast university delivered these maxims. [...]

'Proposition one: time is a man, space is a woman.

Proposition two: time is a killer.

Proposition three: kill time and live forever.'

The gong struck again, and then the same voice delivered the following lecture. 'Oedipus wanted to live backwards. He had a sensible desire to murder his father, who dragged him from the womb in complicity with historicity. His father wanted to send little Oedipus forward on a phallic projector (onwards and upwards!): his father taught him to live in the future, which isn't living at all, and to turn his back on the timeless eternity of interiority.

But Oedipus botched the job. In complicity with phallocentricity, he concludes his trajectory a blind old man, wandering by the seashore in a search for reconciliation.

But Mother won't botch the job.

Man lives in historicity; his phallic projector takes him onwards and upwards – but to where? Where but to the barren sea of infertility, the craters of the moon!

Journey back, journey backwards to the source!'

A click and the transmission was over. I had not understood one word of it, though I was very much more afraid than I had been. The matriarchs, I surmised, had captured me; and they perceived me as a criminal since they did not organize the world on the same terms as I did – the lecture, if it proved nothing else, proved that. I knew I was a criminal because I was imprisoned, although I knew of no crime which I had committed. But as soon as I defined my own status, I was a little comforted.[1]

Novelist, feminist, literary critic, journalist and provocateur, English writer Angela Carter (1940–92) is perhaps most known for her late works of magical realism, *Nights at the Circus* (1984) and *Wise Children* (1991), along with her reworking of traditional fairy tales *The Bloody Chamber* (1979). Angela Carter's *The Passion of New Eve*, published in 1977, is a novel that casts patriarchy into crisis. In this sense, its patriarchal moment is one where patriarchy's might is undermined, castrated, demoted and emasculated. On a literal level, the novel is peopled by male characters who are either sterile (Zero), passing as women (Tristessa), or castrated (Eve/Evelyn). Symbolically and structurally, the novel satirizes and pillories phallogocentricity. Its female characters are often mouthpieces for proclamations regarding the death of progressivist accounts of history and of linear time. However, these proclamations are not free from the sting of Carter's tongue either. Indeed, in *The Passion of New Eve*, one can never be entirely sure which Carter is mocking the most: the maniacal, subjugating diktats of patriarchy? Or the womb-centric, pseudo-mysticism of 1970s French feminist theory and theology?[2] Neither is exempt from Carter's scorn and polemic.

The opening extract comes from a moment where the central character, Evelyn, a misogynist who has fled his pregnant and abused lover, Leilah, is kidnapped in the desert and taken to an all-female compound, Beulah, run by a monstrous, archetypal female named Mother. Mother, who is also a plastic surgeon, rapes and then castrates Evelyn, turning him into a woman, the Eve of the title. Just prior to Evelyn's sex change, he is forced to listen to the 'lecture', quoted in the extract.

The lecture outlines several of *The Passion of New Eve*'s key concerns: the notion of a gendered metaphysics ('time is a man, space is a woman'), the use of myth to police gender norms, here with recourse to *Oedipus Rex*, and the privileging of matriarchy as a corrective to patriarchy: 'Mother won't botch the job'. As Evelyn realizes, the 'matriarchs … did not organize the world on the same terms as I did'. In the novel, he will be made to realize what it feels like to live as a woman. And yet, *The Passion of New Eve* does not champion an essentialist view of gender. Rather, Carter sets social constructivist and essential theories of gender in play with each other, challenging the strict separation and policing of these apparently opposed camps within second wave feminist theory, and beyond.

As a patriarchal moment, *The Passion of New Eve* offers a nuanced, yet polemical reading. Although it absolutely seeks to undermine, deface and raze patriarchy to the ground, as readers we are forced to occupy two bodies: Evelyn's and Eve's. We inhabit both the patriarch and the subjugated body – the boundaries between them undone by the fact that Evelyn is 'turned' into Eve. As David Punter identifies, the novel mounts a key contestation of 'the gendered structure of narrative', one which throws the reader back on their own gendered reading position in disorientating ways.[3] Do we read Evelyn/Eve as male or female? And how might this alter or throw into relief our own gendering as readers? The novel interrogates complicity with forms of gendered violence by interpellating the reader as both victim and perpetrator of gendered violence.

Furthermore, the novel treats both patriarchal and matriarchal mythologies as deeply suspect ideologies. As is evident from the excerpt, Carter satirizes matriarchal, anti-phallic and anti-historical mythologies by presenting them, according to Lorna Sage, 'as consolatory fictions (that) must be exposed and reasoned (and jeered) out of countenance'.[4] This jeering takes the form of an overblown thealogical rhetoric, as in the excerpt. As such, *The Passion of New Eve* is a crucial text for thinking about the ideological excesses of the second wave feminist movement, as well as those of patriarchy. Neither, Carter surmises, should be allowed to stand within western culture.

The novel begins in London, where Evelyn has his last night in the city before moving to New York. He takes a date to the cinema where an old movie is showing, starring Tristessa de St. Ange, a 1940s film actress, idolized by Evelyn in his youth. Tristessa will come to play a pivotal role in the novel when she does appear in the flesh. A transvestite, s/he works in the novel to satirize Hollywood's production of images of perfect and persecuted womanhood, images that collude with women's subjugation and the eroticization of this subjugation.

From this early image of the shimmering fantasy work of the silver screen, the novel lurches, violently, into a dystopian nightmare, when Evelyn lands in New York. Carter's dystopian New York is terrorized by a faction referred to only as 'the Women', who leave their tags on the walls of expensive hotel lobbies: 'the female circle – thus: ♀ with, inside it, a set of bared teeth. Women are angry. Beware Women! Goodness me!' (11). Carter's protagonist, a sex-crazed misogynist who owns, only, that he has 'an ambivalent attitude towards women' which sometimes manifests in him 'tying a girl to the bed before I copulated with her', does not take the threat of these bared teeth entirely seriously as directed at his own manhood (9). However, the novel soon corrects him.

Evelyn embarks upon an affair with an erotic dancer, Leilah. Evelyn exoticizes, eroticizes and defiles Leilah, tying her to the bed when he leaves her in his apartment to go to work. Leilah, as Evelyn depicts her, is 'a born victim' – one who willingly (although with a modicum of, seemingly, staged resistance) subjugates herself to Evelyn's rule. In turn, to Evelyn, Leilah quickly becomes 'an irritation of the flesh, an itch that must be scratched; a response, not a pleasure' (31). When Leilah becomes pregnant, Evelyn refuses to marry her and tells her 'firmly ... that she must have an abortion' (33). After she haemorrhages and, subsequently, is sterilized, Evelyn abandons her 'to the dying city' and flees to the desert (37).

Already surrealistic in tone and imagery, from this point in the novel, *The Passion of New Eve* becomes increasingly so as Evelyn voyages deep into the desert and is kidnapped by a gang who seem, initially, to be 'the Women' from New York, except these captors' symbol looks 'like a broken arrow or truncated column' (45). Following his capture, Evelyn is taken to an underground lair, the 'place they called Beulah' (47). Beulah will be the site of Evelyn's forced sex change – the place where Evelyn will become Eve, ruled over by the monstrous Mother. Beulah's symbol, the broken column, is made manifest in a stone monument:

> A stone cock with testicles, all complete, in a state of massive tumescence. But the cock was broken off clean in the middle .... The top half of the cock, ten feet of it, lay in the sand at my feet but it did not look as if it had fallen accidentally. (48)

The symbolic and the premonitory collide in this edifice. In *The Passion of New Eve*, the phallic is profoundly under threat: patriarchy, rendered as a tyranny at the end of its tether. The novel satirizes the emergence of a new kind of patriarchy (or, at least, a new version of the old kind of patriarch) in 1970s America: one run by the cult leader-guru-sexual mystic, à la Charles Manson, and represented most fully in *The Passion of New Eve* by the impotent Zero and his harem of devoted, subjugated wives.

The edifice is also a very real pre-sentiment of Evelyn's forthcoming castration – itself 'a complicated mix of mythology and technology' (48). The novel moves between these two modes – the seeming timelessness of myth revealed, as Roland Barthes has suggested,[5] to be a complexly encoded set of culturally policing discourses, and the technological, equally revealed as profoundly motivated by ideologies that aim towards myth. That is to say, *The Passion of New Eve* makes a technology out of myth and a myth out of technology, particularly when it comes to turning Evelyn into Eve.

From his arrival at Beulah, Evelyn is locked into a 'simulacrum of the womb' (52), where he is forced to listen to a piped-in female voice which shifts register between apocalyptic end-of-days prophesy and a 'lulling chorus' which murmurs 'NOW YOU ARE AT THE PLACE OF BIRTH' (52). Evelyn is subjected to a series of medical tests, washed and shaved by his 'captress' who looks at him with 'utter contempt' (55). Evelyn is dressed to look like his captress, then taken through a labyrinthine series of passages to meet Mother, 'the Minotaur at heart of the maze' (58).

Carter lingers over the Mother's body, which, as Aidan Day describes, is the result of 'a kind of super plastic surgery', which has rendered her as the archetypal maternal.[6] Mother 'was breasted like a sow – she possessed two tiers of nipples, the result ... of a strenuous programme of grafting, so that, in theory, she could suckle four babies at one time' (59). Mother's physical capacity dwarfs Evelyn's in every sense; he knows that 'there was no way in which I could show her my virility that would astonish her' (60). This is a narrative of masculinity unmanned in the face, and body, of the technologically enhanced female:

> Before this overwhelming woman, the instrument that dangled from my belly was useless. It was nothing but a decorative appendance attached there in a spirit of frivolity by the nature whose terrestrial representative she had, of her own free will, become. Since I had no notion how to approach her with it, she rendered it insignificant; I must deal with her on her own terms. (60)

Here, Carter deals a further blow to the myth of phallic power. 'Free will', in combination with technology, renders the male instrument 'useless' and 'insignificant'. The terms of engagement shift from the patriarchal to the matriarchal: Evelyn must deal with the Mother 'on her own terms', rather than assuming the terms of phallic logic. As throughout *The Passion of New Eve*, this encounter places gendered forms of power under question, specifically via second wave discourses about new reproductive technologies. Evelyn's inability to 'astonish' the Mother is part of a wider conversation regarding men's sexual function once women can, supposedly, deny, grant or control sexual access to their bodies, a conversation which gestures outwards to the free love movement of the 1960s and 1970s.

As 'her own mythological artefact', Mother embodies an anti-essentialist notion of womanhood: one made rather than born, to paraphrase Simone de Beauvoir.[7] The constructedness of Mother's body undoes the 'natural' right to domination presumed by patriarchy generally and Evelyn specifically in the novel. As Mother tells Evelyn: '[t]o be a *man* is not a given condition but a continuous effort' (63). Here, Carter also anticipates social constructivist positions on gender, typified by Judith Butler's ur-text *Gender Trouble* (1990).

But Mother is also a mouthpiece for a combination of thealogical and French feminist readings of gender, prevalent within the second wave. The latter is characterized by the 1970s work of Hélène Cixous.[8] In 'The Laugh of the Medusa' (1976) Cixous proposes that women *need* to speak in a different language to men if they are to be liberated from the structures and strictures of patriarchy.[9] In *The Passion of New Eve*, female characters are frequently rendered illegible to male characters – as with Evelyn's observation at the beginning of the novel that Leilah speaks in a language he cannot comprehend: 'her argot or patois was infinitely strange to me, I could hardly understand a word she said' (26).

French feminist essentialism and social constructivism meet and spar throughout *The Passion of New Eve*, which is one of the reasons it is such a productive text for thinking about the way these two discourses abut. However, neither theorization of gender is portrayed as an absolute or a solution to patriarchy in the novel. Carter does not pillory patriarchy in order to elevate matriarchy, although matriarchy is privileged, in terms of its relative representation, in the novel. Rather, it is 'gender-based determinism' that is under critique – a notion that is rendered a myth by Carter, as Sarah Gamble argues.[10]

So, then, we are not to look to the Mother in *The Passion of New Eve* as a solution or consolation for the smashing of patriarchy. As Evelyn realizes, just before he is raped by the Mother: 'that women are consolation is a man's dream' (60). Elsewhere, Carter argues that any idea of essential maternality is, equally, a myth:

> If women allow themselves to be consoled for their culturally determined lack of access to the modes of intellectual debate by the invocation of hypothetical great goddesses, they are simply flattering themselves into submission (a technique often used on them by men)...Mother goddesses are just as silly a notion as father gods.[11]

The Mother, whilst functioning as a wielding site of power in *The Passion of New Eve* is also, frequently, rendered silly – a parodic embodiment of thealogical cultism, such as became popular in certain second wave quarters in the 1960s and 1970s.

Following Evelyn's raping by Mother, he is led to 'the operating table, where Mother waited with a knife' (69). There in a 'warm, inter-uterine, symmetrical place', watched by 'rows of silent, seated women', Evelyn is castrated by Mother 'with a single blow' (69–71). Over the following two months, Evelyn is turned into Eve. Eve escapes back into the desert, only to be kidnapped again by arch-patriarch 'Zero the poet' and his wives. Rendered as ridiculous as the monstrous Mother, Zero, fittingly for a phallic symbol, is monopedal:

> He had only one eye and that was of an insatiable blue . . . . He was one-legged, to match, and would poke his women with the artificial member when the mood took him . . . . He loved guns almost as much as he cherished misanthropy. (85)

Zero is a quintessential misogynist and works in the novel as a perfect counterpoint to Mother. His first act is to 'unceremoniously' rape Eve and then appoint her as another wife in his harem (86). All of his other wives love Zero 'blindly', utterly subjugated to his will and rule (87). Sexually enslaved to Zero, his wives have swallowed the myth of patriarchy's supremacy, enacted through their marriage contract: 'they believed it predicated their very existence, since they'd decided to believe that sexual intercourse with him guaranteed their continued health and wellbeing' (88). As the quintessential patriarch, Zero '[believes] women were fashioned of a different soul substance from men, a more primitive, animal stuff' (87). Accordingly, he beats and defecates on his wives, showing more care towards his pigs: 'he let the pigs do as they pleased [but] demanded absolute subservience from his women' (95). Here, the novel plays out what Aidan Day, referring to Carter's gender polemic, *The Sadeian Woman*, calls 'a Sadeian structure of relations':

> [T]he vacuity that Zero projects on to his women and which they then internalize lies, in fact, in himself. Carter points to this through his name, but also through presenting him, for all that he loved guns, whips, Wagner and Nietzsche, as deficient in the maleness he himself mythologizes. He is one-eyed, one-legged and infertile.[12]

The Passion of New Eve argues that patriarchy itself is structured on this relation: projecting *its* lack on to women, so as to conceal its own impotency. But Carter also suggests, out of step with other feminist positions of this period that women willingly subjugate themselves to this patriarchal myth and that, in fact, this subjugation may feel very much like pleasure – as enacted by Zero's adoring and defiled wives. As such, the novel is crucial for thinking through the nuances not only in the dynamics of patriarchy but also in the theories that would seek to oppose it.

Conclusion

Gaby Mahlberg

The 'patriarchal moments' discussed in the present collection across genres and centuries broadly cover three different types of patriarchal power relationships: that between fathers/parents and their children, between men and women, and between individuals, families and governments.[1] All three are 'political' in the widest sense of the word, as power relations within the family and relationships between the sexes are governed by unwritten sociopolitical norms and conventions, whose transgression can nevertheless lead to conflict and debate. The last of the three patriarchal power relationships is contingent on the first two and builds these into a complex web, which is 'political' in the narrow institutional sense of the word, in which roles within the family are mirrored or replicated by those in the state, although it remains contested how far the parallels between familial and wider sociopolitical roles go at different points in time and where they might have their limits.

The first of these power relationships between fathers and their children is based on their biological link, with paternal responsibility and duty of care being met by the affection and reverence of their offspring. This biological relationship is best exemplified in the essays on Locke, Wollstonecraft, Sidney and Kafka, where it is not always entirely harmonious but fraught with assumed mutual obligations, the non-observance of which could easily turn into resentment and hatred. Locke's *Thoughts Concerning Education* (1693) considers a dynamic relationship between parents and children that changes in character as the children develop into adults, and J.K. Numao focuses on the patriarchal moment in which a state of relative equality is achieved and parents and children can meet as genuine friends. However, this natural termination of the dependence of children on their parents implicitly only applied to male offspring before the modern period as the same progression to independence was not available to girls and young women. Significantly, therefore, Numao confines his discussion to the relationship between fathers and sons.

In the Western European legal tradition women remained the legal property of their fathers beyond adulthood, and if they married, they became legally dependent on their husbands. Thus they never developed the same status of relative equality to their fathers, as is shown in the case of Wollstonecraft's Mary, whose main pursuit in life becomes the escape from the constraints imposed on her gender. While Faubert focuses on the issue of property-ownership that was denied to women in the patriarchal society of eighteenth-century England, legal and economic constraints could also have serious emotional and psychological consequences, as Wollstonecraft's protagonist is pressured into a loveless marriage for the sake of re-uniting two families divided over a property dispute and, because she remains bound by duty and guilt, she is unable to choose the lifestyle she desires.

Yet, men could also suffer from fraught relations with their fathers, as did Algernon Sidney, who as a younger son of an aristocrat was denied, on the grounds of primogeniture, the same status as his older brother and spent much of his adult life in pursuit of a meaningful social position and an estate he could call his own. Similarly, Franz Kafka struggled with feelings of inferiority, not through the vagaries of birth, but as a consequence of his physical and mental delicacy, which he juxtaposed in his *Letter to his Father* to the latter's intimidating masculinity and strength. The *Letter* reveals the full depth of psychological power a father could exercise over his son beyond adulthood, leaving his son not just full of fear but also with 'this feeling of being nothing' (Jahraus: 155). Throughout his life Kafka would feel like a failure unable to find solace either in his Jewish faith or in marriage – the only thing that would have made him his father's 'equal' (Jahraus: 161). Yet, parental influence over their offspring's person, property and marriage could also affect wider family and social relations.

Wollstonecreaft's Mary shares the prospect of a loveless union with the bride of Lorca's *Blood Wedding* (1933), who is equally forced into marriage for the consolidation of family property, and both stage an elopement of sorts: Mary leaving for Portugal to escape life alongside her husband, while Lorca's bride is abducted by her lover on her wedding day, ending in the brutal revenge killing of both of them in defence of the jilted husband's honour. For, as Federico Bonaddio has shown, in a patriarchal society like that of early twentieth-century Andalusia, the reputation of men was dependent on the honour and submission of women, their 'sexual purity, modesty and restraint', which 'cannot be guaranteed' (166). Constrained less by economic necessity than by bourgeois social convention, meanwhile, Ibsen's Hedda Gabler chooses suicide as her way of rejecting patriarchal norms, while also freeing herself from 'marriage's biological trap' of motherhood (Weinstein: 152).

These literary marriages take us to the second patriarchal power relationship between men and women established by the perceived order of creation, critically assessed in the essays on the Bible and Talmud by Sarra Lev and Deborah W. Rooke. Based on a biased authoritative reading of these key texts which positions woman as the inferior helper of man, marriage has been depicted as the natural union between men and women, so that those distancing themselves or withdrawing from it are in need of justification. Mary Astell thus warns her female readers not to enter into marriage lightly, while nevertheless advocating wifely submission to their husbands, albeit to maintain the due social order rather than in acknowledgement of any natural male superiority. Astell, it seems, would have been amenable to Rousseau's suggestion of limiting a husband's power by informal means such as the manipulation of 'his sexual needs' (Parageau: 111) rather than open rebellion, while Wollstonecraft's Mary refuses to play the game of the sexes by simply withdrawing from all marital duties. An alternative approach was proposed in Tolstoy's *Kreutzer Sonata*, which resonates with Wollstonecraft's concept of '"legal prostitution"' (Faubert: 124) in considering marriage as 'a means of licensing the sexual exploitation of women by men' (Alston: 142). For Tolstoy and his Christian anarchism the only logical way out of this exploitative relationship is 'chastity' and the pursuit of 'selfless brotherhood and love' even though this might lead to the extinction of the human race (Alston: 142).

The third and most complex patriarchal power relationship addressed in this collection concerns individuals, families and governments. Its classical description can be found in Aristotle's *Politics*, which identifies two key partnerships, between 'men and women, indispensable for human reproduction' and between '"natural ruler" and "naturally ruled"' (i.e. masters and slaves), indispensable for human survival'. These two partnerships then 'join to form a household' or family, which becomes one of the building blocks of the city-state (Hall: 37).

Following in the same tradition, the early seventeenth-century London clergyman William Gouge depicted the family as a microcosm of the state, in which children learn to be responsible members of civil society. In a similar way, the family in Rousseau's *Emile* becomes a training ground for the life of an active subject/citizen in the state (Parageau: 108). Yet, it might also be questioned whether or not there is a moment in the life of each individual in which the link between fathers and their children is either broken or fundamentally changes, so that these parallels no longer apply. Sir Robert Filmer's *Patriarcha*, 'the ideological bedrock of patriarchalism', which was 'vehemently attacked at the time of the Exclusion Crisis' (Cuttica: 66) for its rejection of a contractual relationship between rulers and ruled and a denial of parliamentary liberties, thus became a test case for patriarchal political thought. While the Kentish gentleman implied in the early seventeenth century that the ruler's fatherly domination over his subject-children endured into adulthood and thus kept his subjects in a state of permanent sociopolitical immaturity, his opponents in the later seventeenth century suggested (albeit using a caricature of Filmer for their own political purposes) that once adulthood had been reached the relationship between fathers and their offspring fundamentally changed. In response, Locke established in the first of his *Two Treatises of Government* that kings could not claim any authority over their subjects on the basis of a hereditary succession based on primogeniture because the line of succession was many times broken by the vagaries of biology as well as warfare and conquest.[2] His *Thoughts Concerning Education* also suggests that biological maturity and adulthood change the bond between fathers and sons/their children from one of responsibility and care to one of friendship in which adult offspring become the intellectual and civil equals of their fathers.

The relationship between fathers and sons as well as their sons' position in society at large might also be affected by order of birth as we have seen in the case of Sidney. A move away from a patriarchal political system ruled by primogeniture might therefore have been of particular benefit to younger sons who had most to gain from a political order based on personal merit and individual achievement rather than birth. It might therefore be unsurprising that early modern republicanism in particular has sometimes been associated with an uprising of younger sons against the rule of primogeniture in the family and in the state.[3] Yet the association between family and state outlived the early modern period. As we have seen above, Kafka's struggle against his own father within the narrow confines of his family also stood for the wider struggle his generation of German expressionist writers fought against rigid paternalist and patriarchalist structures in society and the state before the First World War, embodied by the government of 'the old Austro-Hungarian monarchy, which had been ruled by the caricature of an old and seemingly benevolent father' (Jahraus: 156).

Another problem for a political system based on patriarchal power and family relationships, meanwhile, is the rule of women as discussed by authors as different as John Knox and Angela Carter, or the political space to be inhabited by women within a patriarchal system, an issue addressed by Aristotle as well as Kant. While Knox objects to the monstrosity of female rule as subversive of the natural sociopolitical order, Carter embraces female rule as a satire on the 'phallogocentricity' of the modern world (Charnock: 172). Arguably, Carter's dystopian matriarchy in *The Passion of New Eve* is the only successful female government presented here, but it is based on the subjection and consequent emasculation of men. While women in Aristotle's *Politics* are citizens of an inferior kind 'incapable of most public activities' (Hall: 36), the women in Kant's political system are depicted as inferior and intellectually immature, yet it is never entirely clear to what extent their 'intellectual immaturity' (Pascoe: 116) is either natural or conventional. Hence both McLaren and Pascoe try to grapple with the issue to what extent their authors should be considered either 'sexist' (Pascoe: 120) or 'misogynist' (McLaren: 50), or just the unreconstructed products of their time. A similar ambiguity can be found in Prosper Enfantin's address to the family of Saint-Simonians of 1831, which supposedly calls for the liberation of women. Yet, Enfantin's idea of liberation does not involve women's equality within the Saint-Simonian family but their (temporary) exclusion from it lest they 'enter into the state of *confused equality*'. The only place open to them remained that of the female leader, a 'maternal figure' (Laqua: 132), alongside Father Enfantin himself. Thus, as Daniel Laqua's essay shows, Saint-Simonism was at the same time 'both patriarchal and anti-patriarchal' (132), conservative and progressive. A similar ambiguity runs through all the essays in the present collection as a latent theme that is there right from the start.

As we have seen in the essays in the present collection, patriarchal power relationships in the western tradition are based on the three great monotheistic world religions as well as ancient political philosophy, in which the origins of mankind and society are discussed and a seemingly 'natural' order is established in the process of creation or the formation of the first human societies. Reverence for creation and the social order emerges from works as disparate as Augustine's *City of God* and Pope's *Essay on Man*, while the contestation of these foundational texts and their wider contexts shows that the perceived 'natural' order of creation might be built on very shaky foundations indeed.

The prime example for this are the different versions of the creation story as outlined both in the Talmud (Lev) and the Bible (Rooke), suggesting that it depends entirely on our preference and translation whether or not we find proof for a hierarchy of the sexes. One-sided interpretations and selective quotations from the Qur'an out of context have also skewed the picture. As Asma Barlas points out, 'it is not just questionable textual practices, but also the failure to contextualize its teachings, that ties the Qur'an in perpetuity to a long defunct patriarchy' (Barlas: 33). The same issue is also addressed in Conybeare's chapter, which questions the extent to which 'Augustine's vision of humans in the world, and of their political organization, is ... hierarchical', before concluding that it is 'far more dynamic and egalitarian, through its recognition of others in their common humanity, than would be suggested by a patriarchalist reading' (48).

The image that emerges from the essays at hand therefore is one of a contested patriarchalism, characterized by tensions between a normative framework and actual sociopolitical practice. While normative authority is exercised or imposed, this same authority is also constantly undermined as the patriarchal power brokers struggle to rise up to their task. The remaining question meanwhile is how this normative authority is created, or why a patriarchal norm is upheld even though all concerned are aware of its fictionality. A normative framework shapes wider power relations and serves the maintenance of hierarchies and the *status quo*, and it is always in the interest of certain individuals and groups to maintain them (cf Baines: 100). Those who shape the interpretation of a text can thus shape ideology, while ideology can also shape the interpretation of a text. The reading and re-reading of texts is therefore a dynamic process that can lead to different results in different contexts and circumstances. The 'patriarchal moments' captured in this collection are records of these processes of definition and contestation.

Suggestions for Further Reading

Given the substantial literature on patriarchalism, this list is highly selective. It focuses on key editions of texts and a few works which should help to contextualize them.

General Works on Patriarchalism

Amussen, Susan D., *An Ordered Society. Gender and Class in Early Modern England* (Oxford: Blackwell, 1988).

Butler, Judith, *Gender Trouble: Feminism and the Subversion of Identity* (New York and London: Routledge, 1990).

Cuttica, Cesare, *Sir Robert Filmer (1588–1653) and the Patriotic Monarch: Patriarchalism in Seventeenth-Century Political Thought* (Manchester: Manchester University Press, 2012).

Roberts, Peters Belinda, *Marriage in Seventeenth-Century English Political Thought* (Basingstoke: Palgrave Macmillan, 2004).

Schochet, Gordon, *Patriarchalism in Political Thought. The Authoritarian Family and Political Speculation and Attitudes Especially in Seventeenth-Century England* (Oxford: Blackwell, 1975).

Walby, Sylvia, *Theorizing Patriarchy* (Oxford: Blackwell, 1990).

The Bible

Rogerson, John W., *Genesis 1–11* (Sheffield: JSOT Press, 1991).

Rooke, Deborah W., 'Feminist Criticism of the Old Testament: Why Bother?', *Feminist Theology*, 15 (2007), pp. 160–74.

Skehan, P. W. and A. A. Di Lella, *The Wisdom of Ben Sira* (Anchor Bible, 39; New York: Doubleday, 1987).

Upton, Bridget Gilfillan, 'Can Stepmothers Be Saved? Another Look at 1 Timothy 2.8–15', *Feminist Theology*, 15 (2007), pp. 175–85.

Whybray, R. N., 'The Immorality of God: Reflections on Some Passages in Genesis, Job, Exodus and Numbers', *Journal for the Study of the Old Testament*, 72 (1996), pp. 89–120.

The Talmud

Aaron, David, 'Imagery of the Divine and the Human: On the Mythology of Genesis Rabba 8§1', *The Journal of Jewish Thought and Philosophy*, 5:1 (1996), pp. 1–62.

Fonrobert, Charlotte Elisheva, *Massekhet Eruvin: Text, Translation, and Commentary. A Feminist Commentary on the Babylonian Talmud*, ed. Tal Ilan and Tamara Or (Tübingen: Mohr Siebeck, forthcoming).

Judah, Hanoch and Theodor Albeck (eds), *Midrash Bereshit Rabbah* (Jerusalem: Wahrmann, 1965).

Scott, Joan, 'Deconstructing Equality-Versus-Difference: Or, the Uses of Poststructuralist Theory for Feminism', in Steven Seidman (ed.), *The Postmodern Turn: New Perspectives on Social Theory* (Cambridge and New York: Cambridge University Press, 1994), pp. 282–98.

The Qur'an

Ahmed, Leila, *Women and Gender in Islam* (New Haven, CT: Yale University Press, 1992).

Barlas, Asma, *Re-Understanding Islam* (Amsterdam: Van Gorcum, 2008).

Rahman, Fazlur, *Major Themes of the Quran* (Minneapolis, MN: Bibliotheca Islamica, 1980).

Aristotle's *Politics*

Freeland, Cynthia, *Feminist Interpretations of Aristotle* (University Park: Pennsylvania State University Press, 1998).

Modrak, Deborah, 'Aristotle: Women, Deliberation, and Nature', in Bat-Ami Bar On (ed.), *Engendering Origins: Critical Feminist Readings in Plato and Aristotle* (Albany, NY: SUNY Press, 1994), pp. 207–21.

Senack, Christine M., 'Aristotle on the Woman's Soul', in Bat-Ami Bar On (ed.), *Engendering Origins: Critical Feminist Readings in Plato and Aristotle* (Albany, NY: SUNY Press, 1994), pp. 223–36.

Smith, Nicholas D., 'Plato and Aristotle on the Nature of Women', *Journal of the History of Philosophy*, 21 (1983), pp. 467–78.

Augustine's *City of God*

Arendt, Hannah, *Love and Saint Augustine*, transl. J. V. Scott and J. C. Stark (Chicago, IL: University of Chicago Press, 1996).

Elshtain, Jean Bethke, *Augustine and the Limits of Politics* (Notre Dame, IN: University of Notre Dame Press, 1995).

O'Daly, Gerard, *Augustine's City of God: A Reader's Guide* (Oxford and New York: Oxford University Press, 1999).

Wetzel, James (ed.), *Augustine's City of God: A Critical Guide* (Cambridge: Cambridge University Press, 2013).

Knox's *First Blast of the Trumpet*

Brammall, Kathryn M., 'Monstrous Metamorphosis: Nature, Morality, and the Rhetoric of Monstrosity in Tudor England', *Sixteenth Century Journal*, 27 (1996), pp. 3–22.

Collinson, Patrick, 'Knox, the Church and the Women of England', in Roger A. Mason (ed.), *John Knox and the British Reformations* (Aldershot: Ashgate, 1998), pp. 74–96.

Dawson, Jane, 'The Two John Knoxes: England Scotland and the 1558 Tracts', *Journal of Ecclesiastical History*, 42 (1991), pp. 555–76.

Healey, Robert M., 'Waiting for Deborah: John Knox and Four Ruling Queens', *Sixteenth Century Journal*, 25 (1994), pp. 371–86.

McLaren, Anne, 'Delineating the Elizabethan Body Politic: Knox, Aylmer and the Definition of Counsel 1558–88', *History of Political Thought*, 17 (1996), pp. 224–52.

Gouge's *Of Domesticall Duties*

Booth, William James, *Households: On the Moral Architecture of the Economy* (Ithaca, NY: Cornell University Press, 1993).

Fletcher, Anthony, *Gender, Sex and Subordination in England 1500–1800* (New Haven, CT and London: Yale University Press, 1995).

Weil, Rachel, *Political Passions: Gender, the Family and Political Argument in England, 1680–1714* (Manchester: Manchester University Press, 1999).

Filmer's *Patriarcha*

Burgess, Glenn, *British Political Thought, 1500–1600. The Politics of the Post-Reformation* (Basingstoke: Macmillan, 2009).

Cuttica, Cesare, 'Kentish Cousins at Odds: Filmer's *Patriarcha* and Thomas Scott's Defence of Freeborn Englishmen', *History of Political Thought*, 28 (2007), pp. 599–616.

Daly, James, *Sir Robert Filmer and English Political Thought* (Toronto: University of Toronto Press, 1979).

Schochet, Gordon, *Patriarchalism in Political Thought. The Authoritarian Family and Political Speculation and Attitudes Especially in Seventeenth-Century England* (Oxford: Blackwell, 1975).

Sommerville, Johann P., *Royalists and Patriots. Politics and Ideology in England 1603–1640* (Harlow: Pearson Education, 1999; ii edn).

Sidney's *Discourses Concerning Government*

Scott, Jonathan, *Algernon Sidney and the English Republic, 1623–77* (Cambridge: Cambridge University Press, 1988).

Scott, Jonathan, *Algernon Sidney and the Restoration Crisis, 1677–83* (Cambridge: Cambridge University Press, 1991).

Winship, Michael P., 'Algernon Sidney's Calvinist Republicanism', *Journal of British Studies*, 49 (2010), pp. 753–73.

Locke's *Thoughts Concerning Education*

Corneanu, Sorana, *Regimens of the Mind* (Chicago, IL: The University of Chicago Press, 2011).

Fliegelman, Jay, *Prodigals and Pilgrims: The American Revolution against Patriarchal Authority, 1750–1800* (Cambridge: Cambridge University Press, 1982).

Schochet, Gordon, *The Authoritarian Family and Political Attitudes in 17th Century England: Patriarchalism in Political Thought* (New Brunswick, NJ: Transaction Books, 1988).

Yeo, Richard, 'Locke on Conversation with Friends and Strangers', *Parergon*, 26 (2009), pp. 11–37.

Astell's *Reflections on Marriage*

Gallagher, Catherine, 'Embracing the Absolute: The Politics of the Female Subject in Seventeenth-Century England', *Genders*, 1 (Spring 1988), pp. 24–39.

Kolbrener, William, and Michal Michelson (eds), *Mary Astell: Reason, Gender, Faith.* (Aldershot and Burlington, VT: Ashgate, 2007).

Perry, Ruth, *The Celebrated Mary Astell: An Early English Feminist* (Chicago, IL: University of Chicago Press, 1986).

Springborg, Patricia, *Mary Astell: Theorist of Freedom from Domination* (New York: Cambridge University Press, 2005).

Weil, Rachel, *Political Passions: Gender, the Family, and Political Argument in England, 1680–1714* (Manchester: Manchester University Press, 1999).

Pope's *Essay on Man*

Hammond, Brean, *Pope and Bolingbroke: A Study of Friendship and Influence* (Columbia: University of Missouri Press, 1984).
Nuttall, A. D., *Pope's 'Essay on Man'* (London: Allen and Unwin, 1984).
Rogers, Pat, *A Political Biography of Alexander Pope* (London: Pickering and Chatto, 2010).

Rousseau's *Emile*

Guénard, Florent, 'L'Etat et la famille', in B. Bernardi (ed.), *Jean-Jacques Rousseau. Discours sur l'économie politique* (Paris: Vrin, 2002), pp. 87–102.
Hunt Botting, Eileen, *Family Feuds: Wollstonecraft, Burke and Rousseau on the Transformation of the Family* (Albany, NY: State University of New York Press, 2006).
Okin Susan, M., *Women in Western Political Thought* (Princeton, NJ: Princeton University Press, 1979).
Spector, Céline., *Au prisme de Rousseau: usages politiques contemporains* (Oxford: Voltaire Foundation, 2011).

Kant's *What is Enlightenment?*

Hippel, Theodor von, *On Improving the Status of Women* (Detroit, MI: Wayne State University Press, 1979).
Langton, Rae, 'Duty and Desolation', *Philosophy*, 67:262 (1992), pp. 481–505.
Schott, Robin May, *Feminist Interpretations of Immanuel Kant* (University Park: Pennsylvania State University Press, 1997).

Wollstonecraft's *Mary*

Frost, Cy, 'Autocracy and the Matrix of Power: Issues of Propriety and Economics in the Work of Mary Wollstonecraft, Jane Austen, and Harriet Martineau', *Tulsa Studies in Women's Literature*, 10:2 (1991), pp. 253–71.
Golightly, Jennifer, *The Family, Marriage, and Radicalism in British Women's Novels of the 1790s: Public Affection and Private Affliction* (Lewisburg, PA: Bucknell University Press, 2012).

Mandell, Laura, 'Bad Marriages, Bad Novels: The "Philosophical Romance"', in Jillian Heydt-Stevenson and Charlotte Sussman (eds), *Recognizing the Romantic Novel: New Histories of British Fiction, 1780–1830* (Liverpool: Liverpool University Press, 2008), pp. 49–76.

Shanley, Mary Lyndon, 'Mary Wollstonecraft on Sensibility, Women's Rights, and Patriarchal Power', in Hilda L. Smith and Carole Pateman (eds), *Women Writers and the Early Modern British Political Tradition* (Cambridge: Cambridge University Press, 1998), pp. 148–67.

Enfantin's *Call to Woman*

Carlisle, Robert B., *The Proffered Crown: Saint-Simonianism and the Doctrine of Hope* (Baltimore, MD: Johns Hopkins University Press, 1987).

Moses, Claire G., *French Feminism in the 19th Century* (Albany: State University of New York Press, 1984).

Pilbeam, Pamela, *French Socialists Before Marx: Workers, Women and the Social Question in France* (Montreal and Kingston: McGill/Queen's University Press, 2000).

Pilbeam, Pamela, *Saint-Simonians in Nineteenth-Century France: From Free Love to Algeria* (Basingstoke: Palgrave, 2014).

Tolstoy's *Kreutzer Sonata*

Alston, Charlotte, *Tolstoy and His Disciples: The History of a Radical International Movement* (London: I B Tauris, 2013).

Bartlett, Rosamund, *Tolstoy: A Russian Life* (London: Profile Books, 2013).

Møller, Peter Ulf, *Postlude to the Kreutzer Sonata: Tolstoj and the Debate on Sexual Morality in Russian Literature in the 1890s* (Leiden and New York: E. J. Brill, 1988).

Tolstoy, Leo, *The Devil and Cognate Tales* (London: Oxford University Press, 1934).

Ibsen's *Hedda Gabler*

Durbach, Errol, '*Ibsen the Romantic': Analogues of Paradise in the Later Plays* (Athens: University of Georgia Press, 1982).

Goldman, Michael, *Ibsen: The Dramaturgy of Fear* (New York: Columbia University Press, 1999).

Meyer, Michael, *Ibsen: A Biography* (New York: Doubleday, 1971).

Moi, Toril, *Henrik Ibsen and the Birth of Modernism* (New York: Oxford University Press, 2006).

Weinstein, Arnold, *Northern Arts: The Breakthrough of Scandinavian Literature and Art from Ibsen to Bergman* (Princeton, NJ: Princeton University Press, 2008).

Young, Robin, *Time's Disinherited Children* (Norwich: Norivk, 1989).

Kafka's *Letter to his Father*

Alt, Peter-André, *Franz Kafka: Der ewige Sohn, Eine Biographie* (München: C.H. Beck, 2003).

Anz, Thomas, *Frank Kafka* (München: C. H. Beck, 1989).

Dienes, Gerhard and Ralf Rother (eds), *Die Gesetze des Vaters. Hans Gross, Otto Gross, Sigmund Freud, Franz Kafka* (Wien, Köln, Weimar: Böhlau, 2003).

Jahraus, Oliver, *Franz Kafka: Leben, Schreiben, Machtapparate, Eine Einführung* (Stuttgart: Reclam, 2006).

Lorca's *Blood Wedding*

Bonaddio, Federico (ed.), *A Companion to Federico García Lorca* (Woodbridge: Tamesis, 2007).

García Lorca, Federico, *Four Major Plays*, Oxford World's Classics; transl. John Edmunds; intro. Nicholas Round; notes Anne MacLaren (Oxford: Oxford University Press, 1997).

García Lorca, Federico, *Blood Wedding*, Aris & Phillips Hispanic Classics; transl. Paul Burns and Salvador Ortiz-Carboneres (Oxford: Oxbow Books, 2009).

Gilmore, David, *Aggression and Community. Paradoxes of Andalusian Culture* (New Haven, CT and London: Yale University Press, 1987).

Morris, C. B., *García Lorca: Bodas de sangre*, Critical Guides to Spanish Texts (London: Grant & Cutler, 1980).

Carter's *The Passion of New Eve*

Day, Aidan, *Angela Carter: The Rational Glass* (Manchester: Manchester University Press, 1998).

Gamble, Sarah (ed.), *The Fiction of Angela Carter: A Reader's Guide to Essential Criticism* (Basingstoke: Palgrave Macmillan, 2001).

Moi, Toril, *Sexual/Textual Politics* (London: Routledge, 1985).

Raphael, Melissa, *Introducing Thealogy: Discourse on the Goddess* (Sheffield: Sheffield Academic Press, 1999).

Sage, Lorna (ed.), *Flesh and the Mirror: Essays on the Art of Angela Carter* (London: Virago, 1994).

Notes

Introduction

1   See e.g. Careen Shannon, 'The Patriarchy Is Dead? Really?' (16 September 2013, http://msmagazine.com/blog/2013/09/16/the-patriarchy-is-dead-really/; accessed on 13 July 2014).

2   See e.g. Allegra Stratton and Jo Adeutnji, 'As the Recession Bites, Will Women Bear the Brunt of Job Losses?', *The Guardian* (Saturday 31 January 2009, http://www.theguardian.com/money/2009/jan/31/recession-women-job-losses; accessed on 13 July 2014).

3   See e.g. Stephanie Nicholl Berberick, 'The Objectification of Women in Mass Media: Female Self-Image in Misogynist Culture', *The New York Sociologist*, 5 (2010), http://newyorksociologist.org/11/Berberick2011.pdf; accessed on 13 July 2014.

4   See e.g. Kira Cochrane, 'The Fourth Wave of Feminism: Meet the Rebel Women', *The Guardian* (Tuesday 10 December 2013, http://www.theguardian.com/world/2013/dec/10/fourth-wave-feminism-rebel-women; accessed on 1 July 2014).

5   With 'power', we refer to a situation where an individual or an institution has the *puissance* (the potential) to act on something or somebody if they want to (see e.g. Cesare Cuttica and Glenn Buress (eds), *Absolutism and Monarchism in Early Modern Europe* (London: Pickering & Chatto, 2012), esp. 'Introduction', pp. 1–17).

6   See e.g. Moi Toril, *Sexual/Textual Politics* (London: Routledge, 1985) and Josephine Donovan (ed.), *Feminist Thought. The Intellectual Traditions* (New York: Bloomsbury, 2012; fourth edition revised and expanded).

7   See Goran Therborn, *Between Sex and Power: Family in the World, 1900–2000* (London and New York: Routledge, 2004).

8   It is worth specifying that a society that is not subject to a patriarchalist system of government or one where the political apparatus does not depend on a patriarch-king can be a society where the rules of patriarchy still apply, for instance to the way in which jobs are allocated, positions of influence (e.g. political, economic) distributed, sexuality perceived and lived, women treated, marriage arranged and gender-related rituals performed.

9   Nicola Matteucci, 'Paternalismo', in Norberto Bobbio, Nicola Matteucci and Gianfranco Pasquino (eds), *Dizionario di Politica* (Turin: UTET, 1983), pp. 804–5, p. 804 (our translation).

10 Susan D. Amussen, *An Ordered Society: Gender and Class in Early Modern England* (Oxford: Blackwell, 1988), p. 55.

11 Gordon Schochet, *Patriarchalism in Political Thought: The Authoritarian Family and Political Speculation and Attitudes Especially in Seventeenth-Century England* (Oxford: Blackwell, 1975), p. 268.

12 See Cesare Cuttica, *Sir Robert Filmer (1588–1653) and the Patriotic Monarch: Patriarchalism in Seventeenth-Century Political Thought* (Manchester: Manchester University Press, 2012), 'Introduction', pp. 1–18.

13 See e.g. Sylvia Walby, *Theorizing Patriarchy* (Oxford: Blackwell, 1990). Relevant feminist classics here are Joan Scott, *Gender and the Politics of History* (New York: Columbia University Press, 1988) and Judith Butler, *Gender Trouble: Feminism and the Subversion of Identity* (New York and London: Routledge, 1990).

14 Mary Beard, 'The Public Voice of Women', *London Review of Books*, 36 (20 March 2014), pp. 11–14.

15 In his Letter to the Corinthians, St Paul called on the congregation, 'Let your women keep silence in the churches: for it is not permitted unto them to speak; but they are commanded to be under obedience, as also saith the law' (1 Corinthians 14:34).

16 Speaking is only one dimension of the process whereby women were barred from expressing themselves and their ideas, and needs to be related to reading, writing and printing. Only over the course of the early modern period would women come to benefit from the opportunity of seeing their work published through the new freedom of print.

17 Beard, 'The Public Voice of Women', p. 14.

18 See Katherine Smits and Susan Bruce (eds), *Feminist Moments* (London: Bloomsbury Academic, forthcoming).

19 See Cesare Cuttica, '*To Use or Not to Use… The Intellectual Historian and the Isms: A Survey and a Proposal*', *Etudes Epistémè*, 13 (2013), Varia (http://episteme.revues.org/268).

Chapter 1

1 Genesis 3.14–19. Bible quotations are taken from the Revised Standard Version.

2 Sirach 25.24.

3 1 Timothy 2.11–15.

4 The outright forbidding of women to speak later in the same letter (1 Cor. 14.34–35) clashes awkwardly with the more permissive attitude; it has more in common with the dogmatic negativity of 1 Timothy, and may well be a gloss.

Chapter 2

1 *Androgynus* is the Greek loanword in rabbinic literature for one born with male and female genitals. In this case, however, the term refers to a body that is half male and half female.

2 See Bereshit Rabbah (*hereafter*: BR) 8:1 for complete text. The translation is my own from the edition of *Midrash Bereshit Rabbah*, ed. Judah Theodor and Hanoch Albeck (Jerusalem: Wahrmann, 1965). I have divided the text into sections for ease of reading and inserted ellipses for brevity. Double quotation marks are used for biblical verses referred to by the rabbis and the verse references supplied in brackets. Italics indicate transliterations and my own emphasis. While I consider only this *petihta*, many of the individual *midrashim* also appear elsewhere in rabbinic literature. See, for example, bBer 60b–61b; bEruv 17b–19a.

3 I have retained both uses in this chapter.

4 The Hebrew Bible is divided into three sections: *Torah* (the Pentateuch, or 'The Five Books of Moses'), *Nevi'im* (lit. Prophets) and *Ketubim* (Writings, or the Hagiographa).

5 More often than not, a *petihta* quotes only a small part of the verse, but refers to a larger text around it. Here, only the words 'Let us make an *adam*' are quoted, but verses Gen. 1:26–27 are referenced.

6 For the sake of clarity, I will refer to the text as a whole as 'the *petihta*' and to each individual part that forms the *petihta* as a '*midrash*'.

7 In his opening to the *petihta*, R. Yohanan offers a particular frame for this apparent inconsistency. In this paper, however, I will concentrate on the individual *midrashim* rather than on the frame. See BR 8:1 for full text.

8 Plato. *Symposium*, transl. Benjamin Jowett (London: Sphere Books, 1970), section 189e.

9 So too, it may object to the story's origins in Greek lore.

10 Although these mini-*midrashim* are compiled into one *petihta*, each is representative of an opinion that may or may not accept the others'. Thus, chances are that this *adam* is regarded as male.

11 For the full text of these *midrashim*, see BR 8:1.

12 A rabbinic adage that explains the non-linear nature of time in midrashic explanations states: 'There is no early or late in Torah.' The fact that in a linear timeline creation precedes praise is thus irrelevant to them in this context.

Chapter 3

1 I use the words read/interpret interchangeably, and by patriarchalism I mean the ideologies and institutions of patriarchy as I define it in the text. For a detailed

analysis of the issues considered in this essay, see Asma Barlas, *'Believing Women' in Islam* (Texas: University of Texas Press, 2002).

2   See Yusuf Ali, *The Holy Qur'an* (New York: Tehrike Tersile Qur'an, 1988), p. 1806. Page references to this edition will be given in parentheses throughout the text.

3   See Amina Wadud, *Qur'an and Woman* (Oxford: Oxford University Press, 1999), p. 70. The exact meaning of *daraba* is contested in literature.

4   See Ali, *The Holy Qur'an*, pp. 1116–17.

5   Riffat Hassan, 'An Islamic Perspective', in Karen Lebacqz (ed.), *Sexuality: A Reader* (Cleveland, OH: Pilgrim Press, 1999), p. 354.

6   Azizah Al-Hibri quoted in Wadud, *Qur'an and Woman*, p. 71 (her emphases).

7   Zainah Anwar and Ziba Mir-Hosseini, 'Decoding the "DNA of Patriarchy" in Muslim Family Laws', *Open Democracy*, 21 May 2012, https://www.opendemocracy.net/5050/zainah-anwar-ziba-mir-hosseini/decoding-%e2%80%9cdna-of-patriarchy%e2%80%9d-in-muslim-family-laws, accessed on 16 February 2015.

8   Azizah Al-Hibri quoted in Wadud, *Qur'an and Woman*, pp. 70–7.

9   Laleh Bakhtiar, *The Sublime Qur'an* (Chicago, IL: Kazi Publications, 2007), p. 94.

10 See Marmaduke M. Pickthall, *The Meaning of the Glorious Koran* (New York: Mentor, n.d.), p. 291.

11 See Mustansir Mir, *Dictionary of Qur'anic Terms and Concepts* (New York: Garland, 1987).

12 See Pickthall, *The Meaning of the Glorious Koran*, p. 81

13 Muhammad Asad, *The Message of the Qur'an* (Gibraltar: Dar al-Andalus, 1980), p. 871.

14 Where I have not quoted an author, it means this is a standard translation of the Qur'an by all translators.

15 Pickthall, *The Meaning of the Glorious Koran*, p. 53 (my emphasis).

16 Ibid., p. 53.

17 See Barlas, *'Believing Women' in Islam*.

18 Caroline W. Bynum, ' "… And Woman his Humanity" ', in Caroline W. Bynum et al. (eds), *Gender and Religion* (Boston, MA: Beacon Press, 1986), p. 1.

19 In Ali, *The Holy Qur'an*, pp. 1083, 1089.

20 See Barlas, *'Believing Women' in Islam*.

21 Kate Millett, *Sexual Politics* (New York: Doubleday, 1970), p. 26.

22 Wadud, *Qur'an and Woman*, p. xxi (her emphasis).

23 Margaret Hodgen uses this phrase for the Bible: see Margaret Hodgen, *Early Anthropology in the Sixteenth and Seventeenth Centuries* (Philadelphia: University of Pennsylvania, 1964), p. 446.

24 In Ali, *The Holy Qur'an*, p. 178.

25 Ibid., p. 461.

26 See, for instance, Kecia Ali, *Sexual Ethics and Islam* (Oxford: Oneworld, 2006) and R. Rhouni, *Secular and Islamic Feminist Critiques* (Leiden: Brill, 2010).

27 In Ali, *The Holy Qur'an*, p. 1241.

28 Kenneth Cragg, *The Event of the Qur'an* (Oxford: Oneworld, 1994), p. 121.

29 Ibid., pp. 114–15.

30 In Ali, *The Holy Qur'an*, p. 38.

Chapter 4

1 Book 1, 1259a-1260a (from the canonical version available online at http://www.perseus.tufts.edu/hopper/text;jsessionid=93F5F166BAD877C4F6D1D4942E034 669?doc=Perseus%3atext%3a1999.01.0057, accessed on 16 February 2015). My own translation. Another version can be found in T. A. Sinclair (transl.), *Aristotle: Politics* (Harmondsworth: Penguin, 1962), pp. 49–50. All subsequent page numbers in the text refer to Sinclair's edition.

2 For a brilliant analysis of Aristotle on slavery, see Sara Monoson, 'Navigating Race, Class, Polis and Empire: The Place of Empirical Analysis in Aristotle's Account of Natural Slavery', in Richard Alston, Edith Hall and Laura Proffitt (eds) *Reading Ancient Slavery* (London: Bristol Classical Press, 2010), pp. 133–51.

3 See Marilyn Katz, 'Women, Children and Men', in Paul Cartledge (ed.), *The Cambridge Illustrated History of Ancient Greece* (Cambridge: Cambridge University Press, 1998), pp. 100–38; Edith Hall, *The Return of Ulysses: A Cultural History of Homer's Odyssey* (London and Baltimore: The Johns Hopkins University Press, 2008), ch. 9; and Edith Hall, *Greek Tragedy: Suffering under the Sun* (Oxford: Oxford University Press, 2010), ch. 3.

4 For the Amazons, see 'Herodotus', in Tom Holland, *Herodotus: The Histories*, with an Introduction by Paul Cartledge (London: Penguin, 2013; transl.), pp. 302–4, 600; for Artemisia, see ibid., p. 481.

5 Edith Hall, 'Deianeira Deliberates: Precipitate Decision-Making and *Trachiniae*', in Simon Goldhill and Edith Hall (eds), *Sophocles and the Greek Tragic Tradition* (Cambridge: Cambridge University Press, 2009), pp. 69–89.

6 Katz, 'Women, Children and Men', pp. 107–20.

7 Darrell Dobbs, 'Family Matters: Aristotle's Appreciation of Women and the Plural Structure of Society', *The American Political Science Review*, 90 (1996), pp. 74–89, p. 78.

8 'Herodotus' in Holland, *Herodotus: The Histories*, pp. 182–3.

9 See Crisp's translation: Roger Crisp, *Aristotle: The Nicomachean Ethics* (Cambridge: Cambridge University Press, 2000; transl.), pp. 92–3.

10 Arlene W. Saxonhouse, 'The Philosopher and the Female in the Political Thought of Plato', in Nancy Tuana (ed.), *Feminist Interpretations of Plato* (University Park, PA: Penn State Press 1994), pp. 67–86.

11 María Luisa Femenías, 'Women and Natural Hierarchy in Aristotle', *Hypatia*, 9 (1994), pp. 164–72, p. 169.

Chapter 5

1 Augustine, 'City of God', in R. W. Dyson (ed.), *Augustine. The City of God against the Pagans* (Cambridge: Cambridge University Press, 1998), 12.22. The Latin text to which I refer is that edited by B. Dombart and A. Kalb, *De Civitate Dei*, Corpus Christianorum Series Latina vols. 47 and 48 (Turnhout: Brepols, 1955). References to the *City of God* are given throughout the essay by abbreviated title (CG), book and chapter number.

2 For more on the intriguing implications of this passage, see Margaret R. Miles, 'From Rape to Resurrection: Sin, Sexual Difference, and Politics', in James Wetzel (ed.), *Augustine's City of God: A Critical Guide* (Cambridge: Cambridge University Press, 2013), pp. 75–92.

3 Note that the Latin here rendered as 'caresses' in fact means something like 'gentle speech': another privileging of conversation.

4 Cicero, *De Re Publica. Selections*, ed. J. E. G. Zetzel (Cambridge: Cambridge University Press, 1995), 1.39.

5 This is my own translation.

6 Note the role played by this notion in the doctoral dissertation of Hannah Arendt, translated as *Love and Saint Augustine* (Chicago, IL: University of Chicago Press, 1996).

7 I have explored this notion more fully in Catherine Conybeare, 'The City of Augustine: On the Interpretation of *Civitas*', in Carol Harrison, Caroline Humfress, and Isabella Sandwell (eds), *Being Christian in Late Antiquity* (Oxford: Oxford University Press, 2014), pp. 139–55.

8 Hannah Arendt, *The Human Condition* (Chicago, IL: University of Chicago Press, 1998), p. 177.

9 Ibid., pp. 177, 178.

10 Charles Taylor, *Sources of the Self: The Making of the Modern Identity* (Cambridge, MA: Harvard University Press, 1989), p. 36.

Chapter 6

1 John Knox, *The First Blast of the Trumpet against the Monstruous Regiment of Women* (Geneva, 1558), 10.v-11.r. Early English Books Online. Web. 26 June 2014. http://eebo.chadwyck.com.ezproxy.liv.ac.uk/search/full_rec?SOURCE=pgimages.cfg&ACTION=ByID&ID=99843818&FILE=../session/1403698001_3794&SEARCHSCREEN=CITATIONS&SEARCHCONFIG=var_spell.cfg&ECCO=default&DISPLAY=AUTHOR. All subsequent quotations refer to this edition.

2   My emphasis.

3   'Dejected' here means 'cast down from high estate or dignity'.

4   Patrick Collinson, 'Knox, the Church and the Women of England', in Roger A. Mason (ed.), *John Knox and the British Reformations* (Aldershot: Ashgate, 1998), pp. 74–96.

Chapter 7

1   William Gouge, *Of Domesticall Duties* (London: Printed by John Havliand for William Bladen, 1622). The extract is from Gouge's dedication to his readers, added to the second edition of his pamphlet. Page references to this edition will be given in brackets within the text.

2   Susan D. Amussen, *An Ordered Society: Gender and Class in Early Modern England* (Oxford: Basil Blackwell, 1988), pp. 7–33. Gordon J. Schochet, *The Authoritarian Family and Political Attitudes in 17th-Century England* (New Brunswick, NJ: Transaction, 1975; 1988).

3   Laura Gowing, *Domestic Dangers: Women, Words, and Sex in Early Modern London* (Oxford: Clarendon Press, 1996), p. 24.

4   Karen Harvey, *The Little Republic: Masculinity & Domestic Authority in Eighteenth-Century Britain* (Oxford: Oxford University Press, 2014), pp. 30–1, 64–72.

5   Brett Usher, 'Gouge, William (1575–1653)', in *Oxford Dictionary of National Biography* (Oxford: Oxford University Press, 2004; online edn, January 2008). [http://www.oxforddnb.com/view/article/11133, accessed 23 May 2014].

6   See the 1634 edition from University of Illinois (Urbana-Champaign Campus), STC12121 and the 1622 edition from the University of Illinois (Urbana-Champaign Campus) (STC12119; reel 1204). The latter is the edition used in this chapter.

7   Laura Gowing, *Common Bodies: Women, Touch and Power in Seventeenth-Century England* (New Haven, CT and London: Yale University Press, 2003), p. 199.

8   Patricia Crawford and Sara Mendelson, *Women in Early Modern England, 1550–1720* (Oxford: Clarendon Press, 1998), p. 135.

9   Amanda Flather, *Gender and Space in Early Modern England* (Woodbridge: The Boydell Press for The Royal Historical Society, 2007), pp. 31–7.

10 Amussen, *An Ordered Society*, p. 47.

11 Victoria Kahn, ' "The Duty to Love": Passion and Obligation in Early Modern Political Theory', *Representations*, 68 (1999), p. 87.

12 Michael J. Braddick and John Walter (2001), 'Introduction. Grids of Power: Order, Hierarchy and Subordination in Early Modern Society', in Michael J. Braddick and John Walter (eds), *Negotiating Power in Early Modern Society: Order, Hierarchy and Subordination in Britain and Ireland* (Cambridge: Cambridge University Press, 2001), pp. 1–42.

Chapter 8

1   Robert Filmer, '*Patriarcha. The Naturall* Power of Kinges Defended against the
    Unnatural Liberty of the People', in Johann P. Sommerville (ed.), *Filmer. Patriarcha and
    Other Writings* (Cambridge: Cambridge University Press, 1991), pp. 1–68, pp. 4–5. Page
    references to this edition will be given in parentheses throughout the text.
2   For an overview see Cesare Cuttica, 'Sir Robert Filmer (1588–1653) and the
    Condescension of Posterity: Historiographical Interpretations', *Intellectual History
    Review*, 21 (2011), pp. 195–208.
3   See ibid., *Sir Robert Filmer (1588–1653) and the Patriotic Monarch: Patriarchalism
    in Seventeenth-Century Political Thought* (Manchester: Manchester University Press,
    2012), 'Introduction', pp. 1–18.
4   See Richard Tuck, 'A New Date for Filmer's Patriarcha', *Historical Journal*, 29
    (1986), pp. 183–6; Sommerville, 'Introduction', in Johann P. Sommerville (ed.),
    Robert Filmer. Patriarcha and Other Writings (Cambridge: Cambridge University
    Press, 1991), pp. vii–xxxvii.
5   See Cuttica, *Sir Robert Filmer*, passim, esp. ch. 2.

Chapter 9

1   Algernon Sidney, *Discourses Concerning Government*, Revised Edition, ed. Thomas
    G. West (Indianapolis, IN: Liberty Fund, 1996). Subsequent references to this text
    will appear in brackets within the body of the chapter.
2   Johann P. Sommerville ed., *Filmer. Patriarcha and Other Writings* (Cambridge:
    Cambridge University Press, 1991), pp. vii–xxxvii.
3   Michael P. Winship, 'Algernon Sidney's Calvinist Republicanism', *Journal of British
    Studies*, 49 (2010), p. 15, pp. 753–73, p. 767.
4   Ibid., pp. 767–8. This paragraph quotes Winship quoting Sidney.
5   Algernon Sidney, 'Apology in the Day of His Death', in Joseph Robertson (ed.)
    Sydney on Government: the Works of Algernon Sydney (London, 1772), p. 30.
6   Algernon Sidney, *The Very Copy of a Paper Delivered to the Sheriffs* (London, 1683),
    p. 40.
7   Jonathan Scott, *Algernon Sidney and the Restoration Crisis 1677–83* (Cambridge:
    Cambridge University Press, 1991).
8   Robert Blencowe, ed. *Sydney Papers* (London, 1823), pp. 270–1; on this context
    in general see Jonathan Scott, *Algernon Sidney and the English Republic 1623–77*
    (Cambridge: Cambridge University Press, 1988), esp. ch. 4, and Scott, *Restoration
    Crisis*, esp. ch. 5.
9   Quoted in Scott, *Restoration Crisis*, p. 91.

10   Gilbert Burnet, *History of My Own Time*, 2 volumes (Oxford: Oxford University Press, 1823), vol. 2, p. 341.

11   Quoted in Scott, *Restoration Crisis*, p. 256 (and see pp. 254–7 in general).

Chapter 10

1   John Locke, 'Some Thoughts Concerning Education', in J. W. Yolton and J. S. Yolton (eds), *Some Thoughts Concerning Education* (Oxford: Clarendon Press, 1989), §41. Hereafter cited in the text by section number.

2   John Locke, 'Two Treatises of Government', in P. Laslett (ed.), *Locke: Two Treatises of Government* (Cambridge: Cambridge University Press, 1988). Hereafter cited in the text by treatise and paragraph number.

3   Jay Fliegelman, *Prodigals and Pilgrims: The American Revolution against Patriarchal Authority, 1750–1800* (Cambridge: Cambridge University Press, 1982), pp. 4, 38.

4   Robert Filmer, 'Patriarcha', in Johann P. Sommerville (ed.), *Filmer. Patriarcha and Other Writings* (Cambridge: Cambridge University Press, 1991), pp. 6–12; Gordon Schochet, *The Authoritarian Family and Political Attitudes in 17th-Century England: Patriarchalism in Political Thought* (New Brunswick, NJ: Transaction Books, 1988), chs. 8, 13.

5   Andrew Franklin-Hall, 'Creation and Authority: The Natural Law Foundations of Locke's Account of Parental Authority', *Canadian Journal of Philosophy*, 42 (2012), pp. 261–6.

6   See, for example, Nancy J. Hirschmann and Kirstie M. McClure (eds), *Feminist Interpretations of John Locke* (University Park, PA: The Pennsylvania State University Press, 2007). See also David Foster, 'Taming the Father: John Locke's Critique of Patriarchal Fatherhood', *Review of Politics*, 56 (1994), pp. 643–4.

7   John Steinbeck, *Of Mice and Men* (London: Penguin, 2000).

8   John Locke, 'An Essay Concerning Human Understanding', in Peter H. Nidditch (ed.), *An Essay Concerning Human Understanding* (Oxford: Clarendon Press, 1979), II.xviii.18, II.xx.18; John Locke, 'Pleasure and Pain. The Passions', in W. von Leyden (ed.), *Essays on the Law of Nature and Associated Writings* (Oxford: Oxford University Press, 2007), p. 266.

9   John Locke, 'Of Study', in James Axtell (ed.), *The Educational Writings of John Locke* (Cambridge: Cambridge University Press, 1968), p. 417; John Locke, 'Of the Conduct of the Understanding', in Ruth Grant and Nathan Tarcov (eds), *Some Thoughts Concerning Education and of the Conduct of the Understanding* (Indianapolis, IN: Hackett, 1996), §3. For the relationship between friendship and conversation see Richard Yeo, 'Locke on Conversation with Friends and Strangers', *Parergon*, 26 (2009), pp. 11–37.

10   Isaac Barrow, 'Sermon VII', in *Sermons Preached upon Several Occasions* (London, 1679), pp. 240–1; Robert Sanderson, 'Sermon X', *Twenty Sermons* (London, 1660), pp. 202–5.

11 For a list of attributes, see Vivienne Brown, 'The "Figure" of God and the Limits to Liberalism: A Rereading of Locke's "Essay" and "Two Treatises"', *Journal of the History of Ideas*, 60 (1999), pp. 83–100.

12 John Locke, 'The Reasonableness of Christianity', in J. C. Higgins-Biddle (ed.), *The Reasonableness of Christianity* (Oxford: Clarendon Press, 1999), p. 129; 'A Paraphrase and Noes on the Epistles of St Paul', in A. W. Wainwright (ed.), *A Paraphrase and Notes on the Epistles of St Paul* (Oxford: Clarendon Press, 1987), vol. 1, p. 127n, and vol. 2, p. 519n.

13 John Locke, 'A Letter Concerning Toleration', in James Tully (ed.), *A Letter Concerning Toleration* (Indianapolis, IN: Hackett, 1983). See Hymn, 'What a Friend We Have in Jesus'.

Chapter 11

1 Mary Astell, 'Reflections on Marriage', in Patricia Springborg (ed.), *Astell: Political Writings*, (New York: Cambridge University Press, 1996), pp. 1–80, p. 61. Subsequent parenthetical citations in this essay refer to this edition.

2 Ibid., pp. 17–18. This passage is taken from the preface to the 3rd edition, 1706. Emphases in original.

3 Mary Astell, *Letters Concerning the Love of God* (London: Printed for Samuel Manship … and Richard Wilkin, 1695), p. 1.

4 Mary Astell, *Moderation Truly Stated, or, a Review of a Late Pamphlet, Entitul'd, Moderation a Vertue* (London: Printed by J. L. for Rich. Wilkin, 1704), p. 59. See also 'An Impartial Enquiry into the Origins of Rebellion', in *Astell: Political Writings*, ed. Springborg, pp. 129–97.

5 John Evelyn, *The Diary of John Evelyn*, ed. John Bowle (New York: Oxford University Press, 1983), p. 405.

6 Mary Wollstonecraft, *A Vindication of the Rights of Men; with, a Vindication of the Rights of Woman* (New York: Cambridge University Press, 1995), pp. 117, 292.

7 Mary Astell, *A Serious Proposal to the Ladies*, ed. Patricia Springborg (Peterborough, ON: Broadview Press, 2002), p. 203.

Chapter 12

1 The passage is transcribed from the original issue of *An Essay on Man*, Epistle IV (London: J. Wilford, 1734), pp. 202–39 in Pope's original numbering. Other quotations from the poem as a whole are also keyed to the first published texts. The most scholarly modern edition is Alexander Pope, *An Essay on Man*, ed. Maynard Mack,

The Twickenham Edition of the Poems of Alexander Pope, III.i. (London: Methuen, 1950). This is based on later, revised texts, with slightly different numbering.

2   See Howard Erskine-Hill, 'Pope on the Origins of Society', in Pat Rogers and G. S. Rousseau (eds), *The Enduring Legacy: Alexander Pope Tercentenary Essays* (Cambridge: Cambridge University Press, 1988), pp. 79–93, p. 93.

Chapter 13

1   Jean-Jacques Rousseau, *Emile or on Education*. Introduction, translation and notes by Allan Bloom (New York: Basic Books, 1979), book V, pp. 407–8. All quotations from Rousseau's *Emile* in this chapter are taken from Allan Bloom's 1979 translation. Page numbers given in parentheses refer to this edition.

2   Jean-Jacques Rousseau, 'Discourses on Political Economy', in Victor Gourevitch ed., *Rousseau. The Social Contract and Other Later Political Writings* (Cambridge: Cambridge University Press, 1997), p. 4.

3   This approach is what Susan Moller Okin has called Rousseau's 'functionalist method', in Susan Moller Okin, *Women in Western Political Thought* (Princeton, NJ: Princeton University Press, 1979), p. 235.

4   Mary Wollstonecraft, *A Vindication of the Rights of Woman* (New York: Everyman's Library, 1992), p. 42.

5   On the various interpretations of Rousseau's apparent contradiction, see E. H. Botting, *Family Feuds: Wollstonecraft, Burke and Rousseau on the Transformation of the Family* (Albany: State University of New York Press, 2006).

6   Rousseau, 'Discourses on Political Economy', p. 5.

7   The distinction between domestic and political economy is made in the preamble to the 'Discourses on Political Economy', pp. 3–5.

8   Rousseau, 'The Social Contract' (I, 2), in Gourevitch (ed.), *Rousseau. The Social Contract*, p. 43.

9   See Aurélie Du Crest, *Modèle familial et pouvoir monarchique (XVIe-XVIIe siècles)* (Aix-en-Provence: Presses Universitaires d'Aix-Marseille, 2002), pp. 353–6.

10 Louis-Sébastien Mercier, *Notions claires sur les gouvernements* (Amsterdam, 1787), p. 150 (my translation).

Chapter 14

1   Immanuel Kant, 'What is Enlightenment?', in Pauline Kleingeld (ed.) *Towards Perpetual Peace and Other Writings on Politics, Peace, and History* (New Haven, CT: Yale University Press, 2006), hereafter: 2006a, pp. 35–6. This translation is based on

the Akademie edition of Kant's works and uses the original pagination. Subsequent page references to this and other works by Kant will appear in brackets within the text.

2 Immanuel Kant, *Anthropology from a Pragmatic Point of View* (Cambridge: Cambridge University Press, 2006), hereafter: 2006b, p. 209. Page numbers refer to the Akademie edition of Kant's works.

3 Immanuel Kant, *The Metaphysics of Morals* (Cambridge: Cambridge University Press, 1996), p. 279. Page numbers refer to the Akademie edition of Kant's works.

4 Immanuel Kant, *Observations on the Feeling of the Beautiful and Sublime* (Cambridge: Cambridge University Press, 2011), p. 229. Page numbers refer to the Akademie edition of Kant's works.

5 Kant contrasts this civilized condition with a barbaric one in which 'the woman is a domestic animal' (2006b: 304). One feature of civilized societies, then, is that they treat women like subjects, rather than objects – even if women's subjecthood is ultimately confined to the household.

6 Kant 2006b, p. 209.

7 There were exceptions, of course: as Pauline Kleingeld has pointed out, we know that Kant was acquainted with learned women like Emilie de Châtelet and Mme Dacier, whom he mentions in *The Beautiful and the Sublime*. Thus, Kleingeld argues, it seems fair to argue that Kant could have thought differently – and the important thing is that he did not (Pauline Kleingeld, 'The Problematic Status of Gender-Neutral Language in the History of Philosophy: The Case of Kant', *The Philosophical Forum*, 25 (1993), pp. 134–50, pp. 143–4).

8 See Rae Langton, 'Duty and Desolation', *Philosophy*, 67 (1992), pp. 481–505.

9 See Theodor von Hippel, *On Marriage* (Detroit, MI: Wayne State University Press, 1994); and ibid., *On Improving the Status of Women* (Detroit, MI: Wayne State University Press, 1979).

Chapter 15

1 Mary Wollstonecraft, *Mary, A Fiction* (London, 1788), p. 86.

2 Ibid., pp. 87–9.

3 Wollstonecraft inserts a 'to' after 'Near' in Chapter IV (87).

4 William Blackstone, *The Commentaries of Sir William Blackstone, Knt. on the Laws and Constitution of England*, ed. William Curry (London: W. Clarke and Son, 1796). ECCO (Eighteenth-Century Collections Online), accessed on 12 December 2013, p. 77.

5 Thomas Paine, *The Age of Reason, Being an Investigation of True and Fabulous Theology* (Barrois: n.p., 1794). ECCO (Eighteenth-Century Collections Online), accessed on 10 February 2010, p. 82.

6   The notion that it is natural for some segments of society to wield power over others developed long before the late eighteenth century. Significantly, Robert Filmer's *Patriarcha; or the Natural Power of Kings* (1680) proposed that the king of a country should be regarded as a beneficent father, naturally disposed to do right by his 'children' and also naturally wiser than the rest of society by being born a patriarch.

7   Ashley Tauchert suggests that *Mary* depicts a lesbian love affair in 'Escaping Discussion: Liminality and the Female-Embodied Couple in Mary Wollstonecraft's *Mary, A Fiction*', *Romanticism on the Net: An Electronic Journal Devoted to Romantic Studies*, 18 (2000), (no pagination), accessed on 21 April 2011. Other critics have found such evidence elsewhere in Wollstonecraft's life and work. See, for example, Claudia Johnson's *Equivocal Beings: Politics, Gender, and Sentimentality in the 1790s* (Chicago: University of Chicago Press, 1995), p. 54; and Katherine Binhammer's 'The "Singular Propensity" of Sensibility's Extremities: Female Same-Sex Desire and the Eroticization of Pain in Late-Eighteenth-Century British Culture', *GLQ: A Journal of Lesbian and Gay Studies*, 9 (2003), pp. 471–98.

8   Oddly, too, Henry's mother seems to consider Henry as a husband, since she claims she will be a 'widow' when he dies.

Chapter 16

1   Prosper Enfantin at a Saint-Simonian meeting, 21 November 1831, in: Religion Saint-Simonienne, *Réunion Générale de la Famille: Séances des 19 et 21 Novembre* (Paris: Imprimerie d'Éverat, 1831), pp. 55–6. Subsequent references to this source will be made in brackets within the text.

2   Robert B. Carlisle, *The Proffered Crown: Saint-Simonianism and the Doctrine of Hope* (Baltimore, MD: Johns Hopkins University Press, 1987), p. 58.

3   Pamela Pilbeam, *Saint-Simonians in Nineteenth-Century France: From Free Love to Algeria* (Basingstoke: Palgrave, 2014), p. 16.

4   Christophe Prochasson, *Saint-Simon ou l'anti-Marx: figures du saint-simonisme français XIXe–XXe siècles* (Paris: Perrin, 2005), p. 127.

5   Carlisle, *The Proffered Crown*, p. 90. See Carlisle's remarks on the 'continuity of thought between Saint-Simon and his disciples': ibid., p. 233.

6   Simon Altmann, David Siminovitch and Barrie Ratcliffe, 'Olinde Rodrigues and His Times', in Simon Altmann and Eduardo Ortiz (eds), *Mathematics and Social Utopias in France: Olinde Rodrigues and His Times* (Providence, RI: American Mathematical Society, 2005), pp. 5–38.

7   See e.g. turnouts of 1,500–2,000 for events in Nancy and Metz: Carlisle, *The Proffered Crown*, p. 141.

8   Claire G. Moses, 'Saint-Simonian Men/Saint-Simonian Women: The Transformation of Feminist Thought in 1830s' France', *Journal of Modern History*, 54 (1982),

pp. 240–67, p. 248. Pilbeam suggests that in September 1841, half of the 220 'faithful' in Paris were female: Pilbeam, *Saint-Simonians in Nineteenth-Century France*, p. 34. On Saint-Simonism's appeal to women, see also Christine Planté, 'Les féministes saint-simoniennes: possibilités et limites d'un mouvement féministe en France au lendemain de 1830', in Jean René Derré (ed.), *Regards sur le Saint-Simonisme et les Saint-Simoniens* (Lyon: Presses Universitaires de Lyon, 1986), pp. 73–102.

9   Naomi J. Andrews, *Socialism's Muse: Gender in the Intellectual Landscape of French Romantic Socialism* (Lanham, MD: Lexington Books, 2006), p. xvi.

10   Pamela Pilbeam, *French Socialists Before Marx: Workers, Women and the Social Question in France* (Montreal and Kingston: McGill/Queen's University Press, 2000), p. 79.

11   Jeremy Jennings, *Revolution and the Republic: A History of Political Thought in France since the Eighteenth Century* (Oxford: Oxford University Press, 2011), p. 351.

12   Paola Ferruta, 'Euphrasie and Olinde Rodrigues: The "Woman Question" within Saint-Simonism', in Altmann and Ortiz, *Mathematics and Social Utopias in France*, p. 87. On 13 February 1832, Rodrigues presented his *Bases de la loi morale proposées à l'acceptation des femmes*. In his approach to women's rights, he differed from Enfantin, who focused on morality and 'had nothing to say about ending the exploitation of women by educating them or by paying women a living wage': Pilbeam, *Saint-Simonians in Nineteneth Century*, p. 51.

13   Moses, 'Saint-Simonian Men/Saint-Simonian Women', p. 258. The former Saint-Simonian Eugénie Niboyet also founded a newspaper: Lucette Czyba, 'L'œuvre lyonnaise d'une ancienne saint-simonienne: Le Conseiller des Femmes (1833–4) d'Eugénie Niboyet', in Derré, *Regards sur le Saint-Simonisme et les Saint-Simoniens*, pp. 103–43.

Chapter 17

1   'The Kreutzer Sonata', in Leo Tolstoy (ed.), *The Devil and Cognate Tales* (London: Oxford University Press, 1934), p. 136, pp. 206–7. Subsequent page references to this edition are made in brackets within the text.

2   Amy Mandelker, *Framing Anna Karenina: Tolstoy, the Woman Question and the Victorian Novel* (Columbus: Ohio University Press, 1993), p. 32.

3   Leo Tolstoy, *What Then Must We Do?* (London: Oxford University Press, 1934), p. 352.

4   Ernest Crosby's Russian Journal, Box 4, MS218, Michigan State University Library.

5   *The Diaries of Sofia Tolstoy*, transl. Cathy Porter (London: Alma Books, 2009), p. 117.

6   Peter Ulf Møller, *Postlude to the Kreutzer Sonata: Tolstoj and the Debate on Sexual Morality in Russian Literature in the 1890s* (Leiden and New York: E. J. Brill, 1988), pp. 93–4.

7   Ibid., pp. 103–4.

8   Ibid., pp. 115–27.

9   Leo Tolstoy, 'On Marriage', *The New Age*, 16 December 1897, pp. 173–4. See also *The New Age* for 23 December 1897, 30 December 1897, and 6 January 1898.

10 Prince Galitzen, 'Thou Shalt Do No Murder', in Mrs James Gregor (ed.), *Whose Was the Blame? A Woman's Version of the Kreutzer Sonata* (London: Swan Sonnenschein & Co, 1894), pp. 3–47.

11 Gregor, *Whose Was the Blame?*, pp. 51–174.

12 Møller, *Postlude*, pp. 177–80. For a survey of 'counter-literature' see ibid., pp. 163–80.

13 Charlotte Alston, *Tolstoy and His Disciples: The History of a Radical International Movement* (London: I B Tauris, 2013), pp. 180–7.

Chapter 18

1   Henrik Ibsen, 'Hedda Gabler', in *Ibsen: The Complete Major Prose Plays*, transl. Rolf Fjelde (New York: New American Library, 1978), p. 762. Subsequent quotations will be drawn from this translation and placed parenthetically in the text.

2   Joan Templeton, *Ibsen's Women* (Cambridge: Cambridge University Press, 1997), p. 231.

3   See ibid., Gail Finney, *Women in Modern Drama: Freud, Feminism, and European Theater at the Turn of the Century* (Ithaca, NY: Cornell University Press, 1989); and Ross Shideler, *Questioning the Father: From Darwin to Zola, Ibsen, Strindberg, and Hardy* (Stanford, CA: Stanford University Press, 1999), as well as Ross Shideler, 'The Patriarchal Prison in *Hedda Gabler* and *Dödsdansen*', in Faith Ingwersen and Mary Kay Norseng (eds), *Fin(s) de Siècle in Scandinavian Perspective: Studies in Honor of Harald S. Naess* (Columbia, SC: Camden House, 1993), pp. 78–90.

4   Thomas H. Johnson (ed.), *The Complete Poems of Emily Dickinson* (Boston, MA: Little, Brown and Col., 1961), p. 370.

5   *The Fact of a Doorframe: Selected Poems 1950–2001* (New York: Norton, 2002), p. 78.

Chapter 19

1   'Pavlatche' is the Czech word for the long balcony in the inner courtyard of old houses in Prague.

2   The English version of Kafka's *Brief an den Vater* follows the translation of Ernst Kaiser and Eithne Wilkins reprinted in: *Franz Kafka: The Sons*, intro. Mark Anderson (New York: Schocken 1980). This passage can be found on p. 119. Subsequent references to this edition will be made in brackets within the text.

3   Thomas Anz, *Franz Kafka* (München: C. H. Beck, 1989), pp. 32 ff.

4 Gerhard Dienes and Ralf Rother (eds), *Die Gesetze des Vaters. Hans Gross. Otto Gross. Sigmund Freud. Franz Kafka* (Wien, Köln, Weimar: Böhlau, 2003).

5 Franz Kafka, *Tagebücher*, ed. Hans-Gerd Koch, Michael Müller and Malcolm Pasley (Frankfurt a. M.: Fischer, 2002), p. 461.

6 See the description in Hans Dieter Zimmermann, *Kafka fürFortgeschrittene* (München: C. H. Beck, 2004), pp. 15 ff. and Peter-André Alt, *Franz Kafka: Der ewigeSohn. EineBiographie* (München: C. H. Beck, 2003), p. 563.

7 Franz Kafka, *Briefe an Milena*, augmented edition by Jürgen Born and Michael Müller (Frankfurt a. M.: Fischer, 1986), p. 85.

8 Kafka, *Tagebücher*, p. 223.

9 Franz Kafka, *BriefeanFelice* (Frankfurt a. M.: Fischer, 1976), p. 598.

10 Klaus Wagenbach, *Franz Kafka* (Reinbek b. Hamburg: Fischer, 1964), p. 81.

Chapter 20

1 *Bodas de sangre/Blood Wedding* by Federico García Lorca copyright © Herederos de Federico García Lorca, from *Obras Completas* (Galaxia/Gutenberg, 1996 edition). English Translations by Federico Bonaddio copyright © Federico Bonaddio and Herederos de Federico García Lorca. All rights reserved. For information regarding rights and permissions of all of Lorca's works in Spanish or in English, please contact *lorca@artslaw.co.uk* or William Peter Kosmas, Esq., 8 Franklin Square, London W14 9UU, England.

2 Federico García Lorca, 'Bodas de sangre', in Federico García Lorca, Obras, III: Teatro, 1. Ed. Miguel García-Posada (Madrid: Akal, 1985), Act I, scene ii, pp. 307–413, pp. 367–8, 379–80. All subsequent page numbers appear in parentheses in the text. All translations are the author's own, although he has also consulted the following published versions: 'Blood Wedding', in *Plays: One*, intro. Gwynne X. Edwards (London: Methuen Drama, 1987); Federico García Lorca, *Blood Wedding*, trans. David X. Johnston (London: Hodder & Stoughton, 1989); Federico García Lorca, *Blood Wedding*, trans. Brendan Kennelly (Newcastle: Bloodaxe Books, 1996); and Federico García Lorca, *Blood Wedding*, trans. Paul Burns and Salvador Ortiz-Carboneres, Aris & Phillips Hispanic Classics (Oxford: Oxbow Books, 2009).

3 David Gilmore, *Aggression and Community. Paradoxes of Andalusian Culture* (New Haven, CT and London: Yale University Press, 1987), pp. 144–5.

4 Ibid., p. 127.

5 See Gilmore, *Aggression and Community*, pp. 134, 140, and Julian Pitt-Rivers, 'Honour and Social Status', in J. G. Peristany (ed.), *Honour and Shame. The Values of Mediterranean Society* (London: Weidenfeld and Nicolson, 1965), pp. 21–77, p. 42.

6 Gilmore, *Aggression and Community*, p. 134.

7 Reed Anderson, 'The Idea of Tragedy in García Lorca's *Bodas de sangre*', *Revista Hispánica Moderna*, 38 (1974–5), pp. 174–88, pp. 182–3.

8 Ibid., p. 186.

Chapter 21

1 Angela Carter, *The Passion of New Eve* (London: Virago, 1976), p. 53. All page references to this text will be given in parentheses throughout the chapter.

2 'Thealogy' refers to a distinct discourse that dates from the mid-1970s: it seeks to challenge patriarchal accounts of divinity and privileges a feminist and female-centred spirituality which worships goddesses rather than gods. For a fuller introduction to this term, see Melissa Raphael, *Introducing Thealogy: Discourse on the Goddess* (Sheffield: Sheffield Academic Press, 1999).

3 David Punter, *The Hidden Script: Writing and the Unconscious* (London: Routledge, 1985), p. 37.

4 Lorna Sage, *Angela Carter* (Plymouth: Northcote House Publishers, 1994), p. 39.

5 See Roland Barthes, *Mythologies* (London: Vintage, 1957).

6 Aidan Day, *Angela Carter: The Rational Glass* (Manchester: Manchester University Press, 1998), p. 113.

7 See Simone de Beauvoir, *The Second Sex* (London: Vintage, 1949).

8 For a fuller digest of French feminism and its differences from Anglo-American feminism see Toril Moi, *Sexual/Textual Politics* (London: Routledge, 1985).

9 Hélène Cixous, 'The Laugh of the Medusa', *Signs*, 1 (1976), pp. 875–93.

10 Sarah Gamble, *The Fiction of Angela Carter: A Reader's Guide to Essential Criticism* (Basingstoke: Palgrave Macmillan, 2001), p. 92.

11 Angela Carter, *The Sadeian Woman: An Exercise in Cultural History* (London: Virago, 1979), p. 5.

12 Day, *Angela Carter: The Rational Glass*, p. 117.

Conclusion

1 In pre-modern texts we also find a fourth, master–slave/servant relationship, as slaves or servants might live within the same household as legal dependants of their masters.

2 John Locke, *Locke: Two Treatises of Government*, ed. Peter Laslett (Cambridge: Cambridge University Press, 1998).

3 Joan Thirsk, 'Younger Sons in the Seventeenth Century', *History*, 54 (1969), pp. 358–77.

Index

www.ingramcontent.com/pod-product-compliance
Lightning Source LLC
Chambersburg PA
CBHW062022270326
41929CB00014B/2282